Samuel L. Clarke

Doctrines of Divine Psychology

Samuel L. Clarke

Doctrines of Divine Psychology

ISBN/EAN: 9783337780241

Printed in Europe, USA, Canada, Australia, Japan

Cover: Foto ©Lupo / pixelio.de

More available books at **www.hansebooks.com**

DOCTRINES

of

DIVINE PSYCHOLOGY,

HOLY EXEGESIS, REVELATION OF THE FUTURE LIFE, RESURRECTION
OF THE DEAD, SALVATION OF THE WICKED, ANNIHILATION
OF DEATH AND HELL, EXTERMINATION OF MORTALITY,
TO TRANSHUMANIZE MANKIND.

By SAMUEL L. CLARKE.

BOSTON, MASS.:
PUBLISHED BY SAMUEL L. CLARKE.
1894.

DOCTRINES OF DIVINE PSYCHOLOGY.

PART I.

INSTRUCTION ON THE DOCTRINES, LAWS, AND COMMANDMENTS OF DIVINE PSYCHOLOGY.

I MAKE a revision and integration of the part of this doctrine heretofore published, so that it be clearly understood and reveal the complete book of the human soul both in atonement, revelation, and doctrine. This book is presented to the people to show the victorious and scientific triumph of divine truth at its second advent to earth, showing and proving by works which have already been accomplished that the perfect divine truth, word, and spirit combined has herein been revealed from heaven to man to reclaim falling and suffering humanity, by the oblique course which this doctrine pursued being predestined of God to fulfil the cycle of time prophesied of in the Holy Bible, concerning the second coming of Christ to reign over and destroy his desperate enemies.

The oblique course which the Son of Righteousness took to fulfil the ancient and modern prophecies is the undeniable proof, and infinite testimony that the horn of salvation has appeared the second time without sin unto salvation, whose power, perfect image, works, judgments, righteousness, and equity are beheld and seen perspicuous in divine truth, word, and spirit combined in the utterance of the hidden secrets of the human soul. The full secrets of divine truth and righteousness, which are herein disclosed to the civilized world, are based wholly on the human soul's solving the different and diverse kinds of righteousness and sin existing in human nature manifested through outward signs of principles, which, in reality, are entirely spiritual in both purity and impurity; still, human flesh was used all through the eventful career of this doctrine to show the power and duration of divine truth and the despotic tyranny of sin and iniquity. This scientific course of revelation will surely and undoubtedly reveal the full hidden secrets of that man of sin, the Son of Perdition, who by knowledge and experience is the predominating spirit of this expiring age of assimilation and pollutions. This revelation shall also disclose to the civilized world the fulness of God's divine truth and righteousness in man, and the fulness of sin and iniquity in man. This revelation will show and prove to the human world that Christ, the redeemer of mankind, has made his second advent to the spiritual, civilized, human world which is situated in the soul of man. This revelation shall locate, describe, and show what is divine truth and righteousness, and what is moral truth and righteousness; and show what is sin and vice; which will disclose and separate divine truth and its righteousness from the truth and righteousness of the moral world's polluted customs and formality of godliness, so that everything that God has created, whether to honor or dishonor him, will forever and eternally hold their creative offices, and perform their creative work perfectly. Then the different kinds and grades of purity and impurity will cease to mingle and intermingle, as hath been done all along through the past dark ages of the world's progress in both corruption and incorruption. This revelation shall make known no new truth, neither strange nor new God; but it presents in word, truth, and spirit combined, the Divine Spiritual God which has always been sought and hoped for by genuine humanity since mankind lost his creative state of holiness, perfection, and felicity. Neither does this revelation reveal and make known a new kind of sin and iniquity; but the sin and iniquity that has always prevailed clandestinely in and over pure human nature since mankind disobeyed the holy commandments of God, contaminated and degenerated humanity; although both sin and divine truth and righteousness will seem new, because it is revealed in its true form and expression. The instrument whom God raised up, purged, and refined and purified to reveal and proclaim these eternal truths is not eminent in the world of great and renowned men of this day; but as the Divine God is the real Author of this revelation, it is useless to seek customary prominence among men before presenting it to the world, because the real Author has a world-wide fame of supremacy; therefore the Author of this book is universally spoken of. The revelation that I shall issue among the people is centred to the soul of both sexes of mankind, and the revelations are based wholly upon the principles of mankind, which is the soul, whether dehumanized, human, or transhumanized.

The tender love which the good Lord has thoroughly wrought and interwoven in my flesh and blood, bone and sinew, has stood firm and substantially upon its holy feet to declare the eternal truths unto the people, to rescue humanity from the cruel clutches and ravenous appetite of animalism. Before making plain the holy doctrine of truth I must first locate the bounds of this doctrine and show the sphere of utter and eternal darkness; in order to do this I shall divulge the hidden realities of the apostolic Bible and locate the prophecies and doctrines therein revealed from heaven to mankind, to lead them gradually into a higher life. By locating the prophecies and doctrines of the apostolic Bible, the black veil of the times and time will be consumed which hangs thickly between man and immortality. Also the true utterance of the mysterious doctrines, prophecies, dreams, and visions of the apostolic Bible, which is clothed in sack-cloth and ashes from mankind, will be made manifest by this revelation. The realities of the apostolic Bible are concealed from mankind because it is written with the language of material and terrestial things, and interpreted in the same tongue, which conceals its pure spiritual language and meaning. Man's hope of obtaining the world of eternal rest, peace, and happiness after death is conveyed to the mind through the material language of the Holy Bible and the misunderstanding of its true interpretation.

The material universe is the express likeness of mankind, which makes man the microcosm of the secular world, because mankind, in characteristics, contains all substances of the universe, both of trees, herbs, cattle, beast, fowl, fish, reptiles, and of creeping things of the earth. The spiritual universe in man, called the world, was polluted when the first man, Adam, sinned; disobedience to his Creator caused him to sin and pollute the spiritual universe within him, which was created in perfect holiness. The polluting of the spiritual world in man did not tarnish the purity of the corporeal world. The polluted world in mankind has revolved from generation to generation through inheritance by the propelling upas of animal propensities, and shows its deadly effect among the human races in dehumanized principles.

As soon as mankind stepped into the current of animal propensities, its propelling current bore him gradually on through the past dispensations; and the words of the Holy Bible were used as ensigns and purgative fountains, both oral and written, to convert man from extreme animalism to be loyal to all the laws, doctrines, and commandments of animal nature, which are founded and established upon materialism. The same world that was polluted in man in the beginning of depravity is present today in nature, still being inherited from heir to heir, to continue its prevalence in the human family as it hath done, if allowed, through the science of stratagem and art.

The Almighty God has deprived this science of corrupt craft in human nature the privilege of exercising power over divine nature as has been done over saints who receive the holy doctrine in the fulness.

All the writings of the apostolic Bible in doctrines, prophecies, revelations, and parables have reference to the soul of mankind; and the different evils which are spoken of refer to characteristics which are situated in the nature of all people. The same truth that will transhumanize one soul will perform the same work with another, providing they all comply with the same conditions in purity and sincerity.

Man's principles, whatever they may be, are found in dark sayings of the Holy Bible, and in order to give the holy Exegesis of the Bible, and make plain the true doctrine of psychology, the revelation of the future life, the resurrection of the dead, the salvation of the wicked, the annihilation of death and hell, the extermination of mortality to transhumanize mankind, I must centre my doctrine and discourse on man's and woman's principles, and prompt my doctrine by Biblical standards, and achieve burning testimonies thereby to substantiate every word written to purge out of mankind the polluted world and burn up the chaff with the unquenchable fire of holy truth. My cause for taking this course to present this revelation unto the people is to cause them to see and understand thoroughly that every word of this revelation is wholly against animal propensities, which means sin and iniquity prevalent in human nature manifesting its power in abominable characteristics and the numerous mortiferous diseases. Every germ of these nefarious principles can and shall eventually, by gradual degrees, be utterly annihilated from human nature to establish divine righteousness in the nature of mankind.

Before going further I shall proclaim the redeeming power of the Lord God, which is stretched forth in his handwriting to raise mankind from the animal world, create and fashion them to attain the transhumanized existence of the righteous man.

Divine truth, word, and spirit combined in man and woman will create holy, happy, and perfect characteristics, which will be manifested in dealing with their fellowmen; this is the transhumanized existence promised to the Israelite races.

Holy truth, word and spirit combined, is the tried stone to cast into the earthly body of humanity according to their desire to create the elements of salvation to annihilate and eject the corrupt principles that secrete themselves in human nature, called the mortal soul, and are so deadly destructive to immortality. Divine truth is the supreme power which shall reign over death and hell unto the perfect salvation by inhaling it into the organs of the mortal soul to annihilate and exterminate the dehumanized powers of the soul, and resurrect the dead elements of divine nature, which slumber beneath the turfy sod of animal propensities.

Divine truth is the power, and will exterminate every corpuscular atom of abomination when annihilated upon its land.

Divine truth, word, and spirit is the power that creates and fashions the soul in substance after the image and likeness of the immortal God.

After the elements of divine truth have ejected every evil and stain of sin from man's flesh and blood, bone and sinew, they breathe into the organs of pure humanity the respiring breath of divine nature, and man becomes a living soul, flesh and blood.

Man's principles, whether righteous or unrighteous, are to be found in the language of the apostolic Bible; and the material world and its many substances, improved patents, and moving creatures, both of trees, herbs, beast, cattle, fish, reptiles, fowl, creeping things, water, land, sun, moon, and stars, are used as metaphors to show the real power and offices of mankind's principles, whether righteous or abominable.

It is declared in the Holy Bible that divine righteousness would subdue the mighty prevailing principles of abomination and lie down in the midst of them in safety.

Divine truth shall soon set everlasting seals upon those mighty prevailing principles of abomination that are loose in dishonorable tangible bodies, and are destroying the lives of their fellowmen.

These nefarious propensities loosened in mankind are caused by the retrogression of the present dispensation coming in collision with all the past ages of antiquities; this is because the people of the late dispensation have reached the profound depth and apex of science and art of materialism.

The modern dispensation is giving birth to both modern and antique abominable glory; therefore the present existing dispensation and laws of animal propensities are running precipitously into the styles, fashions, habits, and customs of the past epochs; and these collisions make a continued upheaval of modern vainglory and antiquities. Men have no further progress in these many worlds which are fast running together, and are causing earthquakes, hurricanes, blizzards, and pestilences of every sort in the human soul; this causes the great conflict between soul and body and animal propensities, overpowering divine nature in mankind. The many dispensations which mankind have passed through were the cleansing and purgative currents, founded and established by the Holy God to raise up seed to be instruments in the hands of his power, according to his purposes and man's glory, to perfect the glory of the terrestial kingdom, by bringing all terrestial things into the state of perfection, in form, art, color, patents, and styles. This shows the supreme and infinite wisdom of the Lord God in using mortal agents to effect his purposes, despite of sin and iniquity, both earthly and heavenly.

After the Holy God has used the mortal man to reach the climax in preparing the glory of the earthly and that of the heavenly, he stretches forth his redeeming handwriting to purge out of man those diluting germs of mortality from mingling with those principles of immortality in man that have been instruments of his glory in a hidden way; by placing his arduous desire in mankind to perform a certain portion of work until the earthly glory was perfected; and now the glory of the earthly is equally compared with that of the heavenly.

Man and woman was the earth that was void of human form when darkness covered the face of the great depth and height of God's mysterious workings and power; while the Holy Spirit moved upon the face of his holy word. It was the distinct thoughts of the three intangible gods in one head, called "Trinity," that uttered the fluent words of life by one holy command at the accomplishment of each purpose that worked reciprocally and harmoniously by the medium of divine nature that mentioned and gave name to everything that was made; which was done only by plain alphabetic sentences. In order to produce light on the future punishment, and happiness of mankind, I shall divulge the hidden secrets of the seven doctrines of the human soul; and these seven doctrines will unfold and reveal to the world the entire hidden realities of the unknown worlds in both abomination, morality, and divinity, and reveal man's forthcoming blessedness, peace, and ecstasy, and also his punishment, misery, and woe before attaining to the perfect world, and state how, where and under what conditions all mankind shall receive the perfect life; which will be done by revealing the office and power of each doctrine, and what light shall be produced, and what work has been and shall be accomplished by each one of the seven doctrines.

This will show the height, width, and length of this doctrine. This will exhibit the universal predominance of its power, and the eternal endurance of divine truth. These doctrines will show and prove that all truth is not divine, neither hath physical truth the power as that of divine: although physical truth may use the same language and method, it will fail to accomplish the same work, and prove itself powerless in divine matters. Physical truth may assume the name of divine, and run in the same system; the work will not be done that it goeth forth to do. The only way to cause both divine and physical things to prosper is to show and prove to the people what is divinity and what is physics; which course of revelation will separate the science of divine psychology from the science of metaphysics. Doctrine of divine psychology is the concentrated focus of the seven doctrines of the human soul, and shows that the soul is the ruler and power of the human corporeal body in every active stage of life. All principles prevailing in human nature discordant with the perfect life are the substances and propensities of different races of low and high bred animals, which, by craft and stealth, crept gradually into human nature and corrupted mankind. These seven doctrines will throw light on the different kinds and grades of nature metaphored as animals, water creatures, reptiles, fowls of the air, and creeping things of the earth, that roam wild upon the green plains, water courses, and wilderness of human nature, and are destructive, degenerative, and impedimental to the development of humanity.

There are no other doctrines in existence nor yet to come that are able to accomplish this work save these seven doctrines. Holy Exegesis is the true interpretation of the apostolic revelations, and prophetic fulfilment of dreams, visions, signs and parables, which interpret the Bible language. The conflicts, hazards, and great tribulations which this doctrine encountered to reach this state and privilege constitute the holy Exegesis of the apostolic Bible. The revelation of the future life is the doctrine to reveal the nigh-approaching life for God's elect, the perfect existence of immortal, tangible, and intangible bodies after death, and also the suffering and punishment of the wicked. The resurrection of the dead is the quickening power of divine truth that illumes the mortal soul and revives both the principles of divine righteousness and the laws and customs of metaphysical science in tangible bodies, so that they all be recompensed according to their works, which fulfils the resurrection of the wicked and righteous. Salvation of the wicked is the doctrine of the conversion of the wicked and moral principles in nature to obedience and submissive to the will, laws, and doctrines of the Divine God, so that human flesh will not have to suffer continually for the crimes of wicked souls. Annihilation of death and hell is the doctrine with sufficient force and power to destroy those despicable creatures in nature that will not consent to the doctrines of divine truth and turn from evil desires and do good. This manner of doctrine sets ablaze the burning flames of hell, while this terrible doctrine destroys the desperadoes in the soul. Extermination of mortality is the doctrine with ample power to remove from the soul the dead and mutilated bodies and débris which fill the soul and body with offensive odor and loathsomeness. All of this work can be accomplished and has already been accomplished by the scientific rod of iron signifying divine truth. Even so shall divine truth redeem falling and suffering humanity. The transhumanized existence of mankind is the full, holy, happy, and perfect state of human entity, which is the doctrine with creative and quickening power; and this doctrine is called the "Lamb's Book of Life," because it is entirely a different doctrine from the others. These six doctrines give light, resurrect, reveal, convert, and destroy, and remove the ruins from the human soul.

Transhumanity is the seventh doctrine of the human soul, the creative power of eternal purity, and the life-giving book wherein all the seven doctrines of the human soul co-ordinate and concentrate and establish the Holy City — the New Jerusalem — in the soul of man. The "Lamb's Book of Life," then, is what I am representing and offering to the inhabitants of the human world, under the title of "Divine Psychology," which is free for all who are governed and will be taught and influenced by the spirit of divine truth, so that its spiritual wisdom, light, and life shall be inherited, realized, enjoyed, and understood in every silent and active stage of life throughout its entire sphere, ever from the minutest to God's infinite power working in the human spiritual world.

And its current of purity shall still continue to flow around the orb of humanity in the finite world in its peaceful and mild efflux; shall carry off all impurity, and wear down its rough substances, and hilly woodlands, and mountainous landscapes; shall refine each layer of its stratum, and improve its architecture; and shall fashion and erect its mansions in the same style and after the same plan which this doctrine makes manifest in wisdom's essential degrees in laconic remarks. It can be understood by the manifest power of God's wisdom in the quickening flesh prepared for this purpose and end, that each time divine wisdom circumvolves the brain lobe of humanity, it makes men and women more and more like God, in love, wisdom, sympathy, adoration, submission, and obedience, by being instrumentally presented to God for the maintenance of his glory and man's present and future progress and happiness. The "Lamb's Book of Life" is the original, and present, and yet to come, divine purity, which is the propelling medium of God's power in man working in its combined elementary constituent forces governed by conscientousness to raise up its members through a gradual spiritual creation to populate the world of transhumanity, which is the real sphere for human entity while they live upon the earth in material bodies. The current of the "Lamb's Book of Life" begins to flow through human nature in its mild and creative efflux as soon as men are fully dead from the world, its established vainglory, and prevailing customs and styles. How can men be dead from the customs of the finite world while they exist in the world? By existing in the finite world materially and living in God's divine kingdom in mental spirituality How can this come to pass? By receiving the integration of divine righteousness, complying with every condition which destroys the mortal hope and earthly craves, its love, glory, and pleasure. And all that flow in *the desire of men with power and glory to use the body will be the perfect image of God's intangible body. The established customs and fashions of the finite world which are not called for to sustain the body and maintain life cannot use a dead body; because a body that is dead from the world cannot receive its glory.

The glory, will, and pleasure of God are the same of all men and women who have been crucified in the lust of the flesh and are dead from the world. Then the things which the dead body receives from the world are not the world, neither of the world, but of God and from God; because all things that men receive who are dead from the world come through God, the cleansing fountain to the once dead but now quickened body in the new life. The truthful understanding and the acknowledgment of God's high and simple workings and power under the full control of fear, submission, and obedience are the rudiments of all human knowledge, peace, prosperity, and happiness.

What is the "Lamb's Book of Life" and what does it consist of? It is that manner of sound and pure doctrinal truth emanating from God through his purified, refined, and consecrated flesh, to give life to his chosen and peculiar people. How shall this manner of life-giving book fluctuate in its life-giving issue among the people in both the personal and great worlds, when it is not written, known, nor manifested in its spiritual government to reach the people who are spread abroad universally in the temporal world?

The Lord God shall keep the life-giving book in that channel near whose shores the people of the Prince of this life live, and have made themselves ready to put on the life of the new era, by heretofore being loyal to the government of the old, leaving the type and shadow of good things behind to constrain others to print by the same. And those who do not dwell close by the waters of life, neither live upon this side of its peaceful shore, the Lord God will draw unto the waters of life by some one of his supernatural powers and supereminent attractions.

The "Lamb's Book of Life" shall emanate in friendship, love, and truth with harmony and acquiescency, both spiritual and material, among his chosen people; which means that every one who adheres to this doctrine with the tenacious substances of sincerity and purity to attain the "Lamb's Book of Life" shall be saved.

How can men relish and have a savoring taste for the "Lamb's Book of Life" when one part of divine psychology is continually warring against them and crucifying the old customs of nature which are fulfilled, that once had a hearty relish for the traditions of the old era.

All people who are godly inclined are composed of two kinds of spiritual substances. One part of the spiritual body will strive to retain the world and its fashions; and this part is envious against God. The divine substance in the spiritual body will rebel against the opponents, to dispose of the polluted world and live wholly for the Divine God, according to his glory, to gain a happier world in nature, the inheritance of the holy kingdom, which shall not pass away, but shall rule over all other kingdoms. Seeing that all this must be done before men can reach this perfect state, it is not good for those to seek the kingdom of God who are inclined to glory in the world, the kingdom of men ; for the suffering will be greater than the flesh can stand ; the combat between soul and body will be too severe to live to put down the world. In this case, the evil deeds or carnal inclinations exceed their righteousness, and they can in no case enter the kingdom of heaven. They are permitted in the kingdoms of men, to live in congruity with their righteousness. This shows that it is not good for integral morals to resist the righteous-like traditions of men to inherit the kingdom of God, when they have no taste for divine righteousness, neither any hope of receiving such precious life. But they are permitted to seek out of the " Lamb's Book of Life " that manner of doctrine to bless them to live successfully according to the righteousness of morals, if they have a taste for the Lamb's doctrine concerning the kingdom of men. This method of doctrine will gradually and eventually convert the moral nature to relish and glory in the doctrines of the higher life.

Men must first be converted, and loyal to the doctrines of men, before they can be faithful and loyal to the laws and doctrines of the Supreme of all beings. The seven scientific doctrines of divine psychology are the consumers of nature in mankind, which have reached the consummate limits in the old era ; so that it may vanish away from those who take pleasure in living apart from the customs of morality, and assumed holy divinity, which are pertaining unto vanity ; such as are not called for to sustain the corporeal and spiritual bodies. All things that mankind desire and seek after, not commanded of God for the sustenance of the bodies, are vanity and vexation to the Divine Spirit.

I am hereby empowered to produce light on the mysterious advent of God's terrible but righteous judgments, and the second coming of his Christ, signifying the second advent of divine truth, word, and spirit combined in the man whom God raised up for this purpose to utter the fulness of his truth in simple, intermediate, and high degrees of language concerning the events which took place to fulfil the prophecies of the modern age and produce the world's greatest marvel. All that have eyes to see and understanding to understand shall see and understand God's mysterious power, which he established to fulfil and repeat Bible history spiritually in brief and pointed ways. There are many denominations, and the Lord God purposed and established them, and each denomination has a small portion of divine truth intermingled with words of theory and false conceptions; but no denomination has the perfect truth in the fulness, because it has not yet been revealed from heaven to all mankind.

The Lord God only can pick out the gold from among the many words of the different denominations, and find all the precions stone, coins, substances, trees, herbs, and harmless creatures, to create another world in the hearts of his elect — which, when accomplished, will be called the kingdom of Christ, the transhumanized existence of mankind corporeally.

The reason why divine truth cannot exist in its fulness with any individual denomination which is established systematically upon the laws of animal nature and materialism is because there are diverse adversities of faiths and opinions concerning the present and future life, and no two agree on everything, neither think alike on the present and future doctrines. And these many diverse adversities of faiths and opinions sever in many parts the full doctrine of divine truth, and establish the different so-called Christian denominations; and this mystery maintains discrimination regarding race prejudice, and is the flaming sword that is placed around the different Christian races and fails to submit and consent to union and brotherly love in honor of one God. These many faiths and opinions have prevailed mightily in human nature and crucified the fulness and realization of Christ, the life and light, since Christ was offered to redeem mankind from the tormenting, woful, and miserable world. If Christ flows not through human nature as the material waters flow through the lands of the terrestial kingdom, to cleanse, salvation, which God has prepared for his people, is a failure; for if they look for a material Christ to appear and give them life, they make themselves antichrists. How readeth the Holy Scriptures on this mystery? "The kingdom of God cometh not with observation: Neither shall they say, Lo here! or, Lo there! for, behold, the kingdom of God is within you."

The kingdoms of the dark and polluted world are also in mankind, at war from time to time with the righteous kingdom. Divine truth substances are sleeping in the nature of all godly people and races, which signifies the holy saints; and these millions and millions of saints are waiting and watching for the divine truth to be given unto them. And the compounding of the pure substances will adhere and agree, and produce a change in the soul called the unquenchable fire of divine truth, and burn up the assumed truth and error deinating the Devil's kingdom, and rescue suffering humanity from the cruel clutches and ravenous appetites of animalism, which is mixed in human nature, and produces another change, which creates serpents, reptiles, ravenous beasts, surreptitious fowl, stinging and biting insects, and blood-thirsty water creatures, poisonous substances, cold blasts, hurricanes, and blizzards, and earthquakes and pestilences of every sort in human nature.

The Lord God established the divine nature in the soul of the revelator of these truths and doctrines, which contains all the gold and precious coins and harmless creatures and substances of every sort from among the many Christian denominations, to reveal the Son of Righteousness unto the world, to redeem his people. In order to accomplish the redemption of the saints, and fulfil the Scriptures of the modern age, the Lord God prepared a man who is assigned to this revelation, the express figure of the sins and abominations of the past and present ages by nature, to reveal the sins and iniquities prevalent in the universal masses of humanity; and in order to bring this about the two kingdoms embodied in these two men's souls were compelled to unite in false friendship, love, and truth.

To make the work a perfect success the Lord God brought the two men together in reciprocal love and mutual agreement, unaware of what would befall them, and this league of friendship established a mute covenant between these two men; and one embodied the righteous dispensations and the other embodied the wickedness which was contained in the past and present dispensations, which united with the present existing dispensation to prefigure both sin and divine righteousness. This means that the wicked and righteous kingdoms stipulated, by a false league of friendship, to work for the same object and end, and looked upon each other as very near the same likeness in nature and propensities; still both were ignorant of what the Almighty God was going to work out of their uniting, but the righteous king knew that the Almighty God would use them to fulfil his pleasure in some way.

When the two kings united in the mute covenant, all plans and means had been prepared to fulfil God's pleasure in the dreadful and terrible war between these kingdoms; so that the righteous kingdom would stand up and rebel in its supreme power, and smite the kingdoms of darkness, misery, and woe, which focalized and concentrated in the wicked figure in its adamantine, substantial, excellent, and brilliant power. When divine truth through judgments smote the corrupt, woful, tormenting, and miserable embodiment of the wicked king, and cast his name out of the holy kingdom, then divine truth had overpowered the entire world of sin and iniquity, which was connected to the holy city and sanctuary, and mingled with it and diluted its strength and power; and now the truth has eclipsed and overpowered the great error, and will gain entrance into the hearts of God's elect people by gradual degrees, just as the past dispensations were established in the people of this age.

The great God will not allow any one else to suffer as the man who embodied the wicked kingdom, neither as the rest of the members who are connected with this doctrine, if the forthcoming members present themselves to God to use forever to his glory, and receive and consent to divine truth, as the first members did and desired to do. The many degrees and different kinds of sin were seated in their nature, so that the revelator would consume and pluck them up and gain practical knowledge of the many different kinds of abomination that exercise the prevailing power over humanity, committing the many desperate deeds with a formality of godliness; which forces and compels the people to serve false gods, who are crafting and destroying human lives.

The dreadful and terrible judgments of the Lord God were pronounced on sin and iniquity, which were in the people connected with this doctrine, to fulfil the Biblical and late prophecies on the second coming of God's Christ to earthy bodies, and to get the entire samples of sin and iniquity, to reveal the man of sin to the world, to rescue humanity from that bituminous lake which substances of science created and erected, — the spiritual and modern Sodom and Egypt. The Almighty God was full of mercy, pity, and sympathy for the suffering flesh which was manifested in the revelator while he passed through the time, fulfilling the Bible and exploring the earthly bodies to search out the fine arts and crafty works of sin.

The Son of Righteousness and the Son of Perdition will both be revealed at the same time, which will be done by revealing the great trials this doctrine has encountered, and the holy transhumanized characteristics of the Divine God, which he instilled firmly and substantially in the soul of the revelator, to defend the second advent of truth which God had clothed him in; also, the characteristics of sin and iniquity, which united in a concrete mass in the man whom God raised up and presented to the revelator to represent the depth, height, width, length, strength, and power of sin and iniquity in simple, intermediate, and the predominating wisdom of abominable science, whose concrete spiritual embodiment is called the "Devil's kingdom," or the man of sin, the "Son of Perdition."

The judgments will be found in the ancient and modern prophecies, which will be uttered in the late tongue, in language such as can be understood by all who desire to understand. The impartial judgments of the Lord God purged the divine truth of Christ's first coming to earth, and purified it so that it can unite with the second advent of Christ, which establishes the doctrines of divine truth to consume all sin and iniquity that reign in human nature, and create therein a new life.

How can divine truth accomplish this work without the use of any material thing?

It is accomplished by the foregoing conditions and commandments of life, which are the fertilizing substances to create purity in human nature, and the river of life to flow through the soul, cleanse the earth, and prepare it for the implanting of the seeds of divine truth and to produce growth. The first step in pressing forward to inherit the perfect life in the material body is to be strict in obeying the voice of the Divine God, who whispers softly and peacefully in the hearts of all godly people in plain and distinct thoughts, which teach his people what he will have them to do that he may be glorified in them. When the Divine God breathes his pure thoughts, will, and way into the hearts of the godly, burdens, griefs, and condemnation are thereby ejected and flee away, if the soul is conformed to the will of God and accepts his teachings and ordinations. The cares, griefs, and burdens which appear in the soul are created through rejecting God's pure thoughts and reasons in teaching the straight and only way to life.

God teaches, commands, and directs his people through the currents of his never-ceasing thoughts and reasons, which he infuses in the mind. Nature, which is the ruler and lawgiver of the material body, must receive God's teachings and agree with his pure thoughts and simple reasoning, before divine truth can give peace and rest to the body. The cares, griefs, and burdens of the soul are manifested on the external part of the body physiognomically; the diseases of the soul, whether curable or incurable, are the curable or incurable diseases of the material body. If the soul is depraved the body is punished and suffers for the crimes of the soul with many kinds of troubles and afflictions, both mental and physical. The desires of the heart are the creative germs and blastema from which cometh both good and evil, which is the controlling power of the many thoughts that flow through the organs of humanity from the nature, whether good or evil.

Then there are two mighty powers working in the human soul for excellency and competition; they are the Son of Righteousness and the Son of Perdition. If human nature is inclined to do godly deeds when the Son of Righteousness whispers his thoughts and desires within the soul, they will have a joyful, peaceful, and flaming desire to heed him and obey his teachings; but if the nature is depraved, the thoughts will flow on depraved things, and the desires of the heart will be to do evil deeds, which shows that the thoughts and desires of mankind proceed from their nature. The heart is already condemned that receives the teachings of the man of sin and rejects the righteous man. Why? Because ye are the temples of the Holy Ghost, and God hast commanded you to be not the servants of sin. The man of sin is already condemned in the godly, because he is trespassing on the grounds of the righteous man. If the godly people hear and hearken unto the voice of God, which speaketh in their thoughts and desires, as they hearkened unto sin, when they were the servants of sin, they will abide in perfect peace and health, and walk in newness of life daily; and whatsoever they consign their hands and hearts to will prosper beyond that of the ungodly. When you were the servants of sin you took no thought of the things sin would have you to do, but lusted after the things of the flesh, which was the glory, honor, and pleasure of sin: and the desire worked continually to please the flesh in the lust thereof.

Sin is the cause of every ailment of both soul and body, originated and inherited from the following evils, which are the abominable principles seated in the nature of all godly inclined people, and these evils are performing their work involuntarily; and these evils number seven, which are the seven chief constituents of sin, called

"Devil" and "Satan," and where the fulness of these seven devils are united in one person, it is called "the dragon." Then there are ten horns upon the head of this mighty, monstrous dragon, called abominable principles, which signify power. The names of the seven united devils which control human nature, called "the dragon," are as follows : — deception, enmity, contemptibleness, disobedience, disbelief, jealousy, and lustfulness. The ten horns upon the dragon's head are, namely, vainglorious pride, unthankfulness, self-esteem, beauty, color, self-will, filthiness, laziness, robbery, and murder. The vast world and the magnificent temples of this venomous serpent are brilliantly erected with gold and silver metaphysical education, male's and female's ravenous desire one for the other, partiality for blood-kin, and excessive and undue love and respect for family circle.

This is the great monstrous beast, the kingdoms of the world, called "mortality," that is so mightily opposed to the full doctrines of divine truth. This monster is the lawgiver, cunning artificer, and inventor of the customs and styles, and is the leading and controlling spirit of this advanced age. There is no real pleasure nor satisfaction to be given to those persons who embody this monster in the fulness ; they are craving after illegitimate pleasures, and things which they cannot obtain, because this lustful monster controls the nature and desires and sends them where he pleases, and doeth according to his own will, and rules humanity with great dominion, and prevails clandestinely. These abominable principles keep human nature, which should be free from animal mixtures, polluted ; and this monster shall be cast out of God's people far and near, to end the misery and woe of the polluted world. There can be no desire in mankind to refuse the evil and accept divine righteousness as long as this great deceiver, called "Devil" and "Satan," slumbers in human nature, despises and rejects the Ransomer, the Light and Life, the eternal progression of mankind. God hath created and established that manner of doctrine that will force this degenerator out of human nature and give in return love, peace, rest, joy, and comfort.

None of the elements of the holy spiritual kingdom can reign in peace and love in human nature as long as the monstrous beast, the kingdom of the world, controls the flesh and forces it to yield to his desire, and partake of the food and delicacies to nourish and fill the bowels of this ravenous beast. The desire of the heart must be against this monster before he will perish from the flesh. God's manifest truth teaches his people to deceive no one, to abuse no one, to speak evil of no one, to accuse no one falsely, to take advantage of no one if you have an opportunity, to hate no one, and if any one should by chance take advantage of you, and you have an opportunity to retaliate, you shall return good for evil; this is the victorious triumph of the saints. The fountain of life which God hath bestowed upon his saints is to love the Lord thy God with all thy heart, mind, soul, and strength. How can this be done? By hearkening unto his commandments, obeying his loving voice, receiving his teachings, and walking in the way he hath commanded, sacrificing all other things to do his biddings, knowing within yourself that God is over all, above all, and rules all substances and creatures.

The second commandment completes the fulness of life which shall rule material bodies in the dispensation of this doctrine and the establishment of this age; which teaches to love your fellowman as yourself, do unto others as you would have them do unto you. The foundation of life is to first obey God in all things; and if you deny yourself to please God, you shall deny your fellowman to do the same.

These are the two combined principles of the perfect life to be wrought in the material bodies of God's people, and to the souls of those who are worthy of drink from this clear and pure stream no evil of any sort can possibly find access; but if this current of life is rejected there is no place found in the person for divine righteousness. A man can be morally righteous, apparently, and yet be desperately opposed to divine righteousness. The rigid and brutal laws of animal nature force and compel a man respectively to be loyal to the established laws of morality, apparently, when the real part of man is bitterly opposed to a united and civil government. You are permitted to turn away from an enemy whom you are convinced that you can never have any fellowship with, and yet entertain no malice against him; because one is a vessel to honor, and the other a vessel to dishonor the Divine God.

There are people who have always lived subject and loyal to the laws and doctrines of morality, and yet who have no taste for the divine laws and doctrines, neither do they desire to learn anything concerning God's mysterious works. Why is this allowed to be so? Because the moral God formed and fashioned them with moral substance to learn of him and live wholly for him. The person of this description is organized for the secular world, and cannot serve the Divine God; but God can use him to carry out his purposes to their unconsciousness, but consisting with their inclination and motives. There are other mortals who profess to love God merely to connect themselves with the formality of religious societies, to be respected and prosper materially among a certain class whom they feel will give them advantage in coming into possession of the wealth of the world; when the thought to know whether they are pleasing God in the different walks of life never enters their minds. Their whole object is to accumulate wealth for themselves, kin and kind, and rob and ruin their fellowman in the shrewdest and most desperate way. You cannot classify a moral man with a divine man, although their outward actions almost agree in civility and system; their spirits, tendencies, and motives cannot mingle, because the moral man is the antidivine spirit, and the divine man is the divine spirit accepting God in his fulness, which means both physical and divine giving to each one his due honor and respect.

To reveal the hidden realities of the righteous man's peace and rest and eternal happiness, and the wicked man's everlasting punishment, misery, and woe, I must find, locate, and describe the indwelling man called "the soul" that makes divine beings higher than the animal race.

The formal and stylish physique surrounding the intangible body of human beings is called "land" and "earth" in Scripture language. The part that makes this stylish physique righteous is divine nature, which is the soul, the part that constitutes manhood. Divine nature consists of eight principal powers, which are, to think, speak, see, hear, taste, smell, feel, and active motion. These are the members of the human soul, the part called "man," inhabiting the earthly and divine bodies. Divine nature controls these members in the people of God, and these members govern the members of the material body. The material body has no power of itself, unless it is given by these eight members, and these eight spiritual members have no power over the material, unless it be given by nature; and divine nature has no power of itself, unless it be quickened by the divine spirit, which completes the soul of mankind. Animal nature hath amalgamated with divine nature, which enabled animal nature to reach the climax in human skill, in art, system, style, and custom, under false names and fictions.

The only way to distinguish divine beings from the developed, subtle, and human statured animals is to reveal the hidden secrets of divine nature, and the hidden secrets of animal nature working in the subtle beast, which imitates the divine spirit and causes it to be blasphemed. Transhumanized beings are philanthropical in generosity, love, mercy, truth, and justice, willing to sacrifice their lives for the general good and welfare of their fellowmen, as far as the Lord gives means to help them; and not only this, but to atone and plead with the Almighty God to look upon the wretched and doomed state of men who are groping about in the dark and execrated worlds, seeking for light, understanding, and redemption where there is none to be obtained. Transhumanity is the light and life, beholding the exceeding darkness and the folly of men; and they that are overwhelmed with darkness are unable to see their ignorance and condition.

Divine nature is the substance and power that compels men to lay down their own lives for the welfare of their fellowmen universal, having no respect of persons, willing to suffer any and every thing to redeem them to life; not only in this day but forever.

This is the difference between divine beings and the beast that has developed up to human stature and skill, in science and art. The human statured beasts are striving to make great and honorable themselves, kin and kind. They are slaughtering, cheating, and robbing their fellowman, so that the inheritance of wealth, honor, and fame shall continue among their kin and kind; while others are left in poverty by being secretly robbed by the wise and honorable of the earth.

All human beings having godly inclinations with pure motives and good intentions are connected in talent, whether their work and faith be materially connected or not, whether physical or divine. The many gifts of talents bestowed upon men honorably are issuing from the same vast body, which is the body of Christ or his members, who is preparing the glory of the earthly and the heavenly, which has attained to the vertical point of the perfect day, to unite both earth and heaven, and produce the divine compound substance which is the creation of mankind in the image and likeness of the Lord God. This causes divine and physical things to unite in brotherly love in honor of one God, which will be the Lord God, dwelling among men in corporeal bodies.

The wicked are also united in talent, skill, art, and science in all professions, by the quickening spirit and power of animal nature which flows from the animal world, the vast body, to animate the sub-members that make up the great, monstrous, king leviathan, and the transcendent lights of Lucifer. There are millions and millions of spirits moving over the surface of humanity, but they all originated from the divine and animal natures.

There are only two different kinds of spirits and natures which shall be maintained and perpetuated, and they are the animal and divine; all others shall be utterly consumed from the land. These two eternal spirits are perfect and undefiled in their proper spheres, but God hath determined and declared that they shall cease to amalgamate, and the creation of sin, vice, and crime will have an end.

It is immaterial and non-injurious to the perfect life whether you dance, sing, play on instruments, play games, practise gymnastics, or any sport for pleasure and pastime, if all you do is to glorify God, and to benefit yourselves and fellowmen. God hath appeared to earth to destroy the formality of godliness, and the straining demons and heresies, from his people, so that they may serve him in love, words, deeds, acts, spirit, and in truth, daily, in their dealings with their fellowmen.

The established formality and customs of godliness have grown wax-cold and vanished away to establish the new life. The old customs and formalities of godliness among the religious, socialistic, and Christian-like worships were established in mankind to convert them to honorable systems, styles, customs, and civil-like governments, which have created and fashioned a number to put on the new life, leaving the shadow behind; which is only a faint thought and representation of the real spiritual and material existence of the godly.

The Lord God herein reveals the swelling current, and the involuntary motion, and the propelling power of the eternal doctrines of divine truth, which shall flow through the land of transhumanized bodies -- transferable from one temple to another -- when the work of the Lord God is finished in each temple on earth in the dispensation of this doctrine. The current of life which shall flow from land to land in the promulgation and demonstration of the doctrine revealed in this chapter from the burning mount shall, through gradual degrees, convert mankind's principles to be subject to the perfect life, in honor of the immortal God.

The continual teachings of the doctrines of divine truth, and the gradual changes in the soil of divine nature, the burning and consuming flames of this doctrine, shall destroy the strong and corrupt doctrines of materialism, which advance the true doctrines, and are also substitutes of the spiritual doctrines. These gradual changes shall be produced through immortal atmospheric actions, which shall be breathed from the souls of transhumanized bodies; which shall redintegrate the elect people of God, and bring them, mentally, into the holy spiritual church, to worship the Divine God, one eternal day.

The doctines of divine truth* which shall be taught unto the people upon the earth shall be taught through words, deeds, works, and dealings among men, showing the reality of the perfect life. This manner of doctrine shall be written on the inward parts of transhumanized bodies in the dispensation and establishment of this age. The perpetuity of these doctrines shall be wholly against the four wicked kingdoms which are rooted in human nature; and these doctrines shall be destructive, and desolating, and a mortiferous curse unto the four wicked kingdoms which contain all the abominations and filthiness of sin, which are deeply rooted in the flesh and blood, bone and sinew, of this generation and those yet to come forth out of their loins. These four wicked kingdoms are the four chief horns of mortality, which signify the finite power of government established in this vainglorious generation. The magnificence and excellence of these four wicked kingdoms force their captive agents to exalt them above the holy kingdom; which makes it a shame to even make mention of the holy kingdom in the presence of these four wicked kingdoms. The glory, honor, and reverence which are above all things highly due unto the immortal God are scorned and condemned by the magnificence and gorgeous display, in method, beauty, and styles, which are ornamentally and gloriously beheld in the scenes of the four wicked kingdoms.

The four wicked kingdoms are as follows, and successive as in power, might, and glory to the mortal man, and the animal life which keeps mankind mortal. Educational science is the transcendent kingdom of mortality, and the head of the mortal image; which is the governing wisdom of the world, and the most magnificent and excellent glory of men. This kingdom produces light for the four kingdoms of the world, which by the eclipse of the divine doctrines are now called "darkness." The power of wisdom's lights is situated in the brains of this generation, and continuated through natural endowance from heir to heir, and generation to generation, through inheritance; and this power of science makes the darkness light, and the true light darkness. And for this cause the brain lobe of man in his mortal state is the formal globe of the mortal world, and the pit of hell, which is the Devil's kingdom, and the microcosm of abomination and woful corruption.

If man is not educated according to the systems, laws, customs, and doctrines of the world, he is ignored and disdained by the leaders and rulers of this day in both divine and physical societies; and this makes the science of education abominable, when it is given to man to perfect his material and spiritual existence, if governed and used properly.

Man and woman combined is the second kingdom of the world; which is the life of the Lucifer worlds, and the leading spirit of the times, and the source of power that rules the mortal orbs so that there is no power in wisdom's mighty lights unless the woman is glorified and united with man in his work. If the woman is glorified over the mighty, modern, and finite wisdom of man, she gives him the animating spirit and the power of intellectuality to accomplish his work by the igniting of the light-fuel, which is wisdom.

Man is devoid of wisdom, understanding, and sound discretion if he does not act and perform his work to woman's glory, when they are associated together. As soon as woman condemns and becomes disinterested in man's work, when they two are associated together matrimonially, she thereby withdraws her spirit from him, and his brain becomes cloudy and dull and disintellectual in its thinking facilities, so that his brain lobe is soon in dense obscurity, and idiosyncrasy sets in, and the man can do no work of any worth.

As soon as man finds that his ways are completely hedged up and darkened, and there is no power in him to accomplish his work, without the glory and life of the woman, he repents and returns to her glory and pleasure. In man's mortal state, he is compelled to subdue to the woman's glory and pleasure in her wicked kingdom, if her pleasure and choice are abominable and the man equipped with integrity, so that he may be enabled by her to do some good thing for the welfare of others who are trusting to him for help and support; because those in the service of the man are trusting him to be recompensed for their labor when it is done. And if man dishonors woman when they are united, she has no care nor pity for any one when her kingdom is contemned by man.

Such is abomination and shall not exist in the members of this dispensation. Man shall obey God by putting on his perfect life, and shall live God's life with ease just as men are prone to sin and have no other life to live in the existing dispensation. Woman shall be fully conformed to man's will, glory, and pleasure, and she shall not usurp power over man. Then the feminine woe and the masculine griefs and burdens will have an end; then also there shall be no more woe-men, nor burden-men, but the feminine shall be called "glory-men" and the masculine, "righteous men."

Money, gold and silver, is the third kingdom of the world; and the excess of love burns for it with incessant flames of aspiration in the lust of all nations, people, kindred, kings, and tongues who live upon the earth. All nations come into possession of gold and silver in abundance by the great sacrifices which they make of all other things, so that they may glorify their souls in its luxuries. And those who do not sacrifice all things unto the gods of gold and silver — the king reigning over this kingdom declares that they shall not continue in friendship, love, and truth in union with the subordinate members, if they do not honor and give glory to the sovereign.

This money sovereign that rules human nature compels the subordinate officers to attribute all glory, honor, and reverence unto him, and kills those, with need, reproaches, and disgrace, who do not worship him. And when he finds that a member, or members, has deserted his kingdom to seek a higher life, to rest from his slavish curse, he then becomes wroth, and spews from his mouth floods of prophecies against the members who have turned against their beloved king; so that they may be swallowed up and carried away by his turbulent and loathsome waters. And when the sovereign finds that he cannot convince them of their error through prophecy, he then prepares the strongest and most dexterous members and officers of his kingdom, and pursues them until they are overtaken; then the whole kingdom gathers together with implements of war, determined to bring them under their subjection materially, or to slay them materially and revengfully with want. The power of this kingdom worketh mentally in those who have a ravenous desire for gold and silver; and this false prophet cannot exercise power over those who use money properly, in receiving it with thanks and disposing of it the same way; for if one is glorified in receiving money he should be the same in exchanging it for what he needs.

Blood-kin and family circle is the fourth kingdom of the world, and the basis of the four wicked kingdoms which are the strength of the cycle of hell, the creator and perpetuator of man's abominable existence; which holds in the glory of its kingdom a corrupt doctrine. This teaches, with much power and authority, that if mankind wants to please God and be blessed while they live upon the earth, and be recompensed for good when they are taken by death to life, they must deny all others for their own blood-kin; and all glory, honor, respect, and benevolence are wholly due to them. The doctrine of this kingdom is a fatal curse and abhorrence to all flesh. The combined focus of these four wicked kingdoms is the burning altar and the supreme mortal god whom all nations burn incense unto, and offer up sacrifices to, to maintain life to live upon the earth. This is the dense blackness of hell in the millennium members that are so mightily opposed to the genuine doctrines; because the pure doctrines are destructive to these four polluted kingdoms in men's and women's natures — which is the existing dispensation.

The unfolding of these mysteries shows this doctrine's mission to mankind; it shows that there is a holy, happy, and perfect dispensation to be wrought and established in the people of God, as soon, and as fast as the present dispensation is consumed from human nature. All the prophecies that the Lord God uttered through the revelator during the troublous times of the saints was to bring swift judgments upon these four wicked kingdoms.

These are the kingdoms that were given to God's Christ, embodied in the man whom God raised up to prefigure and represent sin in the fulness; which brought hasty desolation upon the divine kingdom, and then stood up in the figure in its supreme power and made war with the holy kingdom, after partly mingling with it; so that the words of God might be fulfilled. And the judgments of the Lord God were poured out without mixtures upon the wicked sovereign, princes, and all members of the wicked kingdoms, which are as the sands by the seashore, innumerable.

This shows that the approaching judgments of the Lord God shall not disgrace, nor set a stigma of scorn upon, those who were subjects of sin in no material way, for God determined it to perfect the saving power of his chosen people; and for this cause men shall not look with an eye of scorn upon the flesh that bore the manifest powers of sin during God's terrible judgments, knowing that for this purpose they were raised up.

The Lord God issues the laws, doctrines, and governments herein revealed, to present divine truth freely and publicly unto the notoriety, to fortify the beloved city of Jerusalem, to prevent anything abominable from finding entrance upon its blissful shores to again pollute the holy city and sanctuary as has been done heretofore. The truth drifted in an obscured state during the time of the prophecies, to keep secret the fulfilments of the jeopardy which the truth had to encounter before it could be offered to the public; which hazardous fulfilments ended the 18th of August, 1891.

During the time of these secret and perilous fulfilments, no person not belonging to the holy family was allowed to visit the divine sanctuary freely and willingly. This was done to dry up the current of infamous rumors which were previously carried out from the sanctuary by those who visited it for this purpose. When those spies and busybodies were deprived of this privilege, the reproaches were assuaged from over the truth. This was the sole cause for bringing the sanctuary into a family-like system. And those who were holy enough to become members of the family, to work and supply the material needs of the sanctuary, and take a part in the fulfilments of prophecies and repetition of Bible history, were obliged to be cut loose, and plucked out from the antichrist world even as the Divine Christ was concealed from the world.

The truth was the modern ark or sanctuary which gathered the small flock within the close and confined limits of its walls, with samples of all sins and righteousness that were created to honor and dishonor the Lord God, to carry a sample of every sort over to the new world with the holiest of holiest. And now divine truth has sailed around the old world, and landed in the harbor of the new. The former stipulations, governments, commandments, laws, and doctrines are nullified. And behold, the Lord God establishes a new covenant, governments, commandments, laws, and doctrines to show forth his saving power and infinite handiwork, which shall be marvelled at, to bring mankind into the free, holy, and eternal world.

The stipulations, governments, commandments, laws, and doctrines heretofore executed were to convey the truth and its private members through the past epochs of the world in a spiritual journey, both in righteousness and unrighteousness, to attain to the new but original spiritual world. After reaching the new world, the former system, stipulations, governments, commandments, laws, doctrines, customs, and worships are entirely new; and the old are of no effect, and nefarious to eternity, if allowed to exist in the free, holy, happy, and eternal world. And for this cause the Lord God shall establish his everlasting covenant, commandments, laws, doctrines, customs, and worships of the holy seed; and place the truth in its sempiternal system, and show unto the people his goodness and mercy, and the reality of the eternal truth.

The holy city and sanctuary shall no longer be left to the mercy and will of the merciless judgments, laws and doctrines of other people, which were forced by man's and woman's rigid authority. But it shall be established and governed by the holy name and title which the mouth of the Lord God named and blessed forever; none other power than the agents of truth and judgment shall preside over the land.

The commandments, stipulations, governments, laws, doctrines, habits, and manners of worship that shall hereafter go forth from the mouth of the new name and title shall be the supreme government that shall rule in righteousness. And the prevailing powers of opponents who did not heretofore fully consent to the governments of the new name and title, the Lord God shall speedily cast out, and blot their names out of the "Lamb's Book of Life." No bonds of personal claim, straining and stringent governments, shall longer exist and prosper within the limits of the fortified walls of truth and judgment.

The sanctuary shall not compel nor persuade any person or persons who are unwilling to give up the world, to live in freedom and holiness unto the Lord God, unless they so desire. Those who are determinedly sincere in seeking for the attainance of the perfect life shall have a free and full access thereto. Those who are striving to obtain that of which they are not in need shall not be able to overcome, but they shall go the journey as far as the sincerity in them propels; no further can they go. This class are called "lustful strainers," walking after their own ungodly lust, ever learning and never come to any knowledge of the truth; striving and straining to do what they see others do.

The sanctuary shall move in this system, within the limits of the fortified walls of freedom, blessedness, felicity, and peace. The public sanctum of the sanctuary shall be under the control and protection of both divine and physical laws, orderly. He shall allow no congregation nor settled mass of people to enter upon his premises in a fictitiously honorable way, and subdue themselves to the will of the truth, with the object of deceiving and doing injury to the truth, by creating infamy to excite the nations and place them in vehement commotion.

He will accept no persons to care for their physical diseases specially. The sanctuary will receive all persons who are honorable, and come unto him for divine needs, being troubled and afflicted with diseases of the soul originating from mental disorders, through rebelling against divine truth.

He will allow no person to make long and frequent visits leisurely at the sanctum, with the purpose of hearing the mysteries of truth explained to carry out among the antichrists, to be blasphemed. Each one shall hear and receive for himself, and not to present to others; if they do the like they will receive their power and blessing, and turn upon them, and while they are weak devour them.

All who devote themselves to the perfect life must be persons of honorable characteristics, and superfine qualities, in every degree of life. They must be persons who are heartily obedient to both divine and physical laws, to honorable parents, husbands, and wives. No persons nor person of depraved habits shall be allowed to make frequent visits to the sanctuary in a friendly way. No persons who are seeking wordly pleasure shall be taught the doctrine of the new covenant. There must be a total dissolution of friendship with wordly pleasures, and gorgeous display in life, before they can come nigh unto the sanctuary to be proselytized into the doctrines of eternity. All persons visiting the sanctuary to obtain the truth to sustain them in living an honorable life shall, before receiving benefits, make known to the sanctuary their motive, determination, aim, and desire as pertaining to the higher life, and their present existing circumstances, in full, in every walk of life. They shall state their occupation, with name, whether married or single, whether they have friends or relatives under their care. After they have complied with these rules, they must return to their former homes until the psychologist makes atonements on their cases, according to the testimony which he receives from the persons who desire and are seeking deliverance from the strong bands of sin, through the power of divine truth.

And if errors or false statements are made by the persons who are seeking deliverance, and their motive is not holy in taking such step, their names shall be rejected and renounced until the errors are swerved out, and their motive reaches the holy state of the soul; after which the atonements shall have effect on the first work required. But in cases of errors in consultations, exquisite care will be taken to inquire into each case which has been left on record, to make atonements for deliverance from any burden that conflicts with their progress in living an honorable live; whether married or single, such will be annihilated if fully placed in the hands of the psychologist.

The sanctuary shall advise no person not to marry customarily who wishes to live that life, nor those compelled to marry. But he shall give all who do not wish to marry and serve the flesh, the fulness of divine truth to live in newness of life; these he shall give the straight and direct system to walk in to attain the holy state. He will discipline them to live wholly for the glory of the Divine God in the word, spirit, and truth. The sanctuary shall accept no person's name, to make atonements for, who does not wish to live an honorable, godly life, neither married nor single. Those who are not willing to live in one or the other of these two states in life, in an honorable way, are reprobates, giving themselves over to fornication and uncleanness, having their consciences severed from the truth with red-hot irons of lust, forbidding to marry at all, and leading about silly women and men. If divine truth should be given to such people, their natures would become more ravenous for earthly glory, and they would consume the truth wastefully upon the lust of their flesh, and return to receive more to do the same. If they are brutal, one toward the other, they will be the same toward the truth; and use it blasphemously to satisfy their ravenous lust and never attain a higher degree in life. God, the Lamb, reveals the holy and endless law in plain and simple remarks, establishing perfect freedom, love, and union for male and female in the establishment of this age.

Those who are created, fashioned, and shapened after the holy circumcised of the eternal age, and desire a feminine or masculine companion to make home a secret comfort, shall not take to themselves companions, neither masculine nor feminine, from among the antichristian races. Their affections, desires, and confidence shall be toward those who have entered the circumcised life, governed by the eternal doctrines of divine truth.

Those who are scholars, under the disciplinarian of the holy truth, cannot attain to the perfect state of godliness if they seek companions outside of the perfect life that they are putting on; if they do this, they will be taking off the new man and putting on the old man of sin, which will realize the words of the Lord, aforetime: "For if after they have escaped the pollutions of the world through the knowledge of the Lord and Saviour, Jesus Christ, they are again entangled therein, and overcome, the latter end is worse with them than the beginning." "For it had been better for them not to have known the way of righteousness than, after they have know it, to turn from the holy commandments delivered unto them." "But it is happened unto them according to the true proverb, The dog is turned to his own vomit again, and the sow that was washed to wallowing in the mire."

To fortify and shield those who are sojourning in the higher life, the words of the following commandments shall forever be maintained and perpetuated in the hearts of the righteous seed :—

"And God spake all these words, saying, I am the Lord thy God, which have brought thee out of the land of Egypt, out of the house of bondage.

"Thou shalt have no other gods before me.

"Thou shalt not make unto thee any graven image, or any likeness of anything that is in heaven above, or that is in the earth beneath, or that is in the waters under the earth. Thou shalt not bow down thyself to them, nor serve them : for I, the Lord thy God, am a jealous God, visiting the iniquity of the fathers upon the children unto the third and fourth generation of them that hate me ; and shewing mercy unto thousands of them that love me and keep my commandments.

"Thou shalt not take the name of the Lord thy God in vain; for the Lord will not hold him guiltless that taketh his name in vain.

"Remember the Sabbath day, to keep it holy. Six days shalt thou labour, and do all thy work : but the seventh day is the Sabbath of the Lord thy God : in it thou shalt not do any work, thou, nor thy son, nor thy daughter, thy man servant, nor thy maid servant, nor thy cattle, nor thy stranger that is within thy gates : for in six days the Lord made heaven and earth, the sea, and all that in them is, and rested the seventh day : wherefore the Lord blessed the Sabbath day, and hallowed it.

" Honor thy father and thy mother: that thy days may be long upon the land which the Lord thy God giveth thee.

"Thou shalt not kill.

"Thou shalt not commit adultery.

"Thou shalt not steal.

"Thou shalt not bear false witness against thy neighbour.

"Thou shalt not covet thy neighbour's house, thou shalt not covet thy neighbor's wife, nor his man servant, nor his maid servant, nor his ox, nor his ass, nor anything that is thy neighbour's."

Those that turn back from the Lord, and serve strange gods, shall not be called holy, nor of the circumcised. The curse written in the Mosaic law be upon those who fail to hearken unto all the words of this law and commandments, — with worse things to follow.

When any two, male and female, become equally mated, and devoted to each other, when both have put on the new man in the fulness of the perfect life, it shall be called holy and perfect for them to become united male and female under the licuidated law of matrimony which shall be established and ebullitionized from the holy law of this dispensation. The holy seed shall not be wedded by the laws and customs of the antichristians, when the holy and perfect dispensation becomes the government of the people. They shall be wedded by the matrimonial law of word, spirit, and truth combined, whose law is perfect freedom; not compelling them to remain united longer than it shall be agreeable to both parties, when one wishes to remain and the other wishes to depart.

The party wishing to depart shall state his cause and object for desiring such departure; and if he has not a just cause, and a holy object in view for dissolution of matrimony with his companion, and the Lord of this person cannot establish peace between them in anywise, and the alienated person still contends for separation, unconditional, such person shall be allowed to desert the beloved saint, who will also consent to the same freely and willingly. But the person who demands such freedom shall not any more be numbered with the holy seed, while governed by such characteristics; neither shall he be united again to any one of the holy seed.

And if any one of the holy seed has mated with such person, and influenced him to desert his legal companion with the object of uniting with him in secret comfort, such antisaint, who has influenced such person, and caused his love and affections to be alienated, shall be bereaved of the Israelite's blessings, glory, love, and privileges. And if any one of the holy people becomes united in twain with any of the saints who desert their companions, illegitimately to the liquidated method of the holy dissolution of matrimony, that one shall take upon himself the penalty curse equal to that of the lawless deserter. There is no law against the secret pleasure which might exist between male and female when agreeable to both parties. And if any two should disagree concerning the style of how they shall live, when they have become united in friendship, love, and truth, the opposing party, who cannot contain, shall be hastily excluded from the house of such saint; so that the flesh of the saint be not abused; neither shall the holy spirit be placed under the yoke of bondage to take on the animal spirit and curse. The excluded saint shall be allowed to become united with some saint whose inclinations are equally the same.

But if such person is overtaken in trying to deceive the saint, to become united to him with the object of deceiving the saint, to live to his desire after they have become lawfully united, he shall be brought before the judgment council of the Lord God, and renounced, under the penalty curse, to suffer until the delusive power of stealth and stratagem is destroyed. Such persons shall be called the captives of leviathan unicorn power, which shall be the apex of disgrace upon him or her who doeth the like. Such power shall reign over the subjects of this inclination until they repent and utterly reject this unlawful pleasure, and turn unto the Lord God. And when this is done by the captive of this mighty evil, the unicorn shall be cast into torment, which is the punishment for the ungodly characteristics of mankind.

This is the holy and eternal law of union between male and female in the dispensation of this endless truth and doctrine. And furthermore, to make the existence of the righteous seed abound with joy and freedom in every degree of life, I will declare that no male nor female will be allowed to be lawfully wedded to more than one companion at the same time. If they be allowed to be united with more than one helper and comforter at the same time, it will bring in disharmony, and mixtures of principles, which will abolish friendship, love, and truth, and peace and happiness could find no resting-place. And for this cause, let them be united in the Lord, two and two, male and female, just as their qualifications and propensities equal each other and adhere in talent.

There shall be no distinction made in race nor color as pertaining to preference and partiality among the holy seed. They shall be united, male and female, irrespective of race and color, according to their choice and devotion, and none shall make them afraid. The curse which was imposed upon race and color, and has revolved from generation to generation through inheritance, and is maintained in the flesh and blood, bone and sinew, of the Adamite seed, shall be annihilated in the righteous seed; and every germ shall be exterminated from the souls of the elect.

All who become heirs of the perfect age shall be created, fashioned, and shapened with the same purity, life, and light. I care not what their work may be, all among the holy race shall be on equality, and shall have equal love, glory, honor, and respect. I care not what their color, race, work, or talent may be, they all shall be on a level who are members of the immortal race. The Lord God shall purge out of their blood the nefarious principles which make a vast distinction in race, color, beauty, and wealth, before they can put on the new man. This is the birth for man and woman to pass through, to destroy from their natures the nefarious customs of the antichristian races, to unite with the antislavery race.

No male nor female shall be allowed, and called holy, by the law of this dispensation, to seek adulterous pleasures with those with whom they are not lawfully joined; neither shall there be any sexual commerce between those who are not united male and female. Those who are overtaken in default of this law shall be severed from the Israelite's benefits and privileges until they are fully rewarded for their demeanor, and the unicorn slain.

When the love and devotion of any twain are alienated from the bounds of lawful pleasures, in order to be freed from such power they shall bring their desires before the Lord, and confess in full their reprobativeness and concupiscence; and the Lord will make void the evil, and shall not allow it to exercise power over his chosen and faithful people. No person who has not become sincere, and determined to forsake reprobative desires and concupiscent craves, can receive benefits from the Lord. The Lord God will restore the desires to the perfect existence of life, if persons dissolve friendship with tendencies that make the soul depraved. And if such persons fail to bring their weaknesses before the Lord, and make them known unto him, and continue to adapt themselves to unlawful pleasures with those who are inclined the same way, there shall be no redemption for such persons until the full secrets of their disobedience are by them acknowledged to the Lord God. And if the companion of such abandoned desires dissolution of friendship with such person, it shall be hastily granted, upon the basis of sufficient proof.

The lawless and his illicit companion shall be driven from the presence, blessings, and mercies of the Lord God. If the two lawless continue in the same way after they have been renounced, neither one shall any more be numbered with the righteous seed, until their friendship with the reprobative life is wiped out. In all cases the lawless shall be excluded from the premises of the righteous whom they have wronged and caused to suffer; and such excluded abandoned shall not be allowed to take with them anything of value, excepting their clothing. Under no circumstances whatever shall such persons be allowed to repent of their reprobativeness and concupiscence, nor come before the Lord God, until they forsake their lawless companion, and become fully reconciled with the beloved saint whom they have robbed of their semi-power.

Even so shall it be by making the holy people rulers of the secular world; but this law is not in full force and power in its exoteric system, until there be a revision and redintegration of the physical laws, which shall develop marvellously in the hearts of the people of the notoriety.

The eternal church of the Lord God is spiritually founded and established, and shall be materially established and erected upon truth, love, friendship, and unity, wherein the gospel of this dispensation shall be preached forever; no more shall the true gospel of God be tarnished. The baptism of material waters is made void at the termination of the millennium dispensation. The baptism of the perfect dispensation shall be by word, spirit, and truth. The eucharist commemoration of bread and wine is annulled at the ultimation of the millennium era, and the communion of the righteous era shall be love and unity.

Prayers of the wicked shall not prevail, neither shall there be any promises made unto the people by the Divine God; for this is the age to establish God's promises, which have been made unto the just and the unjust, fulfilling them all. This is the eternal day that the Lord God shall fulfil his pleasure concerning the glory and honor of the righteous, and the gratification of his revenge upon animal nature prevalent in the human family. Songs of praise and thanksgiving shall flow in the channels of humanity which formerly were occupied by prayer and sighing.

The worthy Lamb declares firmly and substantially, by making a holy vow which shall ever be maintained through endless ages, to keep the eternal dispensation pure, holy, and distinguished from the millennium. The vow is made in this wise : the millennium members shall not be classified with the eternal dispensation of righteousness, perfection, beauty, and purity. From this 28th day of January, 1892, the perfect dispensation has raised itself above all mankind that have ever existed, and now exist, and constrains them to follow on and progress into the perfect life gradually. Righteousness shall ever stand in his righteous spiritual sphere with unlimited faithfulness and courage, far beneath and above the millennium gods, who are no gods from this date. This righteous embodiment shall be transmigrated and materialized from tabernacle to tabernacle, and shall continue to be the chief ruler, the Lord of the whole earth, and shall roll on throughout ages of eternity.

When this earthly dwelling that the infinite, omniscient, and omnispective Spirit now occupies is styled and ruled out of use by age, and the material existence becomes incapable of performing the work for the more advanced generation, the entire portion of this spiritual embodiment shall be transferred and conferred upon the like purity of earth ; and so it shall pass on from dwelling to dwelling forever. The days of this material tabernacle shall not be numbered.

The government of the holy age, which is woven in the nature of the revelator, shall continue in him, to establish the same, as long as he desires to embody it, and he shall hold a material existence on earth as long as he so desires. And when he shall reach that period that he desires not to dwell upon the earth any longer, he shall have the privilege of presenting this earthly tabernacle to the father and mother dust, out of which he was created, fashioned, and shapened to establish the endless dispensation of righteousness ; so that the forthcoming generations who shall put on the same life shall have the same privileges conferred upon them in their corporeal and spiritual existence, and end their material existence at the time they so desire, even as he shall do.

There shall be no death nor hell to reign over the righteous seed in this endless day ; and for this cause the names " death " and "hell" shall be erased from God's chronological books in this dispensation. When one ceases to maintain a corporeal existence on earth among the righteous race, it shall be fully agreeable to his desire, and according to choice, in time and season. With the righteous race, there shall be no more pain, sickness, sorrow, griefs, and burdens, neither the sharp sting, and the dread concerning death; for these shall not exist in the minds of the righteous race. None of these shall be present to slay the young child and the youth. Age shall not burden; it shall be peaceful as the youth, and merry as the young child. When the righteous cease their corporeal existence on earth to mingle with the dust, it shall be called "mutual slumber." Even so shall the holy seed exist, and cease to exist, and unite in mutual slumber.

The soul and body shall agree on all things to establish eternal peace and rest while each immortal soul is in its earthly tabernacle. In order to achieve the burning testimonies of the apostolic Bible, and produce the unquenchable fire of holy truth, I will bring in a brief history concerning the trials of the principal persons assigned to this incessant doctrine, disclosing the mighty perils which they have encountered to reach the holy doctrines of the higher life, to cause others to attain the same state. The trials of the material persons involved in this revelation are the testimonies, prompted by Biblical standards, that the horn of the perfect salvation is among the people in his supreme power, to lead mankind, who desires to go, step by step, home. The names of the material persons who bore the memoir of the Holy Scriptures during the period which involves the fulfilments of the prophecies of Christ's second coming to earth, both in righteousness and abomination, will be recorded when the revelation approaches the events wherewith they are connected.

According to Act of Congress of the United States of America, this revelation shall be loyal to all of its laws appertaining to doctrines and copyright privileges, abiding in the co-operative bounds of the given title, and may be printed, published, and issued among the people in any city, town, or county of the United States of America, by any agent empowered by the author of the revelation. This revelation contains the pure doctrinal language of divine science in the sphere of the given title. The doctrines revealed in the limits of the given title are free from all nefarious ideas and false conceptions which work with logical reasoning.

The revelator lived out four consecutive years in retirement from public respect, or honor, reproachfully; and during this time totally refrained from all the enjoyments of earthly pleasures, and lived in a recluse state, in close, confined limits, with a few persons who were devoted to the same life. During this time the revelator was a stigma of scorn while he passed the time to obtain a practical knowledge of the revelation that now makes its advent to earth in its translunary light and power for the bettering of humanity, regardless of race or color, who devote their true virtues to the teaching and correction of this endless revelation.

This revelation is free from all obscene language and utterance of profanity; which will strike the case of every person, whether moral, wicked, or righteous. This revelation is not to be contemned, ignored, nor ostracized by being forced upon abandons of chastity, nor to be blasphemed by men and women of reprobate characteristics; only those who are godly inclined, and thirsting after righteousness, are supposed to adhere to these endless doctrines. It shall be the deliberate aim of the author, by the scrutinizing power of the omniscient, omnispective, and omnipotent God, to direct his every way in issuing the revelation, to use the most exquisite care to furnish those with the revelation who are devotedly inclined to live an honorable life; although it is offered to all. This revelation is prompted with the sustenance of Biblical, prophetic fulfilments, substantiating the revelation, to produce ignitable testimonies, kindling a flame of love in each devoted reader's soul; which flame shall be the unquenchable fire produced by divine truth, setting fire to the fuel of the polluted world which is ready to be harvested, to ransom the soul from misery and woe.

The revelator is normally unlearned in every branch of education, other than this endowment, which is revealed from heaven, as herein narrated, against all unrighteousness, to begin the divine creation of man and women in the perfect image and likeness of the Lord God. The revelator does not exalt himself in a material way to be honored and adored by the public as a material god, other than to declare the hidden realities of divine righteousness, and the crafty works of sin, which continue the suffrages prevalent among the human races. The writer is void of all power, omitting divine truth, to which he is instrumentally consecrated, so that it be revealed to the people. The fulness of divine science is manifested in this revelation through language, spirit, and truth, which issued from the holy standard

Bible, coinciding with all of its writings; and such harmony will only be seen and acknowledged by those who are devoted to divine truth, and love to obey its teachings daily.

This revelation does not speak individually against any particular race, color, sect, religion, nor profession; it is against animal propensities, which prevail over all mankind. The revelator is fully consecrated to the will, glory, and pleasure of the Divine Spirit, so that the Spirit of divine truth may speak through him to the people; which makes the tone of the revelation sound as though it was not revealed by the given name of author.

I have made public, by revealing, the beginning of this marvel, and brought in each hazardous conflict which the principal persons had to encounter to overcome the mighty dragon, and leviathan principles that opposed holy truth when it made its post-millennium to the earth, or tangible body. I also referred to those who took an active part against holy truth, and also to those who in courage and faithfulness stood in defence of it. By bringing in the perilous times of the saints, to overcome the mighty dragon and monstrous leviathan, and his agents, I was compelled to bring in the fulfilments of Scriptures, the latter-day prophecies, which coincide with the great tribulations the spiritual and material saints encountered to overcome animal nature, to present the fulness of divine truth to the civilized notoriety.

This course of revelation gives the doctrines of divine psychology, holy exegesis, revelation of the future life, resurrection of the dead, salvation of the wicked, annihilation of death and hell, extermination of mortality, to transhumanize mankind. To place the original propelling, and creative power of divine truth in the embodied substance of divine psychology, I glanced back to the beginning of the creation of the terrestrial and celestial kingdoms, and revealed the deep hidden things concerning materialism and spiritualism; so that all mysteries that have ever existed in Biblical matters will be involved and disclosed to the notoriety in these doctrines, to give the full doctrine of the human soul. I have revealed the hidden secrets of God in working out man's perfect salvation and his glorification from the beginning of creation, all along through the Adamite world, and into the antediluvian supernaturalism; and through the Abrahamic, and Israelite, Jacobite ages; thence into the mediæval ages through the Jesuit, or Christian, dispensation, called "millennium."

After opening the divine mysteries of the seven worlds, I came over into the most modern age, which is the second coming of Christ, called "post-millennium," which shows only a narrow path for divine righteousness through the seven past dark ages of the world. After sailing into the harbor of the new world, I also show the narrow breadth, width, and length divine righteousness has in this vast macrocosm.

To reward and fortify the chosen and faithful people of God assigned to these incessant doctrines and those yet to come, I would zealously add, in their defence, that they shall be locked upon in a distinguished light, irrespective of the customary fame and honor of men. They shall be elevated and enlarged in the human mind for righteousness' sake; so that this revelation shall reach the remotest parts of human desires and thoughts, lest the writings of this book be of no prosperous effect to this generation.

Then let the people connected with this revelation, whose names are mentioned so often, be honored and respected by all who read; because they were fully consecrated to the will of the Holy God, to accomplish his purpose in the fulfilments of the Scriptures, to save all mankind from the woes and torments of the millennium worlds.

In order to fulfil the Scriptures on the post-millennium of divine truth, word, and spirit, as fore-ordained, the Lord God saw fit to choose the outcast, despised, and rejected people to accomplish the work already done in the souls of this people. To the Holy God give I all the honor, dominion, praises, and thanks, forever, for the victorious triumph of divine truth; and he will confer what he may upon his people. Praises and honor, all nations owe to him for what has been done in secret; and now proclaim it openly, that all may read it, and human hearts be opened to receive just as revealed, without adding or subtracting one atom of its word, spirit, and truth, so that divine truth may find welcome resting-temples in this great universe.

This revelation and doctrine cannot have a friendly and peaceful course in this generation if the members of this doctrine, who abided unto the end of the great tribulations revealed in this book, are ignored, ostracized, and contemned by the people. The Lord God prepared them not to suffer for themselves alone, but to reveal the full doctrines of truth to save all who will accept the fulness of truth.

Hence I say, To give justice where it has not been given, a curse be upon all who know of the divine doctrines and fail to give divine truth and its members due honor and respect, where it can be given, and fail to take warning from this caution. The blessings of prosperity, peace, and happiness be upon all who give this doctrine and its members due honor and respect while dealing with them in any way. These words are placed around this doctrine and its members to shield and fortify them against all opponents.

PART II.

DIVINE PSYCHOLOGY ON THE HIDDEN REALITIES OF THE PAST EPOCHS OF DIVINITY. THE CREATION AND FORMATION OF THE CELESTIAL AND TERRESTRIAL KINGDOMS. THE CREATIVE SUBSTANCES, AND THE CREATIVE SOURCE OF POWER. THE TRANSLUNARY LIGHTS, AND THE STAR CRUCIBLES.

The Lord God is the creator and inventor of all things which have been created and made, and they all were formed by his creative power, which lies in his word, in every way it is spoken by the man of God. Before God created anything that is made, the waters and his Spirit were without beginning, and without an end; and they were all and all; and the waters were the only visible substance. The waters and his Spirit were omnipotent, omnipresent, and informal; and these two were composed of the same substance, which is, namely, the Lord God Almighty.

The waters were God's material body, and the Spirit that moved upon the face of the waters was the fulness of the Almighty God, the Life and Light, which kept these bodies of water alive, and the source of power, that ruled them. The waters were the material creative substance out of which he created everything that was made in the terrestrial kingdom; and the Spirit was the part that uttered the distinct alphabetic sounds, and named the things God wanted to create. And when the word was spoken, the Spirit quickened the word; and that thing which the word had named began to germinate.

The first thing God created, to construct the terrestrial kingdom, was the firmament, which was to divide the waters without the firmament from the waters within the firmament; and the firmament is a bright, hard, crystallized substance to hold and protect its creative substances. The next thing God created was the revolution machinery, to bring the different times and seasons in the terrestrial kingdom; and this was the sun-globe, which is made around the earth within the firmament.

The firmament is created round, and it stands above the waters, under the waters, and in the midst of the waters; for there is nothing but waters to be seen without the firmament. But the Spirit of God still moves upon the face of the waters without the firmament and keeps them alive. Without (on the outside of) the firmament there is no beginning to the depth, neither ending to the width, neither is there any top to the waters that uphold the terrestrial kingdom.

After God had created the firmament and the sun-globe, which is the whole revolution of the terrestrial kingdom, he then created the earth and its case, which is created within the sun-globe. The earth's case is as hard as the firmament, and separates the earth from the sun-globe; and the earth's case forms two spindles on each side, as does a wagon; and these spindles extend through the sun-globe into the firmament, and are therefore imbedded therein. Therefore, the sun-globe revolves around the earth and its axis, and keeps all of its machinery in perpetual motion.

Then God said "Let there be light" and there was light, which was produced by dry electric air, which he created within the air tank of the firmament, and pours forth, a stream, into the sun-cruse when it is perpendicularly over the earth.

The intense heat between the firmament and the sun-globe causes this dry electric air to ignite and produce a perpetual flame, which is the translunary light, because it is composed of the same substances. The sun's crucible is made upon a straight line track, which is fixed within the sun-globe, and it moves back and forth from the centre of the earth to its axis. When the sun's crucible is perpendicularly over the earth, it draws fuel from the air tank of the firmament, which causes it to produce a hotter flame. The firmament is a reflector for the sunlight, which polarizes its light and throws it upon the earth.

The moon-cruse is made within the sun-globe, and runs upon a straight line track, and the crucible moves in the same manner as does the sun, but its cruse cannot, and does not, contain fuel; but the moon-cruse receives the greater luminous rays of the sunlight. The stars' crucibles are also made within the sun-globe, and they receive the lesser rays of the luminous sunlight.

On the first day of the week, which is now recorded Saturday, God finished the creation of the terrestrial kingdom, with all of its glorious lights and wonderful machinery; and it took one thousand years, but God recorded it one day, to conceal his real manner of speech and language from the natural man; therefore the time God recorded seven days in the beginning is now called seven thousand years.

And on the second day God said, "Let the waters under the heaven be gathered together unto one place, and let the dry land appear: and it was so. And God called the dry land Earth; and the gathering together of the waters called he Seas: and God saw that it was good. And God said, Let the earth bring forth grass, the herb yielding seed, ... after his kind, and the trees yielding fruit, whose seed was in itself, after his kind: and God saw that it was good."

On the third day God created every herb and fruit-tree which is upon the earth, and he saw that it was good; "and the evening and the morning were the third day."

On the fourth day the lights which God had created within the firmament of heaven attained the goal of perfection, which gave light and life unto the members of the sun. God created only one kind of air within the terrestrial kingdom, and this was electric air; but that electric air which makes the luminous sunlight is thoroughly dry air; and the electric air within the sun-globe is damp air, which gives life and vigor unto all living substances and creatures within the terrestrial kingdom.

On the fifth day God created every beast of the forest and fish of the sea, and every creeping thing of the earth, and fowl of the air, and told them to multiply seed after their kind, and it was so; "and the evening and the morning were the fifth day."

Thus the terrestrial kingdom was finished with all required necessities for man's glory; he only had to bring its creatures under his subjection, and discover its substances, invent patents, and improve the scenes of the earth for his glory.

On the sixth day of the week the immaterial masculine spoke unto the immaterial feminine, and said: "Let us make man in our image, after our likeness: and let them have dominion over the fish of the sea, and over the fowl of the air, and over the cattle, and over all the earth, and over every creeping thing that creepeth upon the earth." And the figurative Adam was created and formed out of the dust of the earth; and God breathed into the formed dust, Adam, electric air, and he became a living soul, and also flesh and blood.

God knew that it was not good for man to be alone, so he made him an helpmeet from his form and named her Eve; she was the man's helper and comforter. And when God made the woman and gave her unto the man, he then gave the man his holy command, which reads as follows: "Of every tree of the garden thou mayest freely eat: but of the tree of the knowledge of good and evil, thou shalt not eat of it: for in the day that thou eatest thereof thou shalt surely die." The tree that God commanded him not to eat of was the fruits of the woman's flesh; and the man understood what the forbidden fruit was.

And when God gave the man his command, he then gave him his spirit of knowledge to quicken the word, which he placed within him. The word was the light and life to gu.de the man in the way that God would have him to go. The electric air was the spirit and the word was the globe which gave light unto the realms of the celestial kingdom which God placed within him. And since the fall of man God called his name "Adam;" and the name "damnation" was derived from this name. He was called "man" because God gave unto him his command; and when he disobeyed his command he was not a man, neither flesh and blood, but corruptible dust.

God named the land wherein he placed him, "Garden of Eden," because there were all manner of fruits for him to eat; therefore the word "eat" was derived from "Eden." God called the woman's name "Eve," because through her evil came upon all mankind; the name "Eve" was derived from the name "evening," because she was made in the evening. She was called "woman" because she gave birth to all woe, sorrow, sickness, pain, and death; and through her these became a universal deluge. The word "wife" was derived from the noun "woman," and denotes the same; only God changed the noun "woman" into a participial noun, and said "his wife" instead of "his woman."

If the man had not taken of the fruit of the woman's flesh, God would have created them male and female to receive the rays of the Celestial Son light; which was to begin on the first day of the week.

When God said unto man, "Be fruitful, and multiply, and replenish the earth, and subdue it," this was for man to be prosperous in multiplying the improvements upon the earth, to bring it to perfection in beautiful scenes, patents, and styles, and every useful thing for man's glory. God created a tribe of brute beasts before Adam, which he called the pre-adamites, and they were as erect in form and stature as man; and this tribe were servants for the man to use to build and improve the scenes of the terrestrial kingdom.

When man lost his holy, happy, and perfect dominion, God called the pre-adamite tribe "serpent," because they were the original of sin. Adam and Eve amalgamated with the pre-adamite tribe, but the woman degenerated herself first, and then her eyes were open to see the fascinations of the forbidden fruit; and then she seduced Adam to do unto her as did the pre-adamites unto her. And for this cause God put the greater curse upon the pre-adamites, and the next greater curse he put upon the woman.

The name "serpent" was derived from the name "servant;" because the pre-adamites were created for man's servants. The curse that God imputed upon the pre-adamites was greater than they could bear; so they reduced until they reached the unfathomed curse where they are today. Therefore the pre-adamite serpent will soon vanish from the earth and be as though it never was; for the pre-adamites were the original serpent, the Devil, who by stealth crept into human nature and corrupted the human family. They drove the image and likeness of God's person out of human nature, and caused the human family to clothe themselves after the image and likeness of the pre-adamite tribe.

At the close of the seventh day, the Lord God spoke unto Adam in Eden land; and when God's voice fell upon his ears Adam died, because the word killed him. The word that God spoke unto him uncovered his sins, and made them plain, so that he could see clearly what he had done; this is the reason why the man sought clothing for himself and wife, because the word God spoke unto them uncovered their sins and filled them with fear and condemnation. It did not change God's ordinations, in the creative use of man, by his violation of the holy law; for it threw mankind in the channel to raise up crucibles to receive the luminous rays of the Celestial Son light.

The man's condemnation shows that he knew what the forbidden fruit was; for where there is no law there can be no sin; and where there is a law and no understanding of the law, there is no condemnation in the violation of the law; neither can the imputed punishment have its full effect upon the violator. Man's condemnation exhibits his knowledge of a crime, and gives a decisive verdict upon the case. When God's decisive doom of punishment which he owes to mankind is justly imputed upon the Adamite seed, he will speedily erase man's disobedience from his book of memory, and glide away the mist of darkness from his face, and glean out his petrified conscience, and make void his sneaky, ravenous lust, which can never be filled with the fascinating charms of the wicked world.

By God's creative words of power, he will destroy man's ravenous lust and pour into their doomed bodies pure waters of life, which will give them victory over the lust of the world. He will immerse them in the deep fathoms of his life and light, which is power and riches, strength and honor, glory, wisdom, and blessing. God will pour within them these seven streams of life, pure waters, which will forever perpetuate peace and pleasure, love and friendship, toward their fellowmen. Then the woman will retain her creative office with man; and they shall be holy, happy, perfect, and undefiled; and they shall keep God's holy laws forever.

At the close of the seven thousandth era of the Adamite world the Lord God appeared to man in Eden to fulfil the words he had spoken unto him when he gave him his holy command, which was God's holy law. And God imputed a curse upon the man, woman, and his servants; though the man's servants had no command from God, because they were brute beasts. But he imputed a curse upon the pre-adamites to henceforth and forever destroy the relationship which heretofore existed between the pre-adamite tribe and the human family.

The pre-adamite tribe reduced from the human stature until they reached their present state, which is the serpent. But the mortal man contains the invisible stature and characteristics of the pre-adamites. God's elect people will soon take off the image of the pre-adamites and put on the image of God.

The curse that God imputed upon the pre-adamites and the human family reads as follows: "Because thou hast done this, thou art cursed above all cattle, and above every beast of the field;

upon thy belly shalt thou go, and dust shalt thou eat all the days of thy life. And I will put enmity between thee and the woman, and between thy seed and her seed; it shall bruise thy head, and thou shalt bruise his heel.

"Unto the woman he said, I will greatly multiply thy sorrow and thy conception; in sorrow thou shalt bring forth children; and thy desire shall be to thy husband, and he shall rule over thee.

"And unto Adam he said, Because thou has hearkened unto the voice of thy wife, and hast eaten of the tree, of which I commanded thee, saying, Thou shalt not eat of it: cursed is the ground for thy sake; in sorrow shalt thou eat of it all the days of thy life; thorns also and thistles shall it bring forth to thee; and thou shalt eat the herb of the field; in the sweat of thy face shalt thou eat bread, till thou return unto the ground; for out of it wast thou taken: for dust thou art, and unto dust shalt thou return."

When the Lord God pronounced his vengeance upon mankind he prepared them sheep-skins to conceal their nakedness, which was done by giving man the instinct to do it. God created Adam in this American world, which he recorded and called "Garden of Eden." Then it was beautifully arrayed with all manner of fragrant flowers and delicious fruit-trees; and God drove him out of this glorious and beautiful land after he disobeyed his command, and sent him unto that desolate part of the world now called Africa. And he journeyed on day by day until he reached the land where God had fore-ordained him to stop; and he began to till the earth for food. And he reached his home in the eight thousandth era of the Adamite world, and began to raise up seed after his kind.

When Adam reached the desolate sod of Africa, God caused the great river Euphrates to divide and come into four great heads, and surrounded the Garden of Eden, which is materially and now called the American land. And the four heads which surrounded the American land God recorded, and called their names Pison, Gihon, Hiddekel, and Euphrates; these are their antique names. They are now, namely, the Atlantic, the Pacific, the Arctic and Indian oceans; and all seas, rivers, gulfs, and straits are the subdivisions of these four grand divisions, and these four grand divisions are the cherubims and flaming sword which God placed on all sides of Eden to keep the Ethiopians from returning to the Garden of Eden until his purposes were accomplished regarding Ethiopia and Eden.

The animals, fowl of the air, and creeping things, followed Adam to the land of Africa, and they spread abroad over the three great continents, Europe, Asia, and Africa. Adam knew Eve, his wife, and she conceived and bare him a son, and they called his name Cain ; and his skin was white, which led the woman to believe she had gotten a man from God. Adam and Eve were both created dark skinned, and they thought that through their white-skinned man-child they would regain their state of perfection. Adam's wife again conceived and bare him a daughter the same color as Cain, she whom Cain took for wife ; but God did not record this matter in the apostolic Bible, because he did not want the following generations to do as they had done. Yet it was God's ordination for Cain to take his own sister for wife, so as to multiply seed to populate the earth, and carry out the fulfilment of his words spoken in the beginning of creation.

Adam again knew Eve, his wife, and she bare him a dark-skinned son, and they called his name Abel ; and Abel worked every way to glorify God, and did everything that he thought was pleasing in the sight of God. And Abel sacrificed unto God offering of sheep ; and Cain offered up the earth's produce, which was merely formality, and for this cause God had respect unto Abel's offering and accepted it, but he did not accept Cain's offering because he did not offer it sincerely. Therefore Cain saw that his offering was refused and Abel's accepted ; he became enraged with jealousy and slew Abel, and this created enmity between Adam and his white son, Cain, and they turned one against the other, for Adam sought Cain to put him to death to gratify his vengeance, because Abel was the only seed of his color. But the Lord God commanded Adam not to kill him, but to spare his life ; and God avenged Cain seven-fold, and this is the reason why God has hid his face, and refused to speak through the white-skinned man.

The color of the skin is the mark which God set upon the white-skinned man to distinguish him from the dark-skinned Ethiopian. God deafened their ears so that they would be dull of hearing his voice ; and blinded their eyes so that their sight into his mysteries be void until he fulfilled his work concerning Ethiopia. The curse God avenged upon Cain read as follows : "When thou tillest the ground it shall not henceforth yield unto thee her strength ; a fugitive and a vagabond shalt thou be in the earth."

Cain said, " Lord, my punishment is greater than I can bear. Behold, thou hast driven me out this day from the face of the earth ;

and from thy face shall I be hid; and I shall be a fugitive and a vagabond in the earth; and it shall come to pass, that every one that findeth me shall slay me."

The Lord God said unto Cain, "Whosoever slayeth thee, vengeance shall be taken on him seven-fold. And God set a mark upon Cain, lest any finding him should kill him. And Cain went out from God's presence and dwelt in the land of Nod east of Eden;" and this is the country now called Asia. At that time Asia was a desolate country with scarcely any herbs growing out of its soil fit for food.

When Cain reached his desolate Asia-land he began to build and to plant, and raised up seed after his kind; and they spread abroad over this continent. Lamech slew his father, Cain, and his own son, Tubal Cain; and for this crime God avenged Lamech seventy-seven-fold. Then Cain's seed fell in the current of wickedness, which bore them speedily on to the climax of depravity. When Cain left Africa Adam had none other seed, and his wife left off conceiving for a season.

The language which is now called the English is the same language that God's electrical and alphabetic breath uttered before the formation of the terrestrial kingdom. God's alphabetic breath uttered this language when every substance that is now formal was informal, and before anything was made that is made. This language is the distinct alphabetic sounds which God's electrical breath uttered, and gave name unto all substances and creatures before creating them. This was done so that the discoverers of these substances, patents, and creatures be inspired of God to give the creative name to all substances, patents, and creatures, to enable them to distinguish one substance, invention, and creature from another.

Before these things began to create, God's alphabetic and electrical breath named the substance and creature he wanted to create; and that substance named began to germinate. God's alphabetic and electrical breath gave names unto all things created in the beginning; and he gave Adam the names of all creatures and discovered substances of his day; and he wrote them in accord with God's creative names. Noah recorded them from the Adamite names in harmony with the improvements and discovery of his day, and reserved them in the ark and carried them over to the new world. Therefore these names were handed down from generation to generation, and each generation discovered new substances, invented patents, which gradually perfected the glory of the earthly and heavenly; which gradually brought in additional words. The creative name of this language is the Ethiopian language: the name "English" is merely a change in the term of speech; for the name "English" was derived from the name "Ethiopia," and makes a softer and more harmonious expression, and makes the expression more appropriate for use.

God inspired mankind to put this language in different parts of speech, and add additional words suitable for divine and physical matters. But the recorders were ignorant of this truth, that it was God's inspiring wisdom that enabled them to attain the full dimension in ferreting out the Ethiopian language. For this cause, man ascribed all the glory and honor to himself, for the wonderful discoveries and improvements which have been made in the terrestrial kingdom.

God will purge out every harsh and profane word from among his creative language, and will use none other words but those used to create the heavens and earth, and the members and substances therein. The words that God shall purge out from his creative language are the words which man linked on for his physical use. And the additional profane words adulterated the pure words. God will record those glorious, and harmonious, and distinct sounds, of luminous alphabetic sentences, which he uttered in the beginning of creation.

The Ethiopian language was the only language used by mankind from the Adamite world until the overthrow of Babel, which was after the deluge; and the different languages sprung forth miraculously to separate the Ethiopian, to scatter mankind in different parts of the earth, to raise up different colors and races of people. The Ethiopian language partly slumbered until the Mosaic law was written and established with the children of Israel; and the Judites improved the language by copying it from the Mosaic law, and adding other words. Just as they discovered the creative substances of the earth, God inspired them to give the substances their creative names. Before God inspired mankind to explore the earth and discover its creative substances, God's creative languages lay slumbering in the earth's substances, waiting the general resurrection day.

"Adam knew his wife again; and she bore a son, and called his name Seth: For God, said she, hath appointed me another seed instead of Abel, whom Cain slew." There had elapsed one hundred and thirty years since the death of Abel, and Seth was born in the same image after Adam's likeness, which was dark skinned, and had the inclination to call upon the name of God.

Unto Adam was born a daughter of the same kind, she whom Seth took for wife ; this established the godly family in the Adamite world, and men looked steadfastly to God. Therefore from this time righteousness began with the Adamite seed ; and Enoch, who was out of the seed of Seth, was translated and ebullitioned into invisible fluid, to raise up Noah, the first figurative righteous Ethiopian branch. Then the continent Africa was speedily populated by the Adamite seed, and some among them grew to be men of renown, which definates that they were wise in things pertaining unto vanity, and exceedingly rich in the world's luxuries ; and they worked heart and soul for the upbuilding of the terrestrial kingdom, and did all they could to retard the progress of the celestial kingdom, although righteousness blossomed from the first unto the third generation, at which time the earth had made a speedy growth in human population.

Men had begun to discover the substance of the earth, and apparently the world was in a progressive state, in beautiful scenes of man's improvements. Just as men increased in the wisdom of the world, they made a gradual decrease in the wisdom of righteousness : and they worshipped the make of their own hands and skill. and forsook their Creator. They journeyed on in this degenerating state. until they walked into the unfathomed depths of depravity ; and the swiftness of its current bore them speedly on into the doomed state of infidelity, which made them wholly depraved. Therefore righteousness grew wax cold, and evil seducers waxed worse and worse in violent wickedness, and depravity continued to spread its broad wings over the earth, until all wickedness was overthrown from the face of the earth, and the germ left in humanity.

When God could no longer forbear with evil seducers, he said, "' My spirit shall not always strive with man, for that he also is flesh: yet his days shall be an hundred and twenty years." It repented God, and grieved him at his heart that he had made man, while he dwelt in the flesh of Noah, through the great persecutions Noah received from the wicked while building the ark, to carry out his purposes in raising up a tried and suffering people ; and for this cause he said, " I will destroy man whom I have created from the face of the earth ; both man, and beast, and the creeping thing, and the fowls of the air ; for it repenteth me that I have made them.'

And God raised up the righteous branch, Noah, and his faith in the words God spoke unto him were accounted unto him for righteousness. Noah received the invisible being called Enoch, whose body had been consumed by God's fiery power, and translated into a spirit for the specified purpose of raising up Noah, the first righteous Ethiopian branch, to accomplish His marvellous work. Those who had lived godly lives during those years when righteousness was blossoming in the earth, united with Enoch to make up the fuel to enable Noah to carry out God's plans. God endowed Noah with wisdom to bring to sight a portion of his creative hidden realities, and they have been handed down from generation to generation, and kept in store for witness against ungodly men.

Noah's work in building the ark was God's supernatural power wrought in him to destroy depraved men from the face of the earth, and to carry safe into the harbor of the new land Noah and his wife, and his three sons, Ham, Shem, and Japheth, and their wives, and a male and female of every creature created in the sun-globe, to keep them alive with him in the ark. Noah erected his ark upon the free sod of Africa, and the deluge bore it safely on to the new Asialand, and there rested it upon the highest peak of Mount Ararat ; therefore this name was given unto this mountain because it was the harbor where Noah's ark landed after forty days' voyage on the raging and turbulent billows of the deluge.

When God commanded Noah to build an ark, men were so desperately wicked that they mocked him in the most lewd way. Noah was persecuted until the Lord became grieved at heart in Noah, so that it repented him that he had created man to have dominion over the terrestrial kingdom, its members, and substances. Noah execrated every living creature that went not into the ark ; and through Noah's curses the whole creation groaned, and travailed in the greatest agony of excruciating pain, until the breath of life which penetrated their systems was forced to leave.

The seven persons that went into the ark with Noah gave all of their time and labor accomplishing the work in building the ark, wherein they found refuge during the terror of the deluge. The following words are the command that God gave Noah after he had finished the ark. " Of every living thing of all flesh, two of every sort shalt thou bring into the ark, to keep them alive with thee ; they shall be male and female. Of fowls after their kind, and of cattle after their kind, of every creeping thing of the earth after his kind, two of every sort shall come unto thee, to keep them alive. And take thou unto thee of all food that is eaten, and thou shalt gather it to thee; and it shall be for food for thee, and for them."

And Noah did according to all God commanded; and when he had gathered his family and other living creatures into the ark as God commanded him, God caused the windows in the firmament of heaven to open; and the waters poured within the sun-globe from without the firmament until all creatures and substances within the sun-globe were swallowed up by them. The waters prevailed fifteen cubit feet above the highest substance in the sun-globe. When the waters reached this expansion, the windows of the firmament were closed until all flesh in whose nostrils was the breath of life died.

When the deluge had finished its great massacre, the windows of the terrestrial firmament were again opened, and the water began to disappear from within the sun-globe into the open heaven without the firmament. But the usual quantity of waters remained in the sun-globe to again give life unto the members of the Son and sun. The sun, moon, and stars refused to give their light during the days of the deluge. The world was clothed universally in utter darkness until the waters assuaged from off the earth; for the sun did not give its full luminous light for three years from the beginning of the deluge. The revolution of the sun's power ceased during this terrible judgment.

Noah and his family turned heart thankfulness unto God when they trod upon the sod of the new world. This ends the revelation of the hidden realities of the Adamite world from the creation of the heavens and earth, which ended in the fourteen thousandth era of the Adamite world.

It came to pass, after the waters assuaged from off the earth, that Noah and all living creatures that went into the ark went out with him. And God spoke unto Noah, and to his sons with him, saying, "Behold, I establish my covenant with you, and with your seed after you; and with every living creature that is with you, of the fowl, of the cattle, and of every beast of the earth with you; from all that go out of the ark, to every beast of the earth. And I will establish my covenant with you; neither shall all flesh be cut off any more by the waters of a flood; neither shall there any more be a flood to destroy the earth."

"I will not again curse the ground any more for man's sake; for the imagination of man's heart is evil from his youth; neither will I again smite any more every thing living, as I have done. While the earth remaineth, seed time and harvest, and cold and heat, and summer and winter, and day and night, shall not cease." The deluge which came over the whole world did not bring the remnant of mankind into the state of perfection; but it placed them in the channel to convey them speedily on into man's creative state. The deluge destroyed severe depravity from among mankind; it destroyed the seventy-fold curse which was imputed upon the white-skinned man, and left seven-fold. And it made a possible way for the Ethiopian race to attain their creative state, and lend a helping hand to all the godly people of the earth, that they may reach the same state.

After the deluge Noah's three sons, Ham, Shem, and Japheth, increased their seed to a vast number, and they began to grow wise in vanity; then there was only one race, one language, and one color of people existing, and they all dwelt together in Asia, where the ark landed. Before Noah died, he blessed the seed of Shem and Japheth, and cursed the seed of Ham, saying that they should be servants of servants for their brethren. And God used Noah to bless the seed of Shem and Japheth, saying, "Blessed be the Lord. God of Shem; and Canaan shall be his servant. God shall enlarge Japheth, and he shall dwell in the tents of Shem; and Canaan shall be his servant."

When Noah died righteousness folded its arms and slumbered beneath the sod until God raised up the second righteous Ethiopian branch. After the deluge the seed of Noah's sons did not spread abroad over the earth, but dwelt together in one continent; and they thought upon a plan by which to save their lives in case there should be another flood of water as had been. So they all joined in and began to build a haven, called "Babel;" and by God's almighty power he overthrew their haven, and confounded the Ethiopian creative language in their mouths, which caused each family of Noah's three sons to speak in an unknown tongue.

There were born unto Japheth seven sons, of which all had families; and each family of these seven formed a tribe. There were born unto Ham four sons, and each of his sons formed a tribe. There were born unto Shem five sons, and each of his sons formed a tribe. The different tribes that sprung from Japheth are, Gomer,

Magog, Madai, Javan, Tubal, Meshech, and Tiras. The different tribes that sprung from Ham are, Cush, Mizraim, Phut, and Canaan. The different tribes that sprung from Shem are, Elam, Asshur, Arphaxad, Lud, and Aram. When the language of Noah's sons' seed was confounded they spread abroad over the three great continents, Europe, Asia, and Africa; and these different tribes spoke in different tongues, which are, namely, the Kenites, Kenizzites, Kadmonites, Hittites, Perizzites, Rephaims, Amorites, Canaanites, Girgashites, Jebusites, Hivites, Arkites, Sinites, Arvadites, Zemarites, and the Hamathites. These are the different tongues and nations which went abroad over the earth after the overthrow of Babel; each tongue made a distinct race, and their color and habits changed from this time.

As God blessed the God of Shem, he chose the tribe out of the seed of Shem to raise up some among them to dwell close by him in refined characteristics; and God chose the family that sprung from Shem, called "Aram," but they were called, after their tongue, tribe, and nation, "the Amorites;" therefore the Amorites were God's chosen tribe, wherein he held the mark-emblems of Ethiopia.

And God chose one man and woman out of the Amorite tribe, so that he might raise up twelve godly tribes to accomplish his plans. When God chose his two instruments out of the Amorite tribe, he loosened them, and suffered them to degenerate themselves by mingling with the ungodly tribes which numbered sixteen, with the Amorites. The man and woman that God chose out of the Amorite tribe raised up twelve distinct tribes after their then refined qualifications. The seed-bearers of these twelve godly tribes were Abram and Sarah; from these two came forth the twelve tribes called "the children of Israel."

Righteousness therefore became wax cold after the sixteen distinct tribes were formed in the earth, and godliness was null and void. And God raised up Abraham, the second righteous Ethiopian branch, to raise up a godly people to accomplish his plans without destroying all living creatures as he had done. When God spoke unto Abraham, he spoke in the Ethiopian language. The Ethiopian language was used by Abraham and his son Isaac; and from Isaac to his son Jacob.

When these three righteous Ethiopian branches died, then the Ethiopian language slumbered until the Mosaic law was written, and then it circulated among the twelve godly tribes. God established the type of his everlasting covenant with Abraham, Isaac, and Jacob; and Moses established it with Abraham's seed.

These are the words of God's covenant with Abraham, Isaac, and Jacob, " Every man child among you shall be circumcised. And ye shall circumcise the flesh of your foreskin; and it shall be a token of the covenant betwixt me and you. . . . And the uncircumcised man child whose flesh of his foreskin is not circumcised, that soul shall be cut off from his people; he hath broken my covenant."

The names of the twelve distinct godly tribes which came forth out of the loins of Abraham, Isaac, and Jacob, are, namely: Reuben, Simeon, Levi, Judah, Dan, Issachar, Naphtali, Gad, Asher, Zebulun, Joseph, and Benjamin. There were two other tribes that came out of the loins of these righteous branches; they, being dishonorable, were cast off from the godly tribes, because they were not materially organized to mingle with the twelve godly races. And these two dishonorable tribes were the Edomites and the Ishmaelites; and these two tribes came on equality with the other ungodly tribes of the earth.

And God placed within each one of these godly tribes his inspiring intellect and great anxiety to do some kind of work either pertaining to the advancement of the terrestrial or celestial kingdom. And this inspiring power governed them in such way as to keep the terrestrial and celestial kingdoms on equality in growth. God therefore has been using each tribe to do a certain kind and portion of work to improve the two kingdoms ever since the Mosaic law was established with Israel.

The Lord God has used the dark-skinned man for his spokesman ever since mankind came into existence; and through them He has been showing his supernatural power, by doing miraculous things in working signs and wonders, that man may see and know that he is God and none else besides him. This has continued throughout all the past ages of the world, for Ethiopia is His creative people and color.

The name " Ethiopia " was derived from the name " earth," because they were taken from the earth; but the Lord God has no respect for individual color, for he has painted them many colors, which is to his glory and likeness. It is God's ordination for the creative color of man to be reserved forever, so that all creative things may henceforth and forever hold their creative offices in every respect.

After the death of the three righteous Ethiopian branches, the twelve godly tribes were then made servants for the ungodly tribes. And God raised up Moses, the fifth righteous Ethiopian branch, to deliver them out of the hands of the wicked tribes; and for the Israelites to drive out the wicked tribes and have possession of the lands and buildings that the wicked then had under their jurisdiction. Moses came out of the Ethiopian tribe of Israel, called "the Levites;" and Moses wrote the first circulating Ethiopian Bible, and he wrote all of the creative realities which are brought out in the apostolic Bible. Moses wrote the typical law of the apostolic Bible; and all the holy prophets that came after him prophesied on the fulfilment of his law.

Elijah was the sixth righteous Ethiopian branch; and his material body was transformed from matter to spirit to form Jesus in the womb, perceptible to the touch and visible to the eye. This was done for the material to be born submissive to the will of the spiritual, so that the plan of salvation would be finished at Jesus's transformation and ascension; which changed him from a corporeal body into a spiritual body with organic structure. Therefore it was the earthy bodily organic structure of Elijah that caused the figurative Jesus to brew in his mother's womb, by God's almighty power.

Jesus, the figurative Christ, died a literal death at the hands of his enemies, to make a way for God's chosen people among the twelve tribes of Israel to die a spiritual death, and be spiritually resurrected by the spiritual Christ, who is the life and light, and source of power that governs the members of the celestial kingdom. The body of the figurative Christ was literally crucified, and also resurrected, to complete the fuel of the Celestial Son light. The figurative Christ Jesus made the seven righteous Ethiopian branches and the embodiment of the spiritual kingdom which God prepared with genuine human facilities to establish righteousness in the members of the perfect age.

When the figurative body of Christ Jesus was seen ascending into the firmament of the celestial kingdom after the resurrection, it was transformed from a mattery body to a spiritual body; which was the concentration and focalization of the seven righteous Ethiopian branches, called "the Lamb's Book of Life," and the spiritual kingdom of Christ, the life establishing the transhumanized existence of mankind corporeally. When the material body became immaterial, the material produced this change by uniting with the spiritual, and the visible became invisible; which completed the fuel to give life and light unto the material members of the spiritual kingdom by the seven doctrines of the human soul.

When the New Testament was distributed among the godly tribes, then the first coming of Christ became omnipresent with them only, for Christ could only be present where his Testament was received. When the godly tribes received Christ's Testament, then they had received Christ in the hope of putting on his glory, at his post-millennium. And this was for them to continue in the hope of putting on the real life of Christ; which hope was to exist in the hearts of each generation consigned to the millennium doctrine of divinity, until God raised up a generation some among whom would contain substance to receive the doctrine of Christ's second coming.

The saints who have reigned with Christ spiritually have appeared with him the second time, without sin unto salvation, to judge the saints and sinners in the souls of material saints who maintain life to live upon the earth. The office of the spiritual saints in glory, who have passed out of the temples of flesh through the past ages and are messengers of Christ in the spiritual kingdom, is to minister unto the saints embodied in the earthly tabernacles; and they are the minds of the seven spirits of the perfect kingdom, which teaches mankind what is right, and what is evil in every silent and active stage of life.

There are two kinds of death which mankind can die, and are compelled to die, one or the other, in the mortal state, before passing from death unto life; which must be done spiritually in its real power for humanity to enjoy its blessings and privileges according to God's promises, although one is a literal death and the other a spiritual death. The literal death, which the bodies of the figurative saints have been dying, was the way in which God had to make up the rays of the Celestial Son light, so that the translunary Son of the celestial kingdom will cast the reflections of its glorious rays into the corporeal saints and glorify them in his spiritual temple. Therefore the spiritual saints are the star lights which shall shine forth into the bodies of the material saints to glorify the Godhead which is the perfect Christ, and form star lights for the spiritual kingdom.

The spiritual death is, to die from the lust of the flesh, that hungers and thirsts after the luxuries of the animal kingdom. And the material saints who shall die this death will be the star crucibles to receive the glorious rays of the Celestial Son light, which is the second resurrection of the dead. The first resurrection of the dead is the great hope centred in the millennium members, to attain the second resurrection ; which is for the material members of Christ to put on his perfect image and likeness, which is life eternally.

He that is more corruptible than incorruptible cannot inherit eternal life in the material body; for if their dishonorable qualities exceed their honorable qualities, they will return again to the mortal life. And those who are found worthy to inherit the fulness of incorruptibleness are thereby made flesh and blood, because a mortal man is not flesh and blood; he is corruptible dust. There are honorable bodies who have no hope in the second resurrection; and these are they who have not fallen asleep in the hope of receiving Christ at his post-millennium; but over such the second death hath power.

The second death hath no power over those who have a part in the first resurrection, because these died daily by being subject and loyal to the teachings of the millennium doctrine of divinity, and waiting the redemption of their bodies at Christ's coming to reign. God is the potter, and he made vessels to honor, and vessels to dishonor; the vessels to dishonor God created, raised up, and preserved, to purify the vessels to honor, to raise up a tried, purified, and refined people zealous of good works.

This point God never revealed understandingly to the mortal man, for he could not have used them to work out his glorification, and honorable men's eternal salvation; this is the sole cause for not giving them a clear sight into the mysteries of his spiritual kingdom.

God's kingdom shall be set up in his elect. So flesh and blood cannot pass into the kingdom, but the kingdom can appear to flesh and blood, and dwell in flesh and blood; and it shall dwell in flesh and blood forever, to keep humanity from amalgamating with animalism.

The natural birth of the revelator was like unto the brethren, and he lived the same life in the flesh, so that he would have a thorough knowledge of the carnal life, and set an example before the brethren, for them to see a possible way to come out of the flesh and live in perfect holiness unto God. He was joined to a woman in the flesh, so that when God called him from the world it would set an example for the brethren, showing that there are no wives, nor natural blood-kin, claimed nor honored in the second resurrection; for if they are relatives in the world, or millennium, when they start in pursuit of this life, they become separated and strangers in the former friendship, until they unite in God's royal family, and then they are one.

From the example which the revelator has placed before the brethren, no one who is a follower of him can expect any one to inherit eternal life for the sake of relationship. The Lord God will not fall short of fulfilling any of his promises made unto righteousness which has suffered in the flesh of mortal men through the past ages ; but the fallacious imagination of mankind has conceived ideas to please themselves, according to each one's fancy concerning the way God's promises will be fulfilled. But man's leaning to his own understanding in giving the meaning of God's written words, opposite to his ordination, did not change God's course of working ; for mankind have only deceived themselves and fallen short of the glory offered unto them.

Men's own deceitfulness has carried their kind down step by step into the doomful state of pain and agony ; and God has used every moment of time to bring them into the state of perfection. The Lord God could not give unto mankind the rights and privileges which he had prepared for them until he prepared the second tabernacle to embody the Godhead; for mankind could never obtain a full redemption of their bodies from misery and destruction by keeping only the commandments recorded in the apostolic Bible.

This Bible was to keep them in the current of civilization, and to increase the refined qualifications of each generation; therefore, by the continual revolution of honorable and refined characteristics, it has reached a generation materially organized to become wholly incorruptible. There is corruptibleness in every mortal being ; but God's elect shall take off the corruptible image of the pre-adamites, and put on the incorruptible image of God. The saints will draw electrical air from the tabernacle who embodies the supreme power of the Godhead, to maintain life to live in conformity with God's will according to his promises. And when God's elect are gathered home, they all will unite, and be created and composed of the same substance as the light fuel ; which will be channels for the waters of life to flow through to convey the life-giving waters unto all people and nations.

The same Jesus whom the ancient mythologies saw going away in the clouds of the terrestrial kingdom, came in like manner in the clouds of the celestial kingdom ; and all who have divine spiritual discernment shall behold his glory, and see him as he is, when they receive his words just as they are revealed from heaven. All spiritual discernment is not divine; there are moral spirituality, malignant spirituality, spirituality by necromancy, and lascivious spirituality, but none of these have power to mingle with divine spirituality. All spirituality outside of divine nature is abominable to the members of the holy life, and it shall not exist in the members of the spiritual kingdom; all powers of abominable spirituality have their kind and worlds to exist in, so as not to mingle with the holy race.

When God's pure word is received by mankind, righteousness and purity will cover the earth as the waters cover the channels of the great deep. This is the same God that spoke unto you of old by the mouth of the holy prophets; and he comes now to fulfil the words spoken by them, and make a full end of sin. The words which are breathed out in alphabetic and luminous sentences are the ark of life; and he who will can come in and find refuge from the deluge of vengeance which shall prevail against the members of the world, and compel them to turn to God in the dispensation of this doctrine. God will suffer the ark of life to sail in the depth and height of wisdom; so that the poor and needy ascend into the height of God's glory, and the high and haughty man shall stoop to inherit eternal life in the material body.

The Lord God came among you the second time embodied in the flesh in a disguised way, to promulgate the perfect truth, and distribute it in the four quarters of the earth; to fulfil his words concerning his second appearing to the earthy body; to make manifest man's good and evil deeds, and to accomplish his work in bringing to sight the mysteries of salvation before the work of redintegration begins with the elect.

God shall not introduce himself unto men who are desperately wicked, but will show forth his strange acts unto them. By doing this, they will declare a spiritual war against him, which will be fought by the tongue weapon; and by the power of God's creative words, he will destroy depravity from the earth. In order to accomplish this thing in anger he shall show forth vengeance unto formality of righteousness, and renounce the wicked through his strange acts of righteousness; for they shall desire to see and understand, and shall look, and behold, and see, and understand not.

The grievances that shall come upon the world are the signet from which God's people will know that the day of rest dawns for them. Independence is God's course, for he will follow no hewn-out system of organization; and his people will love his course, and follow wheresoever he leads them. The Lord God will hew out and establish his own system of organization, which shall be called "the Lord's free and sacred declaration of divine independence." And no man is admitted into the grand secrets of this order before making his vows to the Lord on this wise: they have forsaken all other societies, and are willing to lay down their lives for the order and brethren, where Christ is your vindicator, and God your righteous judge, whose laws are founded upon friendship, love, and truth, interlaced with divinity, sincerity, and purity.

The Lord will keep his members from the evil that shall come upon those who are fighting against his great and notable day. Before one can become a member of God's united order of word, spirit, and truth, they must first dissolve relative friendship with the world, and all things in harmony with the old life, and make a final sacrifice of all things they possess. All who become members of God's society shall give all their time and labor to improve the growth of the spiritual kingdom; the time and service of their bodies will be used to do the masonry of the kingdom, and those who once become members of the eternal age will desire to go no more out, for the former things they lived to enjoy have all passed away, and behold, all things are new to please the inner man. With the elect, that which remaineth decayeth, and becomes wax cold, and ready to vanish away to put on the new.

The Lord God suffered imitators to come among you, proclaiming the same work, so as to make his name a reproach among all nations; for this cause the nations will rage and imagine a vain thing, for fear the majority of the people will fall victims to God's army.

The Lord shall have strong evidences to arise on the sides of both good and evil, so that the honorable and dishonorable will easily follow their own inclinations; by doing this, every one who maketh and believeth a lie will imagine a vain thing in God's workings. And there will be no possible chance for dishonorable characters to inherit eternal life; for this cause God came among you in a disguised way, and as a thief by night, to prevent any one from putting on his life whose evil deeds exceed their righteousness.

These words are sent from heaven to the elect, to comfort them;

in the hardest of trials he will make a way for their escape before they are overwhelmed by the billows of sorrow, although each one shall pay the price of eternal life before receiving it, for flesh itself shall die. The mortal image of the pre-adamites, which mankind are clothed in, shall be crucified before they can clothe themselves in the immortal image; and he who has entered this state of existence will have no pleasure in those who are striving to retain the body of death, for Christ came to destroy the image of the pre-adamites, which brings upon mankind all manner of suffrages.

And God will give in return the quickening image of the spiritual Christ Jesus, whose flesh is the luminous alphabetic letters which are stamped upon these pages. He who consents not to crucify the pre-adamite image shall lose both soul and body; for the spiritual Jesus Christ is the immortal soul of man. It was the mortal image of the pre-adamites that crucified the corporeal figurative body of Christ; and this is the part in the mortal man that is warring against the eternal souls.

And he who strives to retain the image of the pre-adamites is striving to crucify Christ afresh. He who believes and trusts in God will lay down the body of death to receive eternal life through receiving Christ's second appearing; for the Lord thy God is a jealous God, and if thou love another more than him, and present not all things that are called thine unto him, he will spew thee out of his mouth. For he laid down his life, and forsook all things to give unto thee a free and full redemption of thy body.

If thou wilt surrender all unto God, he will drive out sorrow's rudest tempest, and create within you springs of unceasing peace, and everlasting joy, which can never run dry. The Lord God came among you as a thief, to keep his mysterious workings hid from the builders of the terrestrial kingdom, so that they may continue their work, and make all the glorious and modern improvements in its scenes that can be made; and when the divine kingdom is set up in God's elect, the scenes of the two kingdoms' glory will be equally compared.

If men knew that God's holy kingdom was among them, they would cease to make the modern improvements in the terrestrial kingdom, and things would soon be a total wreck. The kingdom of heaven is so different from the way which men imaginarily pictured it out, nothing will induce desperate men to believe that it is among them supremely. If God multiplied material signs and wonders through the man whom he raised up to proclaim these truths, they would seek him to wreak their vengeance upon just as they did the figurative and material Christ. This is God's cause for keeping the mysteries concealed from the understanding of the mortal, until men receive the life, and then they will have a knowledge of God; therefore, men will continue at their work, and follow the evil imaginations of their hearts.

And the prognosticators and astronomers will still predict the great splendor that Christ shall appear to earth in, and what work will be accomplished when he comes; this they will be ignorant of, that Christ is already on earth doing the very same work, in a poor way, apparently. They are looking for these things to be done so that they can see the power, light, and excellency with their natural eyes, when the mysteries of the holy kingdom are spiritually discerned; and they will say, If this is the eternal Christ the Bible is fiction, and God has deceived the whole world on this mystery. This they are ignorant of, that through the imaginations and deceivableness of their own hearts, they have deceived themselves; therefore just and true are God's ways and judgments, for the assumed teachers have let in legions of depraved spirits through teaching damnable doctrines, which have deceived the entire world. They have let in so many seducing spirits to teach them, that they cannot distinguish the good from the evil.

God came not to seek peace among the wicked tribes of the earth, for there is no peace among them; for this cause he came with a sword to sever the wicked from among the just. Those who have lived deliciously on the fat of the luxuries of the world will have their joy turned into mourning, and their delicacies into wrath of eternal damnation. Christ, the faithful martyr, shall put on such strange acts of righteousness that even the elect will at times wonder whether they are true.

The Lord God has been showing forth his supernatural power through the past dark ages of the world, which was for mankind to gain faith in the words that he spoke unto them; and now they can use the supernatural power for eyeglasses to see the creative power which is in his word. Therefore, God's omnipotent power exists in his words, which are uttered upon these pages in luminous alphabetic forms; and the reunion of these many words is the globe of the celestial kingdom, which polarizes the glorious Son light to give light unto the members of the Son. God used his creative power to create the heavens and earths; and when the first man, Adam, lost his creative state, the creative word in man lost its creative power, because Adam was the word.

Man has again attained his creative state, and the power in the word has retained its creative office. When God's divine instrument speaks the word, that that is spoken through him shall be done. The word is sharper than any two-edged sword, and harder than adamant; it pierces to the marrow, and rends asunder the good and evil intents of man's heart, but no one can see the power in God's words until it is spiritually discerned.

There is no way wrought out for the wicked man to inherit eternal life in the material body: for the truth and the lie have both reached the goal of development. The wisdom which God has made his agent to engrave upon these pages is the manifestation that he contains the embodiment of the Godhead, through which he shall achieve victory over the world of wisdom, and be exalted above all mortal beings, and hereby obtain a far more excellent name than they, and far more exceeding glory. Through the quickening power of God's creative words he has therefore reached the climax of the realms of divine existence.

Before Adam lost his creative state, the sun-globe was filled with pure electric air; after the fall of Adam the mortal and corruptible man began to breathe out of his corruptible gastric system impure air, and by a gradual increase of the poisonous breath has filled the sun-globe with impure air. Mankind have become wholly depraved, and impure air is germinating in greater quantities; and the impure air will find its way back in corruptible men in the name of the modern diseases, and by so doing, corruptibleness will destroy corruptibleness.

The pure air which is in the sun-globe will keep out the poisonous air, and prevent it from mingling with the pure atmosphere which belongs to God's elect, and this shall continue until the deluge of pestilences is assuaged from over the earth; therefore, the greater portion of pure air will find its way into those systems which are more incorruptible than corruptible, and impure air will seek principally those bodies more corruptible than incorruptible, and by so doing will soon destroy wholly depraved men from the earth. Then God's elect will soon breath out purity to fill the sun-globe with pure air, just as it was before the earthly Adam lost his creative state.

All wholly corruptible bodies are members of the earth, and not members of the sun, and nothing more than corruptible dust; from dust they were taken, and unto dust shall they return, where they will cease from troubling the just, and cease from corrupting the earth with their poisonous breath. And the sweet, perfumed breath of God's elect will bring the seasons regularly, and fill the sun-globe with flowers of the sweetest perfume; then mankind will be no more members of the earth, but they will be members of the terrestrial and celestial sun and Son. The earth will be their footstool, and the breath of God's lips, which is breathed upon these pages, shall henceforth and forever swallow up the victory of the grave, and God's elect shall attain the eternal triumphant victory over all sin and iniquity.

The grave attained the victory now exercised over mankind through their ravenous lust; but the omniverous power of God's creative and destructive words shall destroy man's greedy lust, and rule the world with a rod of iron. From the fall of Adam, corruptibleness and incorruptibleness were placed on a revolution, and they revolved from generation to generation; the wicked souls of the dead formed wicked seed as fast as they were destroyed from the earth, while passing from one animal body into another. The disembodied souls that were more incorruptible than corruptible have been continually forming embodied souls after the same substance and kind, and by the continual revolution of corruption and incorruption have kept God's holy kingdom and the kingdoms of men equivolent in growth.

It is not the sins committed by the corrupt that make them corrupt; it is the corruptible souls that were admitted into their parents, and the curse fell on their seed, and those after them. There is no curse beyond corruptibleness. This is why this class of mankind is allowed to enjoy, while they exist materially, all the luxuries the world can afford them. The divine man desires not to walk after the corruptible man; for he will consider that his days are numbered, and, besides, full of trouble.

This ends the revelation declaring and showing God's purposes in the establishment of the past epochs of divinity, which discloses the deep and hidden secrets of God's mysterious workings to convey genuine humanity and divine righteousness to the perfect age.

PART III.

DIVINE PSYCHOLOGY ON THE EXEGETICAL ADVENTURES OF THE SAINTS; FULFILMENT OF ANCIENT AND MODERN PROPHECIES; DIVINE BIRTH AND VOCATION OF THE REVELATOR ON A NEW BEGINNING: SKETCH OF CARNAL LIFE.

Samuel's physical birthplace was Prince-Edward Co., Va. He was born December 23, 1863, and was country born and raised. He was very odd from childhood, which was noticed by all who knew him, and he was remarkably attractive; his peculiarity held its office until God called him from his worldly career.

From childhood he cherished an ardent desire to be converted to God and live a Christian life, for the idea followed him that he had to preach God's gospel, and he spoke of it occasionally until he received this eternal light. During his youthful days he attended church and heard ministers preach concerning an awful hell; they preached of its being so terribly severe that it kept him restless most of the time, for fear he might die and be doomed into the pit of misery and woe.

The Ethiopian race of people in those days preached principally on the great agony souls had to suffer who escaped heaven and went down into the pit, they being ignorant of this truth and proof that the burning pit of hell is situated in their souls, which torment their earthly bodies, although the Ethiopians represent it imaginarily and hideously as being a material subterranean pit situated in the macrocosm; but my pen, the flaming sword, wipes out this hideous superstition.

Samuel found nothing in his carnal life whereon he could rest to abolish the frequent tormenting thoughts concerning the burning pit. During the early stage of his scholastic days, he spent a small portion of his time in country school, but only learned to read and write a little. He left the South, and went to the city of Springfield, Mass., in the year of 1882, where he soon learned in part the trade of hotel cookery; and he developed rapidly at this profession, and became a practical cook in 1883, and was married in the same year.

After marrying he felt as though he had committed some unpardonable sin that would carry him down to ruin; and at times he wished vainly that he had never been born, seeing that he was so differently organized from other people, and feeling himself distinguished from others in superiority in every walk of the carnal life. But his stratum being solid and closely compacted enabled him to keep these excellent qualities concealed until the advent of the perfect life was conferred upon him, and the cohesion of word, spirit, truth, and materialism compounded, which give birth to the postliminy of the Divine Christ, the establishment of the transhumanized existence of mankind in the soul of the man Samuel. This suddenly made him the embodiment of God's spiritual kingdom, the unquenchable fire of divine truth, the ruling sceptre of the new age.

Despite sin and iniquity, Samuel secretly suffered in torment until January 24, 1888, at which time he was drawn to the divine healer by the power of God. Although Samuel was unconverted to the custom and style of religion, he felt it was time to seek a better life, because he would die soon. Death seemed imminent at this time, because the globe of the divine kingdom was rapidly approaching him; which caused a concussion in the natural spiritual body. A vehement thought and an enthusiastic desire revived in him amid these contusions and threatening casualties, to pray; and he felt ashamed to begin while he worked in the Hotel Warwick in the city of Springfield, Mass., fearing that the people with whom he was acquainted would find it out and laugh him to scorn; which shows that his natural body was prescient of what was fast approaching, by feelings.

Samuel thought he would leave the place he then worked at, and secure work in some other city, so that he could pray and get converted. He thought in himself if he went among strangers in a quiet and silent manner they would think that was his natural way, and therefore he could get converted, and no one find it out until he confessed it himself openly. He went straight to an employment office, and applied for a cook's situation in any city except Springfield, Mass.; "For," said he, "I am tired of this city. I am willing to work for less wages if I can leave here, I care not how far I go."

He left the employment office, and bought a bottle of medicine for his cold, to relieve him of his distressing feeling, and before going home, he went to his mother's house, and described to her how he felt. She remarked, "You ought to pray, for you want God in you."

Samuel said, "I know I should pray, for Christ came in the

world, suffered, and died to save sinners, and there must have been a great purpose in his doing this." And as Caroline C. Williams. then known and famed as "the divine healer," lived in the basement underneath Samuel's mother's tenement, Caroline was a very frequent visitor, and they were very warm friends, because of the belief which the majority of the family had in Caroline's mission of healing, which was done by praying for the sick, and thanking the Lord for the health of the afflicted who came unto her and trusted in this method: and many, through her, were healed of different complaints.

Caroline came in at the time that Samuel was in his mother's house, and Samuel's mother told her how he said he felt; and Caroline asked him if he did n't believe God could heal him. He said Yes, by the motion of his head. Caroline said to him, "Come downstairs, in my house," and she went on before him. Samuel arose and followed, and said in his mind, "I will go and see if she can do anything for me."

There were two other women in the room when Samuel went in: one was Caroline's sister, and the other Samuel's sister. Both were strong believers in the mission of healing Caroline was then doing, and they continued after Samuel was called, their faith being transferred in his mission to mankind: and they are, namely, Martha, Samuel's sister, and Georgiana, Caroline's sister. alluding to the natural birth.

Caroline got the Bible and read a portion of Scripture: but Samuel paid no attention to the reading, because the Holy Spirit began to make intercession of prayer in his heart while she read: and these are the words of the prayer: "Lord, enable me to believe on the words she shall speak unto me: draw within my wandering mind and scattered thoughts from the vain things of the world, and put my mind on heaven, and heavenly things: here, Lord, I give myself to thee, it is all that I can do."

These words of prayer and reading lasted about five minutes, and when ended it appeared to Samuel that he had been absent from the place he was sitting during the ceremony: and the divine healer remarked, "Thank God, for you are healed, and tell no one that you are not healed, when you leave here." When Samuel arose from his seat, he saw a great shining light streaming forth from his face: but he returned to his physical work as he usually did, and he felt a miraculous change in his feelings such as he had never enjoyed before, and all of his distressing feelings had fled apace, and he was willing then to remain in the city.

This part of the work took place at eve on the twenty-fourth of January, 1888. At this time Caroline was holding, every night, meetings at her house ; and Samuel commenced, from the time he received the great light, to attend the meetings held by Caroline, and only three days intervened between this time and his calling. During this intervention of time, when Samuel was sitting under the sound of Caroline's voice while preaching, he felt his heart imbibing the words, and bearing testimony to all she said.

On the twenty-fifth of January, the divine power of revelation began to work in Samuel, saying, "I have placed in your mouth a new tongue and a new song that the angels never sung ; you have been redeemed, and washed in the blood of the Lamb. I have wrought a miracle in you to bring sinners to repentance."

Samuel said, "Lord, what doth thou mean by having wrought a miracle in me ? "

"Through the supreme power of God I have forced you to repent ; because you believed on her whom I have sent, I have made you an heir, and a joint heir in Jesus Christ ; go and preach my gospel to a lost and sinking world."

Samuel said, " Lord, how shall I preach your gospel ? I am not learned ; shall I go to a seminary and study ministry ? Teach me what thou wilt have me to do."

"I am a teacher in a seminary ; I have made you a student, and have placed in your heart the divine book of revelation, and have made you a prophet, and will reveal unto you, through that divine revelation, signs and wonders of things that shall come to pass. I have made you a prophet, and placed you in Moses' shoes, and as Moses lifted up the serpent in the wilderness even so shall the son of man be lifted up. The time will come when every knee shall bow, and every tongue confess that I am God and besides me there is none other. I have made you on equality with the angels, have taken away from you your animal nature, and you shall not eat the flesh of swine. Faith comes by hearing, and belief comes through Jesus Christ. Repentance worketh conversion, and conversion confession, and confession redemption, and redemption eternal salvation. I have made Caroline mighty, and I am almighty ; command what she will and it shall be done."

And this power and privilege was given to Caroline while she embodied the millennium doctrine of healing the sick and preaching deliverance to the captives of sin, which was the manifest power of Christ's purity while deserting millennium to establish and realize his spiritual coming; which suddenly and unexpectedly produced post-millennium through a spiritual transmigration of the divine inheritance and endowment that God conferred upon Caroline to fulfil Christ's mission in the millennium age in a simple manner, to prepare for the greater power.

Samuel received the inheritance and endowment of the spiritual kingdom of Christ from God through obeying God in the following commandment, which was given to him to purge him, and try, and refine him, and fulfil, and make him pure white throughout the spiritual body, while enduring and overcoming the flood of unreasonable trials that came upon him in carrying out and fulfilling the commandment that God breathed into his heart.

On the evening of the twenty-seventh of January, 1888, at two o'clock, the voice of the Lord God came unto Samuel, saying, "Today, at half past two o'clock, you shall finish up your hotel career; go and be an helpmeet for Caroline." This commandment was the germ of evil that created all the infamy, trials, and perils Samuel had to encounter in the millennium members, who by nature contained the seven past ages of corruption, and that of the modern times.

After fulfilling God's determination, and seeing his purpose in full, which went to the extreme end to give birth to the seven doctrines of the human soul, the unquenchable flame of fire which streams from my soul through the mouth, and from the sword in my hand, does henceforth and forever utterly consume and wipe out the commandment given to Samuel to be an helpmeet for Caroline; which commandment brought sin and iniquity in the holy city and sanctuary.

I erase this commandment from "the Lamb's Book of Life," so that the forthcoming members of this doctrine may not stumble at it, and follow it for an example, and also to cleanse the holy city and sanctuary, so that these seven doctrines be given to mankind reasonably, and free from animal mixtures and the world's polluted customs of man and wife, which prevailed for many days in the mother city against postliminy; which utterly frees Samuel from Caroline, and from the corrupt personal claim of all women and men forever, and he, the embodiment of the seven doctrines of the human soul, is hereby presented to the entire world of humanity.

The commandment given to Samuel was the propeller that hastily brought the perfect salvation to the people, the children of men, through the victorious triumph of one man, the minister of the perfect age. The cause for the abolishment of this commandment will gradually be revealed, until it reaches the fulness of abomination, and the fulness of divine righteousness; whence the end of the world in the holy city and sanctuary.

When the Lord God gave Samuel the commandment to go and be an helpmeet for Caroline, he understood his work with her as helpmeet would be spiritual, in the true meaning, and that God did not mean for him to make a material desertion of his home and natural family until jealousy established conflict between him and wife, which hastily established enmity and desperate discord between Samuel and wife, which issued from her natural body through false judgment on the commandment given to Samuel, which was unreasonable and out of the reach of men's understanding, to bring about this change to separate him from the natural woman, so that the preternatural power of animal propensities and the spiritual supernatural phenomenalism would exist between Samuel and Caroline. Therefore it was utterly against the ordination of God for Samuel and the natural woman to remain united; still, they had to be united naturally to effect this purpose and end.

But Samuel considered the commandment at first, and began to think how he could support his wife and child if he gave up his work; the Lord refreshed in his mind the following words: "Take no thought for your life, what ye shall eat, nor what ye shall drink; nor yet for your body, what ye shall put on. Is not the life more than meat and the body more than raiment? Behold the fowls of the air: for they sow not, neither do they reap, nor gather into barns; yet your heavenly Father feedeth them. Are ye not much better than they? Which of you by taking thought can add one cubit unto his stature? And why take ye thought for raiment? Consider the lilies of the field, how they grow; they toil not, neither do they spin: and yet I say unto you, that even Solomon in all his glory was not arrayed like one of these."

Samuel did according to all God commanded him, and left his temporal work at the time appointed; but he thought the work he was called to do would soon become famous and honorable among the people, and through that source he would secure means to support his family. As soon as Samuel gave up his temporal occupation the news circulated among the people, and a number of them flocked to Caroline's house to see for surety if such report was true: and at this time Caroline was very eminent among those who believed in her mission of divine healing, and faith curing, and mental healing. And when they found Samuel at Caroline's house, acknowledging his calling to be united with her in the doctrine of truth, they believed every other evil report they heard, because they disbelieved the foundation. Rumor upon rumor circulated in the most reproachful manner. Such clamors changed the real truth of Samuel's calling in the minds of the people into a flood of lies: which was belched up in a short time by abandons of chastity, and men and women of reprobate minds, by which the city of Springfield was soon deluged, and became the most calumnious topic of the day.

This flood of the dragon and leviathan waters took Samuel's wife under full control, and influenced her to be carried away from the real truth and meaning of his calling to a higher life and nature. And she became superstitiously enraged against him, and called in a council of doctors; they heard the commandment of Samuel's calling from his mouth, and the judgment of the doctors numbered him with the insane, and he was sent to the asylum, because they understood not the pure language of the Bible.

While Samuel was in the asylum the voice of the Lord came unto him in a revelation, saying, "I have endowed your head with wisdom from on high, and opened the door of utterance to speak the mysteries of God; and through the instrumentality of his power, and through the book of divine revelation that I have wrought in you, I shall use you an instrument to lead Israel out of Egypt into the promised land, as I did Moses in days of old. I have established in you a new work of covenant, and you are my chosen messenger; and I will go with you in every field of battle, and will front each and every battle, and will suffer no hurt, harm, nor danger to befall you.

"I have established your goings, and have made you a pillar in the temple of the Almighty God, and you shall go out no more forever. You shall pass between the waters, and they shall not close upon you. You shall walk through the fire and you shall not be burned, neither shall the flames kindle upon you. Before I will suffer this new work of covenant that I have wrought in you to be condemned or crushed to death, I will destroy the world ; for I am a strong-armed God ; I hold the world in the hollow of my right hand. I can speak down in this world, and shake creation out of its orbit, and man will become lifeless. I have made you a light unto the Gentiles, that they may see their lost state of depravity ; I have made you a prince unto Israel, and through you they shall receive salvation."

Samuel said, " Lord, I thought thou wert the only God."

The voice of the Lord came unto Samuel, saying, " Whatsoever I doeth pleaseth thee, and whatsoever thou doeth pleaseth me ; for thou art my beloved son, in whom I am well pleased. And those that will not hearken unto the prophecies which you shall proclaim unto them shall be destroyed from among the people. I ordained it from the foundation of the world for this work of miracle to be wrought in you ; and I have preserved your life for this specified purpose. I have given you power over the dragon ; the young lion you shall not fear ; you shall tread upon the adder, and he shall not harm you.

" Men have been studying educational science for years and years, to get into my mysteries ; but they cannot get into my mysteries until they come unto me as a little child. I have made you as Mount Zion, a precious stone, and a tried stone, and a sure foundation ; and he that buildeth upon this stone shall be as a tree planted by a river of water, that bringeth forth its fruit in season. Stand still, until I make your enemies as though they never were ; for those that will not hearken unto your voice — I will send upon them all manner of diseases, destructions, and pestilences of every sort, such as never were upon the Egyptians. And during the years of your prophecies I will change the seasons of the times different from what they ever were before ; for I have made you to eclipse any man living on earth in the wisdom of God."

After Samuel had spent a short time in the asylum, his wife became grieved at heart, and repented of the evil devices she predestined to do to him. The power of repentance forced her to take Samuel from the asylum with the promise that she would never again interfere with his calling, to impede the commandment which had been given him. Samuel agreed to leave the asylum according to her promise ; " But," said he, " if you ever oppose my calling in anywise again, you and I will dissolve friendship forever."

As soon as Samuel returned home the strife began afresh between him and wife, and continued for three days; on the third day he reached the point to speak with burning authority, saying, "You and I have dissolved friendship forever and eternally." This manner of speech from Samuel to her caused her to attempt suicide to reach his sympathy, to cause him to retract from what he had said. Seeing her aim, his words stood firm; and in the meantime she returned him over to the city authorities, and he was again returned to the asylum, because he maintained the commandment. Jealousy and the non-consent of Samuel to live fully after the custom of religion and the fashion of man and wife caused this revenge to be exercised over him.

This has fulfilled the words of the Lord God, saying, "But this I say, brethren, the time is short: it remaineth, that both they that have wives be as though they had none; and they that weep, as though they wept not; and they that rejoice, as though they rejoiced not; and they that buy, as though they possessed not; and they that use this world, as not abusing it: for the fashion of this world passeth away."

The Lord God purposed Samuel's marriage after the will of the flesh, so that he might have a knowledge of the carnal life; and through the channel he has passed, has made the possible way, apparently and in reality, for all honorable people to reach eternal rest. None but God's chosen people will be admitted into his rest; he shall gather those whom he has prepared to be heirs of his glory, although they be in the uttermost parts of the earth, He will bring them home, not by the choice and will of man, but according to his purposes.

The second time Samuel was sent to the asylum, his natural parents succeeded in taking him out, after he had been there a few days. After Samuel was redeemed from the asylum, it was made known to him by the Holy Spirit that his next trial would be to enter into a fast, which was to be alone, without the Holy Spirit, forty days, to be spiritually tempted of the Devil. And when the time approached for Samuel to be without the Holy Spirit, he felt the shame upon him of being sent to the insane asylum, and the apparently disgraceful way in which he had been called to work with Caroline. There were times during this abstinence from the Spirit that the very flesh seemed to be leaving his bones, because of the spiritual trials he encountered while fulfilling this time.

There are many things the truth had to withstand, flowing into one centre, that are not narratable while passing this time ; mockings and intense scorn were on all sides, and hopelessness stood close by and preached continually throughout the time of temptation, trying to make the work established in Samuel different from the way he had proclaimed it. And those who stood in faithfulness, believing that the Holy God would soon make manifest his purpose in summoning Samuel in such mysterious way, wondered with great admiration at the long time that intervened between the summons and the beginning of his work, which caused some of the stars of heaven to fall from the higher hope which was then shining in the minds of corporeal bodies, whose faces was turned toward the spiritual Jerusalem.

When the forty days were fulfilled, it was thought by Samuel and those who stood with him that the Holy Spirit would use him to show forth the work he was called to do by empowering him to go out among the people and declare the eternal truth unto the world. And as the Holy Spirit brought nothing in his reach and power to do out among the people, the tempter appeared to him mentally and said, " There is no God ; and you are only thinking up this revelation coming within you. You are making a fool of yourself, and if you do not leave this city you will never do anything but sit around. The Bible is only a story-book, composed by wise men of the world."

Samuel called him a liar, and he fled from his mind, but soon saw himself in a vast wilderness. Finally Samuel saw himself in a vision floating along upon an ocean ; and by the influx of peace which he inhaled into his soul just then, it was made known to him that this was the ocean of God's peace.

Again Samuel was delivered into the clutches of the law by his wife, for non-support, but the case was dismissed owing to its complicacy. Therefore, twice in the asylum, and once in prison has fulfilled the words of the Lord, saying, ." He was taken from prison and from judgment." When it reached this crisis it ended public seance with Samuel regarding imprisonment.

Then it was made known to Samuel that the healing power of millennium, accomplished through Caroline antecedent to his vocation, would be cut off. This was for the inheritance of divine righteousness, and the endowment of divine wisdom, judgment, and equity to be conferred upon Samuel, so that he would be the leader, governor, and commander of the work to follow ; and the work he did was prophesying of God's judgments upon the wicked world, and, instrumentally to God, pronouncing the judgments. But this was a mystery at that time, not knowing what work would be given him; which fulfils as follows : " But of the times and the seasons, brethren, ye have no need that I write unto you. For yourselves know perfectly that the day of the Lord so cometh as a thief in the night. For when they shall say, Peace and safety; then sudden destruction cometh upon them, as travail upon a woman with child; and they shall not escape."

Samuel and Caroline covenanted as follows : that Samuel should be the leader, governor, and commander of the work they two had to do together; and she would be obedient to him in whatever he said. Caroline agreed that it should be according as Samuel had said; because, said she, he was sent to her to be the leader of the work ; for many promises had been made unto her by the Lord God and Samuel came to fulfil them.

Caroline C. Williams was born in Westbrook, Va., October 16, 1856. She left the city of Richmond, Va., and went to the city of Springfield, Mass., in 1872, and was married in the same year. During her wedded life she gave birth to seven daughters, and four of the seven died, leaving three ; after which her husband died also.

Caroline was a woman who was faithful to the cursed law imputed upon man and woman, and her nature issued stringent laws to carry the curse to the extreme, which made her distinguished from other women. When she was joined to her husband, she had no other god but her own family, and her glory, honor, and pleasure were wholly involved in this lower animal kingdom ; the other higher animal kingdoms were rejected by her, otherwise than to use them to glorify her selfish kingdom. As she contained by nature the essential principles of the curse imputed upon the Adamite seed, the Lord God saw that it was good to choose her to fulfil this purpose in revealing the abominations and stringent laws of sin now reigning over humanity.

When she was left without an earthly husband, she became grieved at heart, and started in search of a place of refuge from the burdens and cares that she had suffered and groaned under from youth ; and she soon reached the land flowing with milk and honey, where she ate, and drank, and made her soul fat.

As Caroline was the embodiment of the lower animal kingdom, she was the focalization of the four animal kingdoms, which made her the mother city of the millennium doctrine, the goddess of metaphysics, and the muse of divinity. This gave power to her to give birth to the seven spirits of divinity, called "the seven Ethiopian branches," which were transmigrated and materialized as much as was spiritual in the man Samuel, from whence cometh his power of wisdom and righteousness, to reveal the Son of Righteousness to the world. She also gave birth to the seven spirits of the Devil's kingdom, which were transmigrated and materialized as much as was spiritual in the man who was used in this revelation to prefigure sin and iniquity, whose spiritual name is the Man of Sin, the Son of Perdition, the God of Metaphysics, and the material John N. West.

Caroline's mission of healing began March 31, 1884, continuing from this time until January 27, 1888, at half past two o'clock, at which time the Divine Christ made his second advent to the earthly body Samuel in God's triniunity power, and utterly destroyed the carnal life of Samuel; so that there was found no place in him for the old era.

When Caroline was started on her mission of healing by the commanding power of the Divine Spirit, she was commanded to go in all the world and preach the gospel to every creature; lay her hand upon the sick and they should recover; the blind should receive their sight, and the deaf should receive their hearing, and the dumb should speak with a new tongue; the dead should be raised to life, and devils should be cast out, and the crippled should walk; and whatever she desired, by prayer, believing, she had.

Soon after she received this commandment and started out among the people fulfilling her mission, she felt that she was alone and had no one to assist her in the work she was commanded to do; and this manner of promise was made unto her by the Lord: "I will give unto you a son." Caroline did not ask who the son would be, nor what he would do, nor when he would be given, nor how he would be given; but she made a verbal promise unto the Lord that it made no difference with her how the son was given; when he came forth she would proclaim unto the people that he was given of God.

And when Samuel was commanded to go and be an helpmeet for her, he went straight to her, and spoke the word as he was commanded; and the Holy Spirit bore testimony to what Samuel said, saying, "This is your first-born son in Zion." Then Caroline knew as well as Samuel that God sent him, and she was quickened there and then to know that Samuel was the promised son, strange as it seemed; although Samuel was ignorant of the promise made to her.

It can be understood by the work that manifests itself in Samuel, that all the great work that the Holy Spirit declared that Caroline should do was fully accomplished when Samuel was cleansed by the power of her doctrine. But when the power of divine truth was conferred upon Samuel to do the perfect work in giving birth to the doctrines of the new age, it left Caroline devoid of divine wisdom and judgment, which left her soul unfortified; this caused the revivification of her natural life, which was deadened by the power of divine truth when she received the gift of divine healing from God, which hastily established disagreement between the doctrines of millennium and postliminy.

Doctrines issued from Caroline's nature preternaturally to withstand the divine doctrines of postliminy; and Samuel's nature that he had put on distilled doctrines to destroy the abominable doctrinal science of millennium that strove in the mother city for competition. This prevailed for many days, on account of her former power, and Samuel's being sent to her, which gave her power and authority, because Samuel's power came through her; which gave her power to say to Samuel, "If I am wrong, then you are wrong also." But the Holy Scripture melted and ran together when Samuel began to speak to her to show her where she had erred from the path of divine rectitude; which threw light on her corruption, and produced the unquenchable fire to consume her woful, tormenting, and miserable embodiment in each freak of preternatural animalism.

Samuel was soon made to know, when the covenant between him and Caroline was established, that he should abstain from all meats; but Samuel was still unaware of what kind of work the Holy God was going to use him to accomplish. This was in the sixth month of his summons, and nothing but trouble had shown itself in the purpose of his calling; while the tokens ahead indicated worse to follow.

John N. West is the next most principal member of this revelation, and the understanding of his mighty work in connection with this revelation will come in when it reaches that event. But I will go on to say that he felt he was to follow Samuel as soon as he heard of his vocation; and he heard of it the same evening Samuel was called, and came to see if such were true. And as soon as he heard Samuel talk, he became dead silent to a certain extent until he ended his natural work.

The object in this course of revelation is to declare the time that the holy truth made its post-millennium to the earthly body to reign over sin and abomination, and to tell why the holy Jerusalem encountered so many grievances before the mighty enemies were conquered and put under his feet. The repetition of Christ's spiritual suffering and crucifixion, and the manifest power of his post-millennium to earth to reign over sin and iniquity, and annihilate the principal germs that create abomination, was in this wise : it was to accomplish the fulfilment of the Holy Scriptures, and to realize the simple and wonderful works of the Lord God in the fulness of salvation in the material bodies of the elect people.

The glorious second, but spiritual, advent of the Lord and Saviour Jesus Christ, accompanied by the angelic host of heaven, was fulfilled in the year 1888, January 27, at half past two o'clock on a Friday evening ; at which time the millennium dispensation was fulfilled, and fled away from the soul and body of Samuel, who, by a miracle, was cleansed by the triniunity power of word, spirit, and truth, which realized in the revelator the fulness of postliminy, the embodiment of the eternal dispensation of righteousness. At the time stated that the holy truth, the New Jerusalem, made its advent to Samuel's flesh there was no more place found in him for the glory of the millennium era.

The fulness of the millennium doctrines began its perfect work in Caroline, March 31, 1884 ; at this time she was started on her mission of healing by the power of the Holy Ghost, and she embodied the millennium doctrines. Unlearned she was, but she was wonderful in speech, which was unpremeditated and involuntary throughout her mission. During the time that intervened, from the beginning of her mission to the post-millennium of the eternal truths and doctrines, the Holy Spirit was using Caroline in different simple and poor-looking ways to perform good works among the people, — such as healing the sick, preaching deliverance to the captives of sin, feeding the hungry beggar, and all other duties belonging to the Christian dispensation.

The millennium doctrines appertaining to a Christian life were fulfilled in Caroline's mission of healing when Samuel was cleansed by her doctrine and divinely stamped with the post-millennium creative doctrines, to reveal the son of man to the world. These eternal truths and doctrines will burn up the formality of godliness in the principles of this generation, and establish in them the righteous era; so that they may love their fellowmen as themselves, and do unto others as they would have others do unto them.

Then the millennium era was fulfilled in Caroline, and ended first in the man Samuel; and this sudden change left Caroline on the vertex of the millennium era, awaiting to unite with her son postliminy. This left Caroline still at the verge of the Abyssinian gulf which brought in disagreement between the millennium doctrines and the post-millennium doctrines, which established war between the old and the new. This established a sealed mystery in the earliest infancy of this doctrine's mission to mankind, which caused all the severe troubles of the holy people embodied in the man Samuel manifested in transhumanized characteristics. And these many saints in the righteous dispensation fought triumphantly upon the rich, divine sod of the man Samuel by the elements of the triniunity power of divinity.

When Samuel began to prophesy, all the words of his prophecies which pointed to material things were to discover and destroy the pollutions in millennium, purge and refine its divine substances, to unite with her son postliminy in the eternal age. The more the two ages rebelled, the more depraved and abominable the Christian dispensation became in Caroline's nature, because she was composed of the most adamantine, substantial, and brilliant stratum of the dark-aged worlds. And all those who united with the holy truth in person to help forward the eternal doctrines were agents chosen by the mother city to rebel against the holy city and sanctuary of truth; but this mystery was concealed from the subjects of this woful, and miserable, and crafty embodiment.

This concealed mystery caused all the perilous times of the saints, and those that followed after; because the polluted dispensation was set up, in the minds of the holy saints and those seeking the holy life, to be on equality with the holy dispensation, because the holy dispensation was commanded to go and be an helpmeet for the embodiment of millennium, whose nature was polluted speedily after Samuel was called and united with her, and intermingled with the doctrines.

The disagreement began, and grew stronger and stronger, between Samuel and Caroline immediately after he was summoned to work with her: and she became disobedient to him in the strongest way. This revived and created in the millennium era all sorts of abominations, sin, and vice; which established the preternatural trio-unity of the Devil's kingdom, in the millennium tabernacle, — the mother city, which was pure in the divine hemisphere of human nature, — to give birth to the post-millennium of divinity, so that millennium would give birth to the highest branch of righteousness, and then pollute the substance in her nature, and give birth to the chief metropolis of abomination, signifying the man of sin, the Son of Perdition, the god of metaphysical science.

Here were the mysterious trials of the saints ; and the language of the prophecies which streamed from Samuel's mouth, when he stood up to lead, govern, and command, was to destroy and purge out the pollutions of the Christian age. The fulfilments of all the latter-day prophecies, as called in days of old, are written on the hidden realities of the man of sin, and the truism of Christ in the establishment of the age of sempiturnity, which is to be established in the material bodies of the elect people among the Israelite races. Christ is truth, and the kingdom of Christ is the transhumanized principles created by divine truth to establish the kingdom of heaven in every godly inclined person.

When the millennium mission of divine healing commenced through Caroline, she was living in a basement tenement on Willow Street, in the city of Springfield, Mass., where she remained until the promised son was given. She held Friday night meetings in her apartment, and preached a full mission of healing. and she went from door to door preaching the same, and she went to other cities and towns where she was called to heal the sick. And during the latter part of her mission, the Lord made her to know through a vision that she had to cross the ocean ; but where, and when, and for what purpose, the Lord saw fit to conceal from her.

Caroline's heart became filled with a fervent desire to start on the journey of which she had been forewarned. Then the Lord God began to make the way possible for her to go the journey to the place he had purposed for her to go. Therefore God prepared a Swede woman, whose name was Christina ; and her original home was Calmar, Sweden. Christina had a very great love for Caroline, and much belief in her power of healing ; and her love for Caroline was so great that the best she could do for her was not great enough.

Christina thought that it would bestow upon Caroline and herself much honor to take Caroline and her three children to her original home in Calmar, Sweden, also thinking that much good might be done there among her people through Caroline. When Christina asked her if she would like to go, Caroline had not thought of going; her reply to Christina was, "I will go if the Lord says so." Caroline made a prayer to God, saying, "If thou will for me to go to Sweden, furnish me with the means thou wantest me to have."

Christina left Caroline's house, and as Caroline did not give her a decided reply about going, Christina thought no more of her proposal; but she returned to Caroline's house in a few days and found her preparing for the journey. Christina was struck with astonishment, but she shrank not from her proposal; therefore they made ready and started on the journey June 9, 1887, and arrived in Calmar, Sweden, July 1. The money they started with gave out before reaching their destination, owing to the long route they took; and this caused them much trouble while on their journey; and when they reached Christina's original home, they found that there was almost a dearth among her relatives. Great was her disappointment, for she forethought a good time for Caroline and her children.

Caroline could not speak in the Swede tongue, and neither could Christina interpret the English language in the Swede tongue understandingly. Here was another trial for Caroline; so she appealed to God to know why, and for what purpose, he had brought her to that country when she could not speak the language, neither could the people understand the doctrine of healing.

To strengthen Caroline to carry out the ordinations, God renewed the promise of the son by saying, "I will give unto you a son." Caroline went and told Christina how God had promised her a son; and Christina asked how the son was going to be given. Caroline said, "I care not if he be given as the other children were given to me; when he comes forth I will proclaim it unto the people that he was given of God."

Christina said, "If he is given in that way I will not believe it." Caroline said, "I care not if no one believes it. I shall own him just the same, and proclaim it unto the people that God gave him to me."

Also a plague of fleas was very great upon Caroline's children on account of their age and their being strangers at that place. The youngest child was bitten terribly, and by scratching became covered with scabs. This was the greatest trial that Caroline had while fulfilling this purpose; there were other children in the same house, and they were not troubled with this plague as Caroline's children were. Then the people began to mock and say, "If she has so much faith in God, why does n't she stop the fleas from biting her children?"

But the Lord was carrying Caroline through trials to harden her to stand the unreasonable trials she had to encounter when the promised son was given, that the Scripture might be fulfilled. Caroline and her three children left Sweden October 18, and arrived home November 2, 1887, and Christina returned soon afterwards. Christina felt under obligations to Caroline because of disappointment in the pleasure she forethought for Caroline at her home; so she made Caroline a volunteer promise that she would pay her rent monthly. Caroline told her that she should not make such a promise, as she knew not what she could do; still, Christina resolved to do all she could.

The circular which contains the conditions of Caroline's mission of healing reads as follows: —

THE DIVINE HEALER;

OR,

OUR SAVIOUR'S SPECIAL MISSION.

By CAROLINE WILLIAMS,

54 Willow Street . . . . . Springfield, Mass.

God created mankind holy, happy, and perfect. — *Gen.* 1: 27-31.

Man's fall, man sinned. — *Gen.* 3: 6-17.

The blessed Saviour came according to promise to redeem us from sin.— *Isa.* 53; *Matt.* 1: 25; *Isa.* 61: 1-4.

Sin is the cause of every ailment, such as sickness, sorrow, pain, disease, and death. — *Rom.* 6: 23; *Job* 5: 19; *Ps.* 60: 11; 1 *Pet.* 5: 7; *Isa.* 26: 3; 2 *Cor.* 7: 10.

Fruits of the Spirit and fruits of the flesh. — *Gal.* 5: 19-24; *Rom.* 8: 1-8.

Christ was manifested to take away our sins, for in Him is no sin. — 1 *John* 3: 5.

Surely He hath borne our sicknesses and carried away our diseases. — *Isa.* 53: 4; *Matt.* 8: 17.

Did Jesus come and redeem His people?—*Matt.* 1 : 21-23 : *Matt.* 2 : 1 : *Luke* 2 : 8-16.

Hath He borne your sorrows and carried away your afflictions?— 1 *Pet.* 3 : 18.

Why then are you sick?—*James* 4.

Do you doubt God's willingness; do you doubt God's ability to meet your case?—*John* 4: 46-54 : *Matt.* 8: 5-13; *Luke* 17 : 11-19; *Matt.* 8: 16, 17; *Matt.* 8: 14. 15; *Matt.* 9: 1-8 : *Matt.* 9: 18-26; *John* 11: 1-54; *John* 5: 1-16; *Matt.* 12 : 9-15 : *John* 9: 10-21 : *Matt.* 9: 20-22 : *Matt.* 15: 21-28; *Matt.* 17: 24-27.

Do you doubt God's word?—*Mark* 11 : 24; 1 *John* 5 : 14, 15; *James* 1 : 5-8.

Will you say with an honest heart, Lord, I believe, help Thou my unbelief?—*Mark* 9 : 24: 1 *John* 3: 19-21; *Heb.* 11.

Faith without works is dead.—*James* 2 : 17, 20, 26.

Herein is the work.—*John* 6 : 28, 29.

I have asked and not received. Why?—*James* 4 : 3: *Heb.* 11 : 6.

Other healings. —*Acts* 3 : 1-9 ; 5 : 15 ; 19: 11, 12 ; 20 : 9-12 : 20 : 1-9.

This circular consists of the circumference of the most essential points of the millennium doctrine of divine truth, which the Holy Spirit uttered through Caroline while on her mission of healing, which gave birth to post-millennium. The millennium world consists of four foundations, which worketh mutually and reciprocally together; but in reality these are subdivided into four kingdoms, which are called "the world," the entire globe of the millennium era.

All who are loyal to the laws, doctrines, commandments, and worships of these four kingdoms are blessed to soar into the height and depth, width and length, of these four kingdoms, and enjoy their luxuries, which is the glory of the flesh. Excessive love and desire for education, money and wealth, blood-kin and family circle, women and men craving each other, is the entire globe of the millennium world; and these four united kingdoms are the profound depth and the apex of man's finite power and strength, glory and honor, riches, and blessings, and wisdom.

By man's being faithful to the laws, doctrines, commandments, and worships of the four kingdoms of the world, it creates in his nature the elementary substances of purity to establish a higher existence for man, the inheritance of the perfect and blissful kingdom. The first advent of Christ was the truth to establish the laws, doctrines, worships, and commandments of the millennium era; which enabled mankind to obtain a higher degree of knowledge to search out, and patent, and discover, the perfect glory of the earthly.

The faithfulness of mankind in the accomplishment of this thing has created in human nature precious coins and substances to establish a higher kingdom in nature, when the base coins and substances are purged out of human nature, and prevented from mingling with the elements of the holy and eternal kingdom. The purging of the base coins and substances, animals and reptiles, fowl and fishes, creeping things and uncivilized races, out of man's nature is tormenting and woful, sorrowful and grievous, and intense misery to human flesh, from whence is derived the name "hell."

While man passes from the millennium world to the post-millennium age, he must journey through the seven stages, called "the doctrines of divine psychology," before his hell ends; which is the journey through the seven mortal worlds, the abolishment of mortality in the human soul, which is the end of the world. The disloyalty that prevails clandestinely in the millennium members maintains and perpetuates the suffering sins of the world, such as lying, enmity, scornfulness, disbelief in divine truth, disobedience to God, jealousy, and lustfulness after unlawful pleasures. Individually these are called "devils;" but united, they are called "the great dragon," who is the degenerator of mankind, who deceives the whole world, creates the innumerable evils now in existence, and causes the human family to suffer.

This degenerator, in many cases of nature, slumbers slyly, and continues in false peace and friendship, and fails to do anything apparently like sin. This dragon worketh in his predominant power where the outward appearance of a person is upright and perfect. This is the power and might that uses the openly lawless and the desperadoes to commit the many crimes and daring deeds that are becoming so numerous in the secular world.

The force of murdering, suiciding, robbery, infidelity, and deceiving, current, is seated in those persons who pretend to be the most upright and exact to obey the right; and this class of mankind is thought to be trustworthy, and is put forward in all important matters. This is the great form of godliness that is classified in the finite kingdom, systematically, in the name of Christian worships, that assumes the names of the churches of Christ which are established according to men's opinions, color, wealth, and their hope and imagination of the blissful life.

Those who commit the desperate crimes and daring deeds openly are forced to do so by their crafty and peaceful brothers, and the material crimes are representing the peaceful and crafty brother in doing his biddings. Those who are open, and act out what is in them, are composed of a deleterious volatile substance, which makes them unable to keep concealed the hidden secrets of their hearts ; while the peaceful and crafty man is able to keep his treasured up to bestow upon the lawless. According to the established laws and doctrines, worships and commandments, of animal nature, that class of mankind which acts outwardly what is in them has to suffer materially, and is punished unmercifully for the sins of their accessory brothers.

The Lord God hath created and established that manner of doctrine and dispensation in the nature of man that will punish every man for his sins, whether he confesses his unrighteousness or not. Divine truth will stand up in the human flesh and condemn every man's and every woman's abomination, which will make a hell for them in some way, to compel them to turn from evil and do good, one for another.

The millennium era, after passing through great tribulations, has been purged by the approaching judgments, and united with her son postliminy to testify to the teachings of the higher doctrines, which is the uniting of the two ages, which produces the exoteric power of the post-millennium doctrines, the beginning of divine creation. This ends the millennium doctrines and its healing, world-wide circular, and the cohesion and compounding of the two ages make up a circular and doctrines with a far greater work, — the abolishment of death and hell, the establishment of man's perfect and eternal salvation.

In early summer, the same year of Samuel's vocation, there broke out an epidemic of diphtheria, and Caroline's three children fell victims to this plague, and the two youngest, who bore testimony to Caroline's mission of healing, and agreed with her to make the work with power in some cases that were healed, died.

Georgia M. Williams, the youngest, was the strongest in bearing testimony of her mother's mission ; and she had the gift of healing by laying on of hands. She was born August 28, 1882 ; died, September 4, 1888.

Theresa B. Williams was the next testifier of her mother's mission; she preached and visited the sick. She would tell the people to thank the Lord for all things; and when she saw any one afflicted, she would tell them to come and see her mother, and would say, "My mamma holds meetings." And when she heard of any one being sick near by, she would go and see them, and return home and get her little sister, who had the gift of healing, and carry her to see them when she could; she was filled with sympathy for the sick. She was born December 4, 1881; died, July 23, 1888.

This power of work was not taught to these two children; they began to preach, and testify to what they heard their mother say, as soon as she was called to preach the gospel and heal the sick by laying on of hands. When the first child was taken sick, no physician was summoned, until the child died, because it was taken sick one day and died the next. The Lord did not put the desire in Caroline to have a physical physician to see the child, neither could she ask the Divine Physician to heal it; so she waited to know the purpose, and the child died and carried the purpose into effect. After the death of the child it was published and rumored far and near that she failed to give the child the medicine it should have had, through trying to heal by faith; and there were many disgraceful publications concerning the death of the child, which is a shame to narrate verbatim, because they were inconsistent with reason and did not agree.

When the other child was taken sick, a physician was hastily summoned, but the child died in a few days; and at this time the healing power was evidently destroyed, which ended Caroline's millennium mission, so that she could come under the higher doctrines of postliminy. This was done to fulfil the words of the Lord, saying, "And there appeared a great wonder in heaven." — Rev. 12 : 1.

These fulfilments unfolded and revealed the cause of the troubles which revived speedily after Samuel ended his worldly career; and this chapter was the first power to throw light on what his work would be, and why he was commanded to work with Caroline; and this light sprang forth in the eighth month of his vocation.

All this time Samuel waited patiently for his Holy Father to command the next course for him to do, to fulfil his purposes. Reproaches and disgrace were on all sides; but Caroline sacrificed all of her former friends and eminence, and as she was moved by the Spirit to speak, she proclaimed, unto all who sought of her to know, what was meant by Samuel's being sent to work with her. She proclaimed that it was God's doings, and who could stop it? This she did with much power and authority; she could not tell what God would bring out of the marvel, but she proclaimed it amid all the calumnious reproaches created by the poisonous blasts of abject and wrangling skeptics.

> Some said that Caroline Williams was nothing but a fraud:
> But the Holy Spirit taught me that she was sent of God.
> He chose her from the many; he gave her power to heal:
> The mysteries of salvation he unto her revealed.
>
> Like Abraham, he tried her by sending her away
> To distant lands. among strangers, so far across the sea.
> Like Job, he gave her patience to bear and endure all things.
> Though Satan should afflict her, she will have power to win.
>
> With Joshua's resolution, on Jericho's mighty wall,
> She will march and sound her trumpet until they shake and fall.
> As in the time of Noah — Do you remember him?
> He preached and told the people to cease from doing sin.
>
> But oh, they mocked and scorned him: they said he was a fool
> For preaching such a doctrine, — that God would send a flood.
> Just so with Caroline Williams; they said she preached in vain.
> God sent another prophet, the same truth to proclaim.
>
> But when the prophet told them about the inner man.
> How Christ had washed and cleansed him, they said he was insane.
> They sent him to the asylum, thinking no God was there:
> But oh, they were mistaken, for God had answered prayer.
>
> For he was there to meet him, to comfort and to cheer,
> Saying, "Samuel, I am with you: the world you need not fear."
> Then wake up, sleepy Christians, all ye who sleep in sin,
> And let us join the army, to serve the Lord, our King.
>
> You must be separated from every trifling toy;
> You must have full salvation, if you want eternal joy.
> I am Alpha and Omega, the beginning and the end,
> And if they will not hear me, I will on them judgment send.

When her children died there was great rejoicing among the envious abjects, who said that God was punishing her for taking a woman's husband and calling him her son, and saying that God sent him to her. The enemies then took council against her to have her imprisoned for homicide. This was the time that the red-head dragon stood up in his finite power to slay the man child and his mother; because the doctrine was but in its infancy, and unable to speak for itself, and show its mission to mankind, and destroy the force, power, and might of the red-head dragon, signifying lies.

The finite power of the red-head dragon forced Caroline into gross darkness speedily after Samuel stood up to prophesy, with wings of love and faith, that the end of the troubles would tell the plain truth why God ordained it for her and Samuel to work together in one consent. The red-head dragon spewed out of his corrupt gastric system floods of lies, which utterly destroyed the power and method of divine healing throughout the finite kingdom; so, from that time henceforth, none shall enjoy full blessings and rich privileges of divine healing in its real meaning and essential degree but those who receive the seven doctrines of postliminy in the fulness thereof.

Samuel's wife swallowed up the first flood of lies, and was carried away by its propelling current speedily after he was called. She interpreted the Holy Scriptures, and the commandment given to Samuel, to please her ravenous lust. She disregarded God's commandment to Samuel, and consented to the pernicious judgment of insanity and adultery to carry her point despitefully, and defeat God's ordination. Those seven united principles that lead to degenerate mankind empowered her to rule the city of Springfield to gratify her revenge. All that she said was truth to her kind, and all that Samuel said was rejected; and Samuel shut his mouth, and gave himself into their hands, to do with him as they thought best. If they thought him insane they could put him with the insane, and if they thought that he was feigning himself called of God merely to change wives he was willing they should put him with the lawless and impostors.

While Samuel was passing through these different stages of infamy, his eternal peace and rest were unutterable; he felt satisfied, and willing that the people should do with him all that they had power to do. It never entered his heart to find fault with anything the people were empowered to do to him. He knew by the intangible body of God's manifest power in him, of which his enemies knew not, that his Father was fulfilling his purpose in every dark occurrence; for he knew that the work wrought in him was too great to be received by the people before going through trials to prove its eternal power and purity.

Still, Samuel did not desire war and opposition; he was striving to make peace in every step he took, all the way through the troublous times; and when the trouble came he was willing that the pleasure of his Holy Father should be fulfilled through him in all things. When the millennium mission was destroyed, a gloomy feeling came over Samuel, which made him feel as though the work he was called to do was dead. He appealed unto his Father for something to do, because everything that once was life seemed dead; and Samuel was commanded to prophesy, which was the beginning of the work in him as God had declared it should be.

Samuel said, "Lord, what shall I prophesy, and how shall I prophesy?" He was commanded to write the prophecies that God would reveal unto him. These prophecies, which contain the contents of the seven seals of abominations upon which God poured out his fierce wrath and vengeance, are as follows:—

Through the supreme power of God, and through the book of divine revelation that God has wrought in me, he is using me an instrument to proclaim unto the people the troubles that shall befall men in the last days. These troubles shall visit the world, and be fulfilled in three years' time, commencing with its rapid spread the twenty-seventh of October, 1888. During this time all tribes of the earth shall moan, but that that is determined shall be.

These prophecies that I shall proclaim are given by the inspiration of God, which comes by his revealing power; therefore I am chosen, and ordained a prophet unto the nations, and it shall be made known through the prophecies that I shall proclaim to verify my statements, for God has made this prophet to eclipse any man on earth in the wisdom of God.

These are the troubles that shall befall men in time above mentioned:—

There shall be all manner of diseases such as never were before; the earth's produce shall be cut off, and the earth shall not bring forth food to supply the people's needs. In grain-growing season some days will be so hot that grain growing will be scorched by the sun, and men and cattle will be sunstruck, while other days will be so cold that stuff growing will not prosper, and a famine will go over the earth; and in these three years of trouble men will not have the seasons regularly, as they once have had. There will be thunder and lightning, hurricanes and blizzards and earthquakes in divers places, such as never were before.

Men and women will burn for each other to such an extent that it will be the cause of more murders and suicides than there ever were before. Men will be disappointed with their aims in life ; and there will be more thievery, and robbery, and accidents, and men deceiving and being deceived, than there ever were before. Men will be despisers of good and lovers of evil ; the wicked will do wickedly, and the world will go speedily into infidelity.

There will be a time of trouble such as there never was since there was a nation on earth, for the Devil has come among you having great power, because he knoweth that he hath but a short time. In this time of trouble, the third part of the men of the earth shall be destroyed ; and in this time of trouble the tribulations for God's saints will be greater than they ever were before ; but if they continue in faith they shall have a crown of life that fadeth not away, for their reward is sure and even now at the door.

This prophet Samuel is the man child spoken of in the twelfth chapter of Revelation. He shall rule all nations with a rod of iron, which is the truth ; and at the end, or fulfilment of these prophecies, God will use this prophet Samuel to preach salvation unto the world ; he will proclaim the hidden realities which have been hid from men since the foundation of the world.

This is the second coming of Christ, and the end of the world, and harvest time. The truth that shall go forth out of this prophet's mouth will be a consuming fire to the wicked. This is the day that Malachi said would burn as an oven; this is a spiritual fire, and will burn up all wickedness in men. The truth shall judge the world; and this is the time that every knee shall bow, and every tongue confess that I am God, and besides me there is none other. Then there will be no more going from door to door teaching every man to be your neighbor, nor to know God ; for they all shall know him, from the least to the greatest.

It will be made known through the prophecies I shall proclaim that this prophet Samuel is the second coming of Christ spiritually ; but he will sit on the right hand of his Father spiritually until his enemies are made his footstool, and that will be at the end, or fulfilment, of these prophecies.

Because of the speedy growth of infidelity, God will be on the seat of justice, in this time of trouble, rewarding the wicked according as their works have been. The ungodly will call upon him in this time of trouble, and he will not hear them. They must hear this prophet, or be destroyed; for God will speak to the people through this prophet who is his son throughout all ages of eternity, for Moses truly said unto the fathers, " A prophet shall the Lord thy God raise up unto thee, of your brethren, like unto me; him shall ye hear in all things whatsoever he shall say unto you. And it shall come to pass every soul which will not hear that prophet shall be destroyed from among the people."

Yea, and all the prophets from Samuel and those who followed after, as many as have spoken, have likewise foretold of these days. The prophet Moses spoke of is the second coming of Christ, but those who are saints indeed will have victory over these troubles. Samuel prophesies signs and wonders yet to come, and then cometh the end quickly, the last days, the end of the world.

After these prophecies were written Samuel was moved to carry them to the press to be published; but they refused to publish them. Samuel was then moved by the Holy Spirit to send them out by letters to a few who he thought would like to read them; and this privilege was soon taken away, because the majority of those who heard the reading of the prophecies grew wroth and raged with blasphemous comments about the prophecies. All these things came to pass to fulfil the words of the Lord God, saying, " And there was given me a reed like unto a rod." — Rev. 11 : 1. These fulfilments contained the cycle enclosing the kingdoms of this world, which became the kingdoms of God's Christ, or truth, and shows how the righteous kingdom and the wicked kingdom united, so that the ancient and modern prophecies might be fulfilled.

The second advent of the Devil's kingdom was spiritually embodied in the man John N. West, whose power, office, and work in prefiguring spiritual wickedness was like unto the man Samuel in prefiguring righteousness, the spiritual kingdom of Christ, which shall reign on earth in God's elect. Many material things are mentioned in comparison with the divine spiritual truth, the elementary substances, which shall be used to establish the kingdom of Christ in the hearts of his elect, which is wrought in the flesh and blood, bone and sinew, of the revelator, and will be found in the fulfilments of prophecies harmonizing with this revelation and doctrine.

Many comparisons will be found, in the fulfilments of prophecies, to show the power and might and despotic tyranny which was wrought and interwoven in the flesh and blood, bone and sinew, of the man John, who fulfilled his time warring against the holy kingdom through peaceful stratagem, the art of imitation, and the corrupt science of sage and craft. Many ravenous beasts and venomous reptiles, wicked and wise kings and princes of old, wicked cities, thunder and lightning, deleterious substances, dead and loathsome waters and water creatures, and every thing that moves upon the earth destructive to humanity, materially, is a comparison of the wicked cycle.

In the modern prophecies the American crimes, diseases, accidents, and numerous troubles were used to show the changes and different degrees, crimes, diseases, and accidents which were performed spiritually between humanity, animalism, and divinity, which were at war in the cycle of perdition, during the perils of the saints. The changes in the seasons and nature of material things were used as eyeglasses to see into the changes of the seasons and nature of the wicked cycle, and also the cycle of life eternal. Many of those despotic and tyrannical degrees of animalism which at first were seated secretly and motionless in the Son of Perdition, signify men, who, it was declared, would be destroyed in many parts of the fulfilments of the ancient and late prophecies.

When divine truth annihilated so many of those secret, dexterous, and desperate freaks of animalism which intermingled with human chastity and divinity in the earthly body of the cycle of perdition, then as many men of the earth had been destroyed as was prophesied in the late prophecies. The revolution and resurrection of each dispensation of sin and vice in the orb of perdition contained so many thousand corpuscular freaks of animalism intermingled with humanity and divinity, and so many of these wicked freaks were converted to believe on the Divine God, and so many to the moral gods, that sinners were brought to salvation in each freak; while the desperadoes had to be annihilated and exterminated from the soul.

Every material desperado, wicked, moral, and every kind of ungodly being that has ever existed on earth, or that now exists, stood before the judgment seat of Christ in the freaks of the nature of perdition and were judged according to their deeds, and were rewarded according to their works, while each freak dwelt in an individual corporeal body on earth, — all who have sinned against the Holy God since mankind lost his holy, happy, and perfect state. The same wickedness that raged in the cycle of perdition against the holy saints in the sphere of light and life, is the same sin and vice that prevails pseudonymously over all nations, kindred, people, kings, and tongues who live on earth.

But the time was far spent before the revelator was able to see into the spiritual fulfilments of the ancient and late prophecies, concerning how they were being fulfilled, although he felt confident that the work was being accomplished in some hidden way, and would manifest itself in some way just as he was moved by the Spirit of prophecy to utter. This then concealed mystery caused the prophecies to be ignored by those who gained faith in Samuel's vocation when the prophecies were first uttered and made public among the adversaries of divine truth; and this trial revolved, and resurrected, and awoke the dead and sleepy powers of animal nature which at first were silent and motionless in the orb of perdition.

When the first modern prophecies were written, which involve the contents of the seven seals of God's vengeance against sin, Samuel was prescient to know that his next work would be to prophesy on seven successive waves of trouble, which contained God's vengeance and terrible judgments against sin in corporeal bodies. It was not made known to him whether they would be fulfilled figuratively, spiritually, or materially, although God had determined to execute vengeance through judgments against the pollutions of the world embodied in the man whom he had fashioned and prepared to use, a figure of the entire world's sins and abominations seated by nature in all human beings, — in all who have ever existed, and those who now exist, and those yet to come. This figure contained the most essential, and lucid, and polished principles of abominations, by nature; and this could not be distinguished from divine righteousness by the closest human observer. God only could distinguish his kind, which he had prepared for his people, from among the many samples, and reveal the plain truth of sin and vice and divine righteousness.

All this time the polished figure whom God had raised up to purge and try the saints was visiting the revelator, hearing the mysteries of divine righteousness explained to him. Having an acute sight and a quick understanding into the things explained to him, he became more and more interested in the doctrine of the revelator, which was then based on the judgments, which appeared to be entirely material at that time. This caused the cycle of perdition to stand in great awe of the prophecies, being unaware of the judgments coming upon his soul.

The first plague executed upon the resurrected freaks of nature in the figure reads as follows:—

The prophet Samuel prophesies on the first vial of the wrath of God to be poured out upon the wicked; and this plague will fall upon all who have the mark of the beast.

Through the inspiration of God and by the ordination of his Holy Spirit, he is using me an instrument to foretell of a universal trouble upon the world. This trouble will come upon all who have not the seal of God in their foreheads, those who are not fit vessels for Christ's kingdom; for Christ has appeared on earth to set up his spiritual kingdom. There are seven vials of the wrath of God to be poured out upon the wicked, and through my prophesying of these troubles, the saints will know that this prophet is the second advent of Christ, who has appeared to earth to reward the saints.

There shall fall a grievous sore on men. This disease will break out in boils, and turn to running sores; and this disease will continue five months, commencing November 1, 1888, and the seven vials of the wrath of God will be poured out in three years' time from the twenty-seventh of October, 1888. This plague that shall fall upon men is a torment for the wicked. Some will desire to die, and death shall flee away from them; this will cause intense suffering, such as never was seen before, but it is determined and it shall be. The suffering list will be far greater than the death list, and over three thousand will die in America with this plague. There is nothing that man can do to prevent its spread, for this is a universal trouble, and all tribes of the earth shall moan during the time of the pouring out of these seven plagues because of their severity, and all nations shall know that this prophet Samuel is the second advent of Christ spiritually, and the son of man hath power on earth.

Samuel prophesies on the first plague upon the wicked; for through these prophecies are God's judgments made manifest.

When the time approached for the first vial of wrath to make a material manifestation as it dwelt in the tenor of the prophecies, the enemies were set in rage afresh, with blasphemous sayings against the prophet and those who had verbally published the prophecies and declared that they should be manifested upon those who had sought to injure the truth and its members without a cause. The enemies were very wroth because the grievous sore, which was spiritual, essentially, did not make a material manifestation upon the bodies of all who had opposed and scoffed at the basis of the work.

At that time, which was the third of November, 1888, the Holy Spirit revealed unto Samuel the following words of explanation to read only to those who continued to believe that the prophecies were working to fulfil God's purposes. This explanation was the reed like unto a rod, for those who did not believe in the prophecies were deprived of hearing them read or explained from this time onward.

The seven vials of God's wrath are in the first form of prophecy, which states all the troubles that shall befall the wicked. The seven plagues will be manifested during these three years of prophecy, which is determined of God, that his judgments may make desolate the desperadoes ; and this will destroy violent wickedness from the earth.

The meaning of these prophecies being clothed in sackcloth, they will be prophesied to be seen at a certain time, and they will not be seen at the time prophesied. They will work in an opposite direction, so that every one who is watching my words to be fulfilled will see nothing but errors in my prophecies. For this cause God will send them strong delusions, so that this character of mankind will be destroyed by these plagues ; for nothing that defileth, or maketh a lie, or worketh abomination, will be able to enter this pure, holy, and happy land. None but my royal priesthood shall partake of its treasures of gold and other precious coins and lustrous substances prepared for them in the beginning of creation ; though I shall land many thousands, after smiting the seven streams of the Egyptians, with the rod of my mouth.

This interpretation was only read to those who believed on the prophet by words and acts, which was the court measured within the temple. Then the adversaries were more wroth, and mocked and blasphemed, and made threats of what they would do with the prophet if they had things their way. But the prophet and none of his followers explained the mysteries of the prophecies, because at that time they did not fully understand. This commandment, forbidding to explain the prophecies to the adversaries, was the court without the temple, which gave power to the Gentiles to tread down the holy city and sanctuary through blaspheming God's truth, which he had foreordained to keep concealed until his purposes were fulfilled in these things.

When the prophet wrote and explained why the prophecies were clothed in sackcloth, he remained silent from any work in the outside world from November 3, 1888, until February 28, 1889; which was the time that the Lord God drilled and blasted cut from the world the family of Mary C. West, which consisted of two other members, the third son being isolated, to a certain extent, through marriage. The unmarried sons are, namely, John N. West and Isaac C. West; and the married son is Winston A. West.

Mary C. West left her home, located in the city of Richmond, Va., in 1884, and being a widow, she removed to the city of Springfield, Mass., where she could be with her three sons, all of whom were quite devoted to her as a mother. When Mary reached Springfield, and heard Caroline preach on the doctrine of healing, she believed in the doctrine and was healed of a chronic cough, and in a short time Caroline became a shining light and a great blessing to Mary's family. Mary labored in constant prayer for her three sons to take Caroline for their physician, which they finally did, and they were all healed of different complaints. This was God's purpose, to assemble the kingdoms of the world to pour upon them all of his fierce wrath and vengeance.

Mary owned property in Richmond, Va., and bought another home in Springfield, Mass., and her three sons were in partnership in the retail fruit business, which eventually became the leading and most attractive retail fruit store in the city. When Samuel was chosen to work with Caroline, John and Isaac became deeply interested in him; and this force of interest worked involuntarily, and they felt that they had to follow Samuel and Caroline, although no inducements had been placed before them to compel or influence them to follow the doctrine.

Finally, Mary leaned the same way as her two sons, although she was baffled at Samuel's strange vocation; but she pursued on after her two sons. Winston was rather secretly inclined the other way, and opposed Samuel's prophecies; and his wife, who had been healed by Caroline, finally opposed the prophecies also, through being skeptical on the point concerning Samuel's mission to mankind, involved in the post-millennium of Christ, which was strongly proclaimed when the prophecies were first made public.

John was the business manager of the store, and Isaac, the assistant manager. At length the love that existed between the members of this family began to grow wax cold, because they did not believe, nor think alike, on the doctrine, which at that time had no established method; and they became divided one from the other, which established a private war which was soon made public.

By and by the business began to run behind, so that they were unable to pay their indebtedness, which brought John under severe reprimand from his brother Winston; and as John's love and devotion adhered to the revelator, he brought before him the grievances that he was compelled to succumb to in order to keep peace at the store and shun public disgrace. Then John placed himself and business in the hands of the revelator by making a complete sacrifice of all he possessed. He had no desire to see the business prosper under his supervision, and his desire was to desert the store, as he felt that his work with Samuel was fast approaching, which caused him rapidly to lose interest in the business. Finally the revelator became burdened with John's trials and responsibilities at the store; and he was instructed not to retaliate if he was envied, because God had a purpose in it, which purpose was to try and purge him.

When the revelator became responsible for John's troubles, he appealed unto God to direct him to the Scripture touching on John's work with him; for Samuel felt assured that John would soon be connected with him in some kind of work, and he felt that God was preparing John to be his recording secretary. He found the proof of this to carry God's purposes into a brief and hasty effect concerning the four kingdoms of the world, which were beautifully wrought and interwoven in the members of this family.

This fulfils God's words, saying, "And I looked, and, lo, a Lamb stood on the mount Sion, and with him an hundred forty and four thousand, having his Father's name written in their foreheads." — Rev. 14: 1. Samuel found the strong testimony in this chapter to substantiate his feelings, and John's, also, that John would be his recording secretary during the days of his prophecies; and Samuel sought to know of God the time and season that this matter would go into effect and come to pass.

He found the exact time in the ninth chapter of Revelation, the thirteenth, fourteenth, and fifteenth verses, as follows: "And the sixth angel sounded, and I heard a voice from the four horns of the golden altar which is before God, saying to the sixth angel which had the trumpet, Loose the four angels which are bound in the great river Euphrates. And the four angels were loosed, which were prepared for an hour, and a day, and a month, and a year, for to slay the third part of men."

Samuel was moved and inspired by the Holy Spirit to count the time that intervened from the ending of his physical occupation until it harmonized with the time declared and limited in these three verses. The four principal persons, and first in order, which the Lord God used to do a certain kind of work in connection with these doctrines, to make a brief fulfilment of the Holy Scriptures on the second advent of Christ, are, namely, Samuel L. Clark, Caroline C. Williams, John N. West, and Isaac C. West.

Samuel was the spiritual focus of the divine Euphrates, composed of the seven righteous Ethiopian branches, the medium of life, the land of Canaan, and the state of felicity. And the grand division Euphrates emanated from the principal man Samuel with quickening power, and used the three persons with irresistible power to accomplish their work, which was called "the loosening of the four angels." These four persons were the cherubims and flaming sword which the Lord God prepared to turn any and every way to prevent any one from taking of the tree of life until the seven plagues of the seven angels were fulfilled.

Samuel and Caroline were first prepared for the approaching purposes; but the Lord God concealed his ordinances from these agents while doing their portion of work, so that the Scriptures might be fulfilled without their taking a thought concerning them, until they were fulfilled and opened to the principal man. When the time drew near for Samuel's first work to begin out among the people, he urged his Holy Father to make him to know how John should end his physical work in his store, since he was the most important member of the firm, for he saw no one capable of filling John's place at his store. And as Isaac worked for a firm of wholesale fruit dealers, and had left the matter with Samuel concerning leaving the firm and going to work in his own store in the busy season, the plans were all prepared to fulfil God's pleasure at the time appointed.

Samuel was commanded to go into a fast, which was to abstain from material food, to carry the purpose into effect concerning Isaac and John. During this fast Samuel was commanded to advise Isaac to give the firm for which he worked one week's notice and to go to work in his own store the first of March, 1889.

This advice was given to Isaac before his mother, Mary, and his brother John; but it was kept secret from his married brother, because Samuel was warned by the Holy Spirit not to notify him, because he would oppose the purpose.

Isaac did not know that John was going to leave the store, and at that time there was sufficient help in his store if John remained; but, as Isaac was frightened exceedingly over the judgments which had been prophesied of at that time, he would hearken unto whatever Samuel advised him to do, without stopping to count the cost. Isaac did according as Samuel advised him, which was to carry out God's ordinances; but no one knew, save God, what would follow from this simple change.

Samuel was led to let the other part of the work, concerning John's leaving the store, work in him to leave at the time appointed, without telling him when to leave; this was for God to end John's work at the store to harmonize with his time and purposes. To bring this to pass, God commanded Samuel to set watch for the loosening of the four angels; and this watch began February 28, 1889, at half past three o'clock in the evening, and ended the first of March, at six o'clock in the morning.

There were four times mentioned, scripturally, in this watch for the advent of the Spirit of power to be manifested to begin the mission of Christ publicly. The time stated for the Holy Spirit to be manifested in some marvellous way was at eve, at midnight, at cockcrowing, and at morn. The strongest believers of the work were invited, and were present during this watch; and the time was spent in reading the Bible, and singing songs of praise. Samuel felt a mild reflux of the Holy Spirit at each specified time, and just at six o'clock in the morning the Holy Spirit struck Samuel upon the crown of his head, with exceeding glory, and passed down to the soles of his feet, and all who firmly believed that God would manifest himself, whether they realized it or not, were filled with great glory.

Samuel said nothing about the change at that moment, but started each one who was compelled to go about his daily work. John gave up to Isaac the keys and other things which he had with him belonging to the store, so that he would succeed him in managing the business affairs of the store. Soon after each one who had felt the power of the Holy Spirit began to confess it, they were, so filled with glory that words could not express it; therefore songs of praise flowed out in living streams from those who remained, because they were filled with glory that could not be uttered, neither manifested except in noisy songs of praise. This was done to fulfil God's words of old, saying, "And after these things I heard a great voice of much people in heaven, saying, Alleluia; salvation, and glory, and honor, and power, unto the Lord our God." — Rev. 19 : 1.

March 1, 1889, was the time that the four angels were loosed; and this was the time that the holy city and sanctuary were lifted up among the nations of the earth, so that the Lord God would make a quick work on earth in the fulfilments of prophecies. When Isaac entered his store to succeed John, he felt that there was great trouble for him to encounter, which would spring forth from the change which had taken place ; because the whole matter concerning John's leaving the store had been kept secret from his brother Winston, who was then working in the store and a member of the firm. When Winston came into the store and found that John was absent, and could get no satisfaction from Isaac concerning his whereabouts, he suspected where he was, and began to rage and blaspheme the work that John had left the store to do with Samuel ; and from this time the great war began in this family, and prevailed desperately for many days.

This has fulfilled the words of the Lord God, saying, "Think not that I am come to send peace on earth : 1 came not to send peace, but a sword. For I am come to set a man at variance against his father, . . . and the daughter in law against her mother in law. And a man's foes shall be they of his own household. He that loveth father or mother more than me is not worthy of me : and he that loveth son or daughter more than me is not worthy of me. And he that taketh not his cross, and followeth after me, is not worthy of me. He that findeth his life shall lose it : and he that loseth his life for my sake shall find it. He that receiveth you receiveth me, and he that receiveth me receiveth him that sent me. He that receiveth a prophet in the name of a prophet shall receive a prophet's reward ; and he that receiveth a righteous man in the name of a righteous man shall receive a righteous man's reward. And whosoever shall give to drink unto one of these little ones a cup of cold water only in the name of a disciple, verily I say unto you, he shall in no wise lose his reward."

When Isaac succeeded John in the management of the business at the store, the wholesale fruit dealers, and others besides, grew wroth and uneasy, because it was published that John had left his store, and had taken all the money from the store to help the new work. This calumnious rumor stirred up John's creditors and caused them to push Isaac for cash payments. Isaac was filled with great enthusiasm to defend the work that John had sacrificed the store to do, and was empowered by speech to destroy the requickened power of the red-head dragon at that time, which was the angel that went out from the altar, having power over fire.

The two angels that went out with sharp sickles, mentioned in the fourteenth chapter of Revelation, signify the power of the seven spirits of Christ that used the two writing pens during the second seal, when the books of the apostolic Bible were opened, and revealed God's purposes, which were sealed up from men, concerning the establishment of the past epochs of divinity. Samuel did the revealing, John did the recording, and Caroline did the cooking, washing, sewing, and housekeeping in general.

Isaac became so enthusiastic in defence of the step his brother John had taken that he even cursed those who came to him inquiring after John dishonorably. In a few days Isaac had almost deserted his mother's house, to be with the members of the truth; and Samuel appealed unto the Lord God for a blessing to be imputed upon Isaac, because he declared by actions and words that he had the members of the truth at heart. This is the blessing that the Holy King imputed upon Isaac : —

"Because thou hast obeyed my commandment, and hast not denied my name in the presence of raging and vile men, in blessings I will bless you. You shall have good health, and your burdens shall be light ; and whatsoever you put your hand to, it shall prosper beyond others. I shall give you great wisdom to manage this blessing, so great that there shall be none like unto you. The whole blessing of prosperity shall rest upon you, and you shall abide in the will of the prophet Samuel, and you shall have wisdom to know the will. If any man devise evil against you, he shall fall; and when the time of cleansing takes place, you shall have a crown of life which shall not fade away nor grow dim. Therefore continue in my words, and I will bring them to pass. I will rule this fountain of blessing put upon you with power, and this work shall rest upon this blessing for the whole wealth of the world is in my charge and keeping. I will bless whom I will, and curse whom I will, for in righteousness do I judge and make war."

Business made such rapid increase in a short time after this blessing was imputed upon Isaac, and it was so marvellous and pleasing in Isaac's sight to see his patronage making such progress, that he felt he should do more for the members of the truth ; so he wanted Samuel and Caroline to remove to his mother's house and make it their home, that the members of the doctrine of prosperity be united and all work for one aim in honor of one God.

When Mary, the mother of John and Isaac, found that they were alienated from home, and had lost interest in her, she saw no other way to redeem their fondness for home and mother than to receive Caroline and Samuel, and to take the same interest in the doctrine as her sons took. She invited Samuel and Caroline into her house, to take full control; and she presented herself, property, and all she possessed to Samuel. When the covenant of the people reached this standpoint and privilege, then the kingdoms of the world had become the kingdoms of God's Christ, so that he might cleanse them, to set up his spiritual kingdom, and reign on earth over the abominations and pollutions of the kingdoms of the world.

Samuel accepted Mary's sacrifice and invitation, regardless of its genuineness, and removed into her house and took possession of all that she and her sons held a legal claim over, which was voluntarily presented to him. When Samuel and his members entered her house and began his work, nothing of any worth could be done in connection with Mary's family except by Samuel's commandments, and this privilege and authority were given to him by them, without his demand. It worked in each one of the three members of the family to place all business affairs in Samuel's care and supervision, after discovering that nothing could be accomplished without his command.

As Mary was not taught in Samuel's method of housekeeping and mode of cookery, she was glad to put Caroline over the housework, fearing that she was unable to please Samuel in diet; because he and members subsisted upon herbs, eggs, and vegetables, instead of meats, which continued throughout his days of prophesying. When Mary did not put Caroline forward in everything pertaining to the housework, the work went wrong, which compelled Mary to relax her claim as mistress over the housework by gradual degrees just as time wore away.

Samuel's doctrines and teachings made, by gradual degrees, just as occasion demanded, a complete conflict with every tenet of doctrine and mode of living in the old life. This changed everything around, and worked contrary to the established method of living and teachings. Being of very great age, Mary's life and hope, trust and understanding, were deeply rooted and interwoven in the natural life, both spiritual and physical: and it puzzled her to understand Samuel's mission and doctrines. and at last confounded her to the uttermost, in striving to please, against her will, the principal members of 'the covenant. It was her aim and ardent desire to build on to the old life, and increase the value of her worldly estate, fame, and honor among the physical gods, but the matter was secreted in her heart.

Samuel was striving only to fulfil God's pleasure and determination in the work that he was called to do, in building the kingdom of Christ, which then was in its early infancy. Every step the revelator took, and every course he pursued, was to raise the divine kingdom in honor among the honorable nations of the earth; because then the divine kingdom was greatly dishonored because of the vacancy of the revelations, atonements, and doctrines contained in this book.

Samuel showed Mary the great error she was making in attempting to classify him with the old life to satisfy her avaricious desire and concupiscent craves. Samuel gently, gradually, and briefly declared and revealed unto her his mission to mankind, which gradually compelled him to pronounce hasty and acute judgments against her old life and dogmatical doctrines, and her attempts to build the natural family which he came to purge, cleanse, and refine, by the divine doctrines, and establish one family, called "the family of Christ," so that divine righteousness would exist only among its kind, unmixed with the tenets of doctrines, upon the free and blessed sod of this vast macrocosm.

When Mary attempted to do anything after the mode of the covenant, it was mere assimilation of the real servants of Christ, which issued from the real animal body, working craft and all deceivableness, and caused the divine spirit to be blasphemed. The phenomenal power of assimilation and deceivableness issued from the animal soul, while the real spiritual body was desperately opposed to Samuel's mission and doctrine. This worked continually throughout the time Samuel was fulfilling his mission in the Babylonian kingdom, which revolved around and revived in her to fulfil and give the holy exegesis of the Holy Scriptures during the cycle of time prophesied of concerning the spiritual Babylon and the spiritual Jerusalem and other holy and wicked kingdoms.

Through the holy prince's receiving and involving the natural family in with the royal family of Christ, the globe of the finite world, the animal kingdom, with all its pollutions and abominations, gained entrance into the holy city and sanctuary, and attained power, glory, honor, and dominion over God's elect, owing to the office and public claim each member of the finite kingdom held legitimately over the base upon which the throne of the holy city and sanctuary chose to sit to accomplish his first work when he lifted himself up publicly among the nations, to fulfil his mission to mankind.

When the king of Jerusalem accepted Mary's offer, and went into her house and stipulated with her to take full possession, then the holy kingdom had entered the chief spiritual metropolis empire of all the ancient wicked kingdoms, called "Babylon," which was situated in Mary's antique characteristics and the modern idolatry of the devil's kingdom, which were seated in the branches out of her roots. Then the purposes of God were placed in the propelling current where his Christ could fulfil his pleasure in the great rebellion he had determined against the wicked kings and princes, queens and presidents, of the antique Babylon, and the modern rulers of the existing time in the animal kingdom.

As the holy king was sitting upon his own throne, erected upon the basis of the Babylonian empire, which was supported by the late statutes of metaphysics, and gorgeously embellished with modern idolatry in its grandeur, there was no way possible for the divine kingdom to make war against the animal kingdoms and fulfil the Holy Scriptures on this matter without laying himself waste and entering into solitary desolation. This caused the revolution and resurrection of all the kingdoms upon the face of the earth; which caused kingdom to rise against kingdom, and nation against nation, by being divided in faith and opinion.

This war upon civil terms slaughtered, figuratively and phenomenally, all the officers, governors, and members of depraved nature, who would not subdue materially and spiritually to the statutes of the divine kingdom, which at that time were partly mingling with statutes of the animal kingdom, in order to get judgment against its nefarious laws and stringent government. The reason the temporal world is involved in these revelations and doctrines is to show what fellowship, under the present conditions, physical things have with the Supreme Divine in his existing mission to mankind. Therefore the secular gods and goddesses were involved in these doctrines to show the power and purity of the divine kingdom, and the nefarious laws and stringent government contained in the animal kingdom.

It was so wrought out and established for the supreme power of divinity and the supreme power of animalism to flow together and amalgamate, to show the corruption contained in the finite kingdom, and also the purity that exists in the supreme divine kingdom which must flow through materialism to destroy its pernicious blastemas, which are sent out into the world by the commandments of the gods of metaphysics to continue the increase of mortality in the human family. I am impowered by wisdom's infinite judgment, discretion, and equity, to find, locate, and describe every venomous germ contained in the physical world, and the root and fœtus will be destroyed, so that the Supreme Divine can unite and mingle with the physical government, and continue in the original purity and brotherly love, as was done in the creation of the material universe. Then the Lord God will be polytheistical in the government of materialism and spiritualism.

The Lord God will, by his creative words of power, purge, cleanse, and refine physical things, which he has inspired men to discover and invent, and use them for the glory, honor, and promotion of the material body; and purge, cleanse, and refine the spiritual, and use it for the maintenance and promotion of the indwelling man. Then the Lord God will have no need to destroy utterly either spirit or matter, but to purge out the part which belongs to other kinds, and place both divine and physical gases and substances with that kind with which they were created to mingle and support. Then the judgments which the Lord God pronounced upon the natural family with whom his Christ mingled are not distinguished from the judgments of the Lord God upon all families, — all nations, peoples, kings, and tongues that exist in the animal kingdom; and there are no persons in existence outside the animal kingdom, for all mankind have put on the animal spirit and nature, which have, through all ages, intermingled with humanity, and could not be changed until divine righteousness and animal propensities reached the consummate limits in the human family.

Now the fulness of truth has power over animal propensities, by the power of divine wisdom, judgment, and equity, to throw out of humanity the subtle image of the pre-adamites. The Lord God saw fit to prepare one family out of the pre-adamite world to perform the proof-work, figuratively and phenomenally, so that the full book of sin and abomination be presented to the world, that they who are blinded by their own bitumen may see where they stand and hope in the promise of life which God has prepared for all who receive divine truth in the fulness, — both spiritual and material, — by using the physical science in the proper place, which is to sustain the material ; and using the spiritual in its proper place, which was created and established to sustain and maintain the spiritual existence of man's immortal soul.

PART IV.

THE ABOLISHMENT OF THE BAPTISM OF LIQUID WATERS: THE ESTABLISHMENT OF THE FIERY BAPTISM: THE SECOND VIAL OF GOD'S WRATH; THE BEGINNING OF THE GREAT WAR IN BABYLON.

In order to declare the fulness of the immortal life which is centred in the seven united powers of the kingdom of Christ, I do herein name them as they heretofore existed materially, and now exist spiritually, — obedience and faith, love and hope, charity, patience, and truth. The eighth is of the seventh and is, namely, righteousness. By the supernatural power of God and his love and mercy for the human family, Noah was made the author and restorer of divine obedience ; Abraham, the author and restorer of divine faith ; Isaac, the author and restorer of divine hope ; Jacob, the author and restorer of divine love ; Moses, the author and restorer of divine charity ; Elijah, the author and restorer of divine patience, and Jesus, the author and restorer of divine truth.

These are the seven tried stones and authors of righteousness, and the creative source of divine righteousness, the strength and power of the holy kingdom. All righteousness in the divine kingdom is the co-ordinate of these seven tried principles called "the kingdom of Christ." And all righteousness shall henceforth, through knowledge, spring forth from this head and chief stone, which is the church of Christ. The union of the seven stones is wrought in the eighth, which is composed of the seventh, and constructs the golden and burning altar whereupon all holy spiritual sacrifices shall be placed to burn incense unto the Lord God.

These are the seven scientific principles of eternal life, the embodiment of wisdom, the fertilizing substances to prepare the human soil for the implanting of divinity. These are no longer called by their individual names, neither corporeal nor incorporeal, for their second advent is the Lord God of heaven. The Lord God is the pure thoughts, peace, and rest of the body called "the mind," which is an invisible electric fluid, and brings the different changes to soothe the body, and to perpetuate life eternal; and man inhales this incessant being, and the knowledge of his amiable life, through imbibing the revelation of divine righteousness in the fulness thereof.

I speak comparatively of the past that the people of God may behold and see the spiritual door which he has opened, through the knowledge and discretion with which he has endowed and impowered the revelator, to usher his people into eternal blessedness. The revelator is endowed with the express image and likeness of God's person, making him the embodiment of the entire divine kingdom, while he contains, in substance, all of God's holy principles, love, mercy, and sympathy for the human family, and also his judgments and equity and fierce wrath and vengeance against the brutes, and creeping things, and flying things, and reptile races, which have amalgamated with humanity. He was born materially and carnally, after the will of the earthly Adam, to be in the likeness of his brethren; and through the power which God wrought for his redemption from the animal kingdom, he has opened the door of heaven for his people.

He was changed from the will of the earthly to the will of the heavenly, so that God might use him a full and free subject to accomplish his work in giving birth to the perfect salvation, and convey it to the people. He is declared, firmly and substantially, to be the anthropomorphism of the perfect age, and the propitiator, to make the final atonements for man's redemption from the animal kingdom to obtain the inheritance of the holy kingdom.

When the revelator was born in the spiritual Bethlehem of Judea, which is invisible to the carnal eye and beyond the understanding of the carnal mind, the spirits of the ancient ungodly kings who were in corporeal bodies were troubled and wroth about his birth; and all the chief priests of the ancient spirits gathered themselves in figurative bodies to slay the man child as soon as he was born.

When they sought the man child and could not find him, they were more wroth, and came and slew all the babes nearest to Bethlehem. This was done to make a spiritual repetition of the Bible history, and also to fulfil God's words spoken by John, saying, "I indeed baptize you with water unto repentance: but he that cometh after me is mightier than I, whose shoes I am not worthy to bear: he shall baptize you with the Holy Ghost, and with fire: whose fan is in his hand, and he will thoroughly purge his floor, and gather his wheat into the garner; but he will burn up the chaff with unquenchable fire."

This prophecy, which was spoken by the Holy Spirit through John the Baptist, concerning the baptism of the Holy Ghost, is thought by some to have already been fulfilled at Christ's first advent to earth; but this point the natural man did not understand, although Christ at that time appeared in a natural body, but did not make a complete fulfilment of the prophecy on the spiritual baptism. At that time Jesus only set the type for the real baptism. The material man Jesus had to receive a literal baptism of water, and a visible manifestation of the Holy Spirit. The use of the water through emersion was a type of the real baptism in its purity and cleansing power. The dove was also used as a symbol of the tranquillity and serenity of the spiritual body, and the man whom God would raise up to receive the baptism of the Holy Ghost and fire, and consume by fire the type, and establish the real and eternal baptism, — which is accomplished now by being emerged into the triniunity of word, spirit, and truth.

I declare this to be the genuine baptism of the sempiternal age; and the type is fulfilled and made void, and is of none effect in the perfect age. Those who believed on the millennium Christ and his literal baptism followed on in his precepts by receiving the baptism by water, which was to keep humanity in the current of purity, to convey them on into the state of pure godliness. Christ has appeared the second time to the earthly body, and his body has received the baptism of the Holy Ghost and fire; and all who enter into the city of the New Jerusalem shall be baptized by the same doctrines.

This has fulfilled God's words, saying, "After this I looked, and, behold, a door was opened in heaven." — Rev. 4: 1. "And I saw in the right hand of him that sat on the throne a book written within and on the backside, sealed with seven seals." — Rev. 5: 1.

The Lord God has sowed and reaped seven harvests from the beginning of the world, and is now in the eighth, which is the full repetition and the entire accomplishment of the seven in the eighth, through a spiritual circumvolution. At the end of each harvest he gathered in the grain and chaff, mixed. The origin of purity has passed through these seven harvests, and was greatly increased at the ingathering of each harvest, in both righteousness and unrighteousness.

Noah and the building of the ark was the first harvest of the world; for all the righteousness which was in the antediluvian world was manifested and sealed in Noah, and all the wickedness was sealed in Ham. Both righteousness and wickedness were placed on a revolution, and they revolved from harvest to harvest. At the ingathering of each harvest the righteousness of God was blessed, and the wickedness of men, looked upon in their judgment as righteousness, was cursed; and the curse imputed upon wickedness made also an increase of wickedness at the next harvest. Abraham was the second harvest; and Isaac the third, and Jacob the fourth, and Moses the fifth, and Elijah the sixth, and Jesus the seventh.

These seven righteous branches were the seething process through which materialism had to pass for ebullition; which was to change the solid and material substances of righteousness into electrical fluid. The great and severe trials which the seven righteous branches had to encounter and overcome were the fervent heat that produced the change from the solid to the fluid state, which is the infinite, omnipresent, and Almighty God. The nature of God's elect had to be permeated with divine characteristics to hew out channels in humanity for them to inhale his image, so that he might become universally received, and magnified, and adored in the human family.

The imbibing of this divine electrical fluid is called "the land of

Canaan," typified in days of old to get the language and expression of the spiritual Canaan, flowing with milk and honey. The throne of this fluid and infinite being is based upon justice and judgment, discretion and righteousness; which is the formal globe of the human kingdom with all of its divine substances for the creation and formation of its mansions and other improvements.

The seven co-ordinating lights of the divine kingdom are the seven doctrines of the human soul, the focus of which is the translunary light of the human world. These seven co-ordinates shine in the seven brief principles of humanity, concentrate into one supreme head, make up righteousness, the divine aeriform fluid, and make a visible manifestation through the alphabets. The uniting of these seven prime substances in human nature produces the full power of adhesion and affinity, which changes the name from "righteousness" by converting it into another substance called "fire;" which is the unquenchable fire to consume the entire image of mortality, — which deeds of the mortal man were accounted unto him for righteousness, as have been reserved unto the judgments through the past dark ages of the world for the harvest at the end of the world.

The corrupt spiritual world is destroyed by fire from the holy land; and the holy seed are being sowed in the earth for a perpetual harvest, which shall have no end. This is the new heaven and new earth, wherein dwelleth righteousness. Before the Lord God chose the mother of postliminy, the word, spirit, and truth, the creative substances were omnipresent and informal in humanity, and darkness prevailed over God's mysterious workings, which he had performed through the agency of the mortal man. Therefore God called the divine substances together, and formed and fashioned his kingdom out of his being when he chose the mother of postliminy. God sealed within her the firmament, light, and life of his kingdom, which is the holy city. He formed it the exact measurement of a man, which is the Son of Righteousness, man's holy, happy, and perfect state.

This incorporeal being appeared suddenly to the land, prepared for postliminy by the power of word, spirit, and truth uttered by the Lord God through millennium; and the mortal heaven and earthly characteristics fled away from the holy land, and it was permeated with the entire characteristics of the holy kingdom.

In order to be preserved fully, accomplish his mission to man, and realize the divine birth, the child who passed through the bowels of millennium, after reaching the holy land and fulfilling its birth, had to be taken away from the holy land by being caught up unto the Lord God and his judgment throne to rest upon the informal and infinite substances of divinity, in order to pronounce the judgments, and make his appearance in the holy land just as the judgments were received and adored there, and pronounced upon the members of the holy city and sanctuary.

When the Lord God formed the lunar crucible, he then formed the Son crucible, to complete and perfect the other light crucibles. He then began to form the crucibles to realize the star lights, — the moon, to receive the greater luminous rays of the Son light; the stars, to receive the lesser rays.

God made the Divine Son to be ruler over the day, and the moon to rule the night, — which fulfilled its work while darkness prevailed upon the face of God's mysterious words and works, — and the stars to rule the night when the moon was hid and on the change. The greater stars, which ruled a third part of the night while the moon was passing through her spheral degrees, are called " the constellations of heaven ; " these, being grouped, are called " the blessings of prosperity." This fulfils God's words, saying, "I saw a new heaven and a new earth." — Rev. 21 : 1.

The holy Jerusalem, which was seen phantasmatical in days of old descending out of heaven from God, was the spiritual Jerusalem, the kingdom of God. The bride, the Lamb's wife, is the feminine qualities contained in the fulness of manhood involved in the Son of Righteousness, which brought forth the holy city and sanctuary. The immense, high walls to the spiritual city, and the twelve gates to the city, are the twelve courts of judgment and equity through which the people of the perfect age have to pass to be tried and judged in order to receive a just compensation.

The twelve courts of equity through which man must pass to inherit eternal life are the great and high walls to the holy city. The twelve angels at each gate are the marked emblems of divinity with which God's people must be stamped while passing through the court of equity. The twelve manner of precious stones to the city are the pure and fundamental principles of divinity, which are the precious stones to the building of the walls of the spiritual Jerusalem.

The gates, each being of a single pearl, are the different judgments and justice through which God's people must pass to inherit eternal life; these are involved in the twelve principal judgments. The natural life of man is judged and condemned while passing through the grand jury. The tree of life, on each side of the river of life, bears twelve manner of fruit, whose leaves, for the healing of the nations, are the humane masculine and feminine principles of the holy kingdom, which shall be taught to the members of the perfect age, so that they may gradually come into the perfect existence for mankind. All who accept and adhere to the doctrines which the Lord God shall proclaim through them shall be saved; and those who hear them not shall be damned. Those who believe, and receive the words contained in the doctrines of the perfect age, which the Lord God shall proclaim through the masculine and feminine, shall be healed of all manner of disease of the soul and body.

These two trees of righteousness contain the entire principles of the perfect life, so that they may teach others the same. The doctrines which the Lord God shall teach to all nations through them is the pure river of life, which is clear as crystal. The purity, plainness, and simplicity of the doctrines which shall be taught to the people is the clearness of the river. This fulfils God's words, saying, " And he shewed me a pure river of water of life." — Rev. 22 : 1. " And I saw another sign in heaven, great and marvellous." — Rev. 15 : 1.

THE OPENING OF THE SECOND SEAL.

The prophet Samuel prophesies on the second vial of the wrath of God, which will come upon all who have the mark of the beast, those who have not the seal of God in their foreheads, and those who are not fit vessels for Christ's kingdom ; for Christ has appeared to his temple Samuel, to deliver his elect people out of the hands of the Egyptians, and give them the life which is eternal salvation. After graduating from the divine seminary which contains seven branches of study, I am, therefore, a professor of divinity, qualified to bring to sight the hidden things of darkness from the beginning of creation, also to proclaim unto the people the troubles which shall befall the wicked in the future days, and also that which is even now upon them.

These troubles will also try the saints, to bring them out as pure gold which has been tried in the refiner's fire ; for those who receive eternal life must be thoroughly tried before the life is given unto them. The trials are great tribulations, such as were not since there was a nation; but every one who is found written in the "Lamb's Book of Life" shall be delivered. This second vial of God's wrath will fall upon the oceans, seas, and all fountains of waters; they will become as the blood of a dead man, an offensive smell, and the third part of every living creature in the fountains of waters will die because of this plague.

This will cause the waters to stink, and those who have not the seal of God will loathe and die because of the plague upon the waters. Those who meet the fate of this dreadful plague will feel dizziness of the head, and an offensive breath; and the last stage of these victims will be excruciating pains in the head, causing almost instantaneous death. Decomposition will take place in these victims very soon after the first symptoms are seen. The efforts in medical treatment to relieve these sufferers will seem useless, for a large number will die in all inhabited parts of the globe. The victims of this plague will die so fast, and the smell will be so offensive, that there will not be time to bury all of the dead; some will have to be cremated. This fulfils God's words, spoken by Malachi, saying: "Ye shall tread down the wicked; for they shall be ashes under the soles of your feet in the day that I shall do this, saith the Lord of Hosts."

The time for the commencing of this plague will be the first of June, 1889, and it will last until the first of September in the same year, at which time the waters will begin to return to their creative state. Samuel prophesies on the second vial of the wrath of God, and, behold, five others cometh quickly. This fulfils God's words, saying, "And the second angel poured out his vial upon the sea; and it became as the blood of a dead man: and every living soul died in the sea." "And the second angel sounded, and as it were a great mountain burning with fire was cast into the sea: and the third part of the sea became blood; and the third part of the creatures which were in the sea, and had life, died; and the third part of the ships was destroyed."

Samuel and Caroline accepted the invitation so warmly extended to them by Mary and Isaac, and removed into their home the first of June, which was the commencement of the second vial of wrath. In a very short time after Samuel and Caroline removed to Mary's house, jealousy awoke in the two women by each one's holding a claim over John and Isaac. Mary became very jealous of John and Isaac, and more so of Isaac, because she was afraid that he loved Caroline better than he did her. Caroline was jealous because Mary maintained the natural claim which she formerly held over her two sons, who had presented themselves instruments unto God, both being of full age.

By and by the two women began to annoy each other in acts, and by giving each other word for word, and so on, until war commenced between them. This increased until it became very grievous and painful for Caroline to endure, because she was in Mary's house and detested the idea of taking possession of it; but Mary had given her the privilege of being the mistress of the house.

The contention became so grievous that Samuel chastened Caroline, to re-establish peace between the two women — but to no avail. Then he commenced to search the Holy Scriptures, mentally, to find out the mystery of the trouble into which he had gone unawares; and through searching the word, spirit, and truth, discovered that he had been led blindly into captivity, into the wicked city of Babylon, for some great purpose.

The Scriptures which God quickened and disclosed to Samuel read as follows : " But in the last days it shall come to pass, that the mountain of the house of the Lord shall be established in the top of the mountains." — Micah 4. 1.

Caroline's work at that time was to represent and defend the daughter of Zion, while Mary's work was to represent and defend the daughter of Babylon. The words of the Lord God contained in this chapter of old are the weapons through which the daughter of Zion achieved victory over the daughter of Babylon; but the time of the revealing of this chapter was the beginning of trouble. This has fulfilled the words of God at his Christ's first appearance to earth, saying, " And he looked up, and saw the rich men casting their gifts into the treasury. And he saw also a certain poor widow casting in thither two mites." — Luke 21 : 1, 2.

It did not abolish the war in Babylon when the Lord God opened the Holy Scriptures, locating and describing the cause of it; for it only uncovered the wickedness in the presence of the Holy Lamb, which made it more restless and tormented in seeking a hiding-place from the presence of the holy angels and the Lamb. This caused all the wickedness of Babylon to rise from the dead state and come upon the earth and exercise power over divine righteousness until the Holy Scriptures were fulfilled; and this prevailing power of abomination worked from land to land, interchangeably, to fulfil and carry the trials of the Holy Christ and the saints to the consummation.

Samuel still chastened Caroline, to cause her wrath to cease against the daughter of Babylon, because he saw himself on the point of being driven into the street: and at that time, almost if not the entire city who had heard the rumors concerning the Christ were in great commotion. Those who had property to let would refuse to let them a tenement to live in, because of disgrace; and for this cause Samuel saw that the holy Jerusalem was in jeopardy, and fully compassed with the armies of the wicked, and trodden down by the Gentile world.

At that time there was great war between Isaac and his brother Winston, who owned a share in the same store wherein the blessing of prosperity was planted, that it might bring forth much fruit to sustain the truth materially. This caused Isaac to repent in his heart that he had been so foolish as to take the step which brought him all the trouble he was facing and compelled to endure for the kingdom of heaven's sake. At that time there was a continual stir and an uproar, among the merchants of Springfield, about John and Isaac's believing on Samuel and Caroline; and they opposed Isaac in every way they were able, and predicted a failure in business.

Isaac execrated all who opposed him unreasonably, and imprecated a curse upon his own business, also; and Mary did the same, if any one came to her house and spoke blasphemously against the covenant. In spite of the war between the two women, the Lord God used Mary at the proper time for each purpose he wanted to carry into effect in defence of the holy covenant.

It came to pass that Isaac learned from his mother, Mary, that Caroline and she did not agree, and that she was imposed upon by Caroline; and Isaac's heart turned against Caroline from that time. This empowered Isaac to say to Samuel that they had better separate, if they could not live together in peace; but Samuel gave him no reply. Such was his thought, but God had willed it otherwise.

From this time the blessing of prosperity which Samuel had imputed upon Isaac began to lose its power, and the trade at the store decreased rapidly, because he had turned against his Creator to defend his natural blood. In a short time the store became burdened with indebtedness; the goods, from that time, were not settled for, after the proper traffic system; and everything in connection with the business went pell-mell.

Isaac gradually lost interest in the business, and sought in many ways to dispose of it and exempt himself from its trouble. As he found no way to satisfy his aim, he turned and urged Samuel to do something for his deliverance from the store, requesting, from time to time, that Samuel would command what to do, and he would do anything Samuel said.

During all this time Samuel and John were busy writing and revealing the part of the work which was already fulfilled, and were secluded from the world for this purpose. John did not interfere with the trouble that prevailed between his mother and Caroline; as Samuel was the principal person, he left it for him to perform.

Isaac sought in many ways to be released from the store, and, also, how he might best get Samuel and Caroline out of his mother's house. He did not make his desire fully known at that time, but confessed it when the purgative fountain was opened for the cleansing of the inhabiters of Jerusalem. One great cause of Mary and Caroline's trouble was that they did not agree in the cooking. Mary wanted it done one way, and Caroline wanted it done another way; they were inconsistent in all the housework.

When Samuel imputed the blessing of prosperity upon Isaac, great devotion awoke in Caroline for Isaac, because she was led to believe that he had sold himself a servant unto righteousness, and that his pleasure was stayed in obeying God's commandments issued through Samuel. And Caroline devoted herself to the pleasure of waiting upon Isaac in preference to the other members; and she bestowed upon him great honor; and it was joy and life to her to satisfy and honor him in every way she could. But when she discovered that his love toward her was fictitious, and that he was uncircumcised in heart from the natural mother, and earthly things, she turned to be as great and faithful an enemy to him as she had ever been a friend.

The Lord God quickened in the revelator the chapters of the apocalypse to which I shall refer: these were prepared to turn the two witnesses against the uncircumcised family, to exhort the feminine candlestick to be submissive to the teaching and correction of the masculine candlestick, and to strengthen Samuel in faithfulness. These words are the preamble of the revelations and the phantasmatical scenes which were presented to the sight of the prophet apocalypse John. This showed the involuntary power of sin, and for what purpose he was exiled from home, and shows that God ordained it for the apocalypse John to be cast into the Isle Patmos, to see and hear these dark sayings for the last days of sin, which were loosened in humanity, to war against his Christ.

"The revelation of Jesus Christ, which God gave unto him, to show unto his servants things which must shortly come to pass." — Rev. 1 : 1. "Unto the angel of the church of Ephesus write." — Rev. 2 : 1. Samuel, seeing the hazardous state and conditions of the covenant, continued in severe chastisement of Caroline, to create peace between the daughter of Zion and the daughter of Babylon, the mother city of abominations. But the Lord God performed the work which he had determined, by disguised ways revenging Caroline upon the Babylonian spiritual embodiment. The testimony of Samuel's chastisement reads as follows : "And unto the angel of the church in Sardis write." — Rev. 3 : 1.

It came to pass, after the war had prevailed many days between the daughter of Zion and the daughter of Babylon, that the strife was greatly increased, because the two women became filled with wrath and indignation concerning how the cooking should be done. Mary wanted to cook to John's and Isaac's taste, as she formerly had done ; Caroline wanted to cook to Samuel's taste. This and many other things concerning how it should be done brought in the mighty disagreeing tyrant.

Samuel made many changes in the work about the house, to annihilate the mighty tyrant and quicken and raise from the dead the king of peace and reconciliation. Each change he made increased the enmity for a time, and made it more troublous ; but each change brought victory nearer.

A veil of intense darkness enveloped Samuel, concerning his non-understanding of how reconciliation should be created between the two women ; and the Lord God revealed to Samuel the cause of the non-unity between them, and why they could not agree, which reads as follows : "Then I turned and lifted up mine eyes, and looked, and behold a flying roll." — Zech. 5 : 1. "And he shewed me Joshua the high priest standing before the angel of the Lord, and Satan standing at his right hand to resist him." — Zech. 3 : 1. "And the angel that talked with me came again, and waked me, as a man that is wakened out of his sleep." — Zech. 4 : 1.

Soon after these ancient prophecies opened and explained themselves in the divine brain lobe of Samuel, the daughter of Babylon lost her speech, so that she could not use the material lips and tongue to war against the daughter of Zion as freely as she had done before. The daughter of Babylon did the baking in the cookery; and as they subsisted upon vegetables instead of meats, the daughter of Zion did the vegetable cooking, and the two women ceased from talking back to each other, as they had been doing, but the strife continued through malignant acts toward each other, such as slam-banging of things around, revengefully.

The store, which contained the blessing of prosperity, was on the verge of being foreclosed, by reason of indebtedness; and Isaac, in trying to pay the bills and promote the interest of the new covenant, was entirely lost. His brother Winston, who was in partnership with him, was not dealing squarely with him concerning the business affairs, for fear that he would not be justly dealt with by his mother and brothers, because he imagined a vain thing in Samuel's mission.

Mary was secretly and desperately envious of Samuel and Caroline, because of the war which prevailed between Isaac and Winston; and she sought secretly in many ways how she might best deprive them of the privilege of abiding at her house, without turning against John and Isaac, her two sons. Every attempt and plan which she thought upon was against her sons, also; and this was the power that kept her still and silent in thought, and from doing mischief to the covenant, so that God's purposes would be accomplished concerning the Babylonian principles.

The war became grievous to Samuel; so much so, that the Lord God instructed him to go into a fast, which was to abstain from material food, to prepare for the approaching troubles and perils which he had to face. This fast lasted thirty-nine days, ending on the twenty-third day of the seventh month of the year 1889. At the end of this fast Samuel gave Isaac the command for dissolution of partnership with his brother Winston; and this commandment was given to Isaac in the month of August, the same year.

The commandment to Isaac, for dissolution of partnership, reads as follows: You must tell Winston that as you and he cannot agree, you will dissolve partnership with him September 1, 1889; and you will give him his share, after paying the indebtedness of the store. Isaac held the largest share in the business, and Winston's was of small value, but he refused to relax his minute claim, to establish peace and prevent a failure in business.

Winston's reply to Isaac was that if he did not wish to work with him he could get out, and he would take charge of the store and pay the bills; and therefore he overcame Isaac in giving this commandment, and Isaac did not fully agree within himself with the commandment.

Isaac returned home when his daily task was done, and told Samuel how Winston overpowered him when he gave him the command for separation; and how weak he felt while giving it. Then Samuel saw no way for Isaac to overpower his opponent but by sending John to the store to give the command with power, and compel Winston to desert the store at the time appointed; because John was a man possessed of great power of speech, and very affluent in language.

John refused, upon oath, to go to the store; and said in his heart that if God could not save Israel without his going to the store to work, they could go to perdition; and at this time John cursed the whole frame of the work as it then existed. This caused John to think in his heart how to do mischief to the covenant. He made an attempt to desert the holy city and sanctuary, but found his way completely besieged, so that he was compelled to relent.

On the evening of August 27, 1889, Winston's wife came to call on Mary, her mother-in-law; and Mary appeared to be more friendly, at this time, than usual, because she detested her, for they had previously lived together in the same house and were compelled to separate because they could not live together agreeably. As this was a time of trouble and perplexities, it was inexpedient to make peace with Winston's wife. John, being present, and hearing Samuel's judgment on the false friendship between the mother and daughter-in-law, filled with wrath and indignation, and said to Samuel that he would drive Winston's wife from his mother's house, if he was willing; and Samuel empowered John to execrate Winston's wife, and drive her from his mother's house, the base of the sanctuary.

Immediately after this was done, John came to Samuel and said, "If you will turn me loose, I will go down to the store tonight and blow it to shivers, and compel Winston to desert the store; and Isaac and I will take charge of the store and pay the bills." Samuel turned John loose with mighty force and power of the Spirit to carry out the commandment which had been given to Isaac concerning dissolution of partnership. And John went to the store and gave Winston the commandment with great authority concerning how he should relinquish his claim September 1, 1889, and Isaac and himself would take charge of the store and exempt it from indebtedness.

John warned Winston not to fight against him, for he was not the same man he was when he worked with him in the store ; he warned Winston not to get in his way, for he was dreadful and terrible. But Winston, being urged and influenced by others, failed to take warning, but gathered a re-enforcement and made war against John and Isaac, saying that he would not forfeit his claim, but would appeal to law for his rights. John told him that he would willingly meet him to fight the matter through, it mattered not what step he took.

John cut the time short for dissolution of partnership from the first of September, and told Winston not to come into the store any more after that night, which was August 27, 1889. John warned Winston of great danger if he returned to the store on the following day ; but Winston failed to take warning, and went as far as to put an advertisement in the papers that he would take charge of the store the next day, and be the responsible party for the payment of bills against the store.

On the following day John and Isaac returned to the store, with the hope that Winston had accepted the warning and would not return to the store with his old claim. But Winston gathered his army together the next morning and began the feud-rebellion at Mary's house, and thence to the store. This lasted, severely, until the twenty-ninth of August, 1889, at which time Winston and his host overcame John and Isaac at the store, the battle being fought with the tongue only, through desperate imprecations.

John and Isaac lost all hope, and saw no way to gain victory in the battle ; so the Lord God poured out his spirit of vengeance with power upon John, and prophesied against Winston and his host, by declaring what would befall him and those who followed after. The spirit of vengeance was poured upon John with such power that he lost control of himself, and unconsciousness hastened in, which caused him to be arrested ; but he was released immediately from prison, and the next day was the Sabbath.

Then Samuel saw that he was completely overcome by the Satanic host, and saw no way to finish the work at the store unless he went himself; and he had no share in the store that was legal in the physical law. As the city had laid the cause of the trouble to Samuel, he felt that his going to the store to finish the work would increase the trouble, and verify the accusations brought against him as being the origin of the family war. Here was a great trial for the commander.

John had decided within himself that he would not return to the store the following Monday; and Samuel saw no way to overcome, but to take John and Isaac and go to the store and work with them, to finish up the rebellion. Therefore Samuel went to the store to finish the work; but after he had been in the store a few hours, Winston, his adversary, brought in an officer and ejected Samuel from the store.

This was the first of September, 1889; and this was the time that the power of the blessing of prosperity of the holy kingdom was destroyed, and the beginning of the second period of desolation. This was the time the Messiah was cut off from the temporal world, and the time that the people of the prince destroyed the power of the holy city and sanctuary by the influx of the fulness of the pollutions of the world.

When the trouble reached this standpoint, the creditors made attachments on all property belonging to John and Isaac, and favored the rebellious brother. John and Isaac owned two horses and wagons, which were used at the store; and also had a barn, built on their mother's lot, by Samuel's command, a few months before the feud-rebellion. When the horses and wagons were attached, Samuel's brother of the natural family paid the attachment, and the horses and wagons came into his possession: and he presented them to Samuel for the advancement of his work, if he went into business so that he could use them. Samuel agreed to sell the property and refund the money if he could not use them in business of some kind.

From the first day of Samuel's vocation into the higher life and doctrines, the kingdom of darkness, which was prefiguratively embodied in John, was set up in the minds of the people of the holy prince as being a great and holy divine; and was honored and looked upon, reverently, as equal to and beyond Samuel, because of John's business ability and the fame of his family, which originated from the property they owned. John was the sanctuary belonging to the kingdom of darkness; he was by nature the burning altar upon which all sacrifices were placed to burn incense unto Baal, or the gods of gold and silver, and all precious things belonging thereto.

While John was working in the store and visiting the two witnesses, Caroline had very great love for him, and he had increscent love for her; and Caroline's very heart lusted and burned for Isaac and John, and she proclaimed that they were her sons, also, which stirred the jealous minds of many people among their acquaintances. As time wore away, love increased on both sides, one for the other, until John and Isaac finished up their mission in the world.

John and Isaac received Samuel, believed on him, and followed him, because of the love they had in store for Caroline; but this they did not confess until they appeared before the judgment seat of Christ. John and Isaac contained the fruits of the woman's flesh, which she lusted after to amalgamate with the seed of men, which adulterated the pure and holy word of the Lord God; and they were by nature the second advent of the serpent, the Devil, working in his subtlety to degenerate the second Adam and Eve from their perfect state, so that they would be driven from the spiritual land of Eden.

When Samuel was commanded to go and be a companion for Caroline in her mission, it made such stir, and created such disgraceful rumors concerning her work, that it caused her to make petition to God, to know why he did not send John, who was unmarried, to be a companion with her in the work assigned to her. She received no reply, but by works; and God fulfilled her request, not to her glory and conception, but according to his glory and purposes in bringing salvation to his people.

This was the beginning of the infatuation between the second woman and the pre-adamites. It did not change the ordinations of God in the creative use of man, because he violated the holy laws; neither did it conflict with God's purposes, for it threw man in the channel to raise up crucibles to receive the luminous rays of the Celestial Son light. All of this was done to fulfil God's words spoken by the prophets, and also to make acute repetitions of Bible history in all its different important courses of workings through the past epochs of the dark-aged worlds. It has made spiritual fulfilments of all the essential prophecies in the apostolic Bible, and in some of the prophecies has made material fulfilments.

The holy Jerusalem was led in such way as to make spiritual fulfilments of all the disobedience and sins committed by the holy people aforetime, in the most abstract way. The kingdom of utter and eternal darkness was endowed with just such inclinations and corruptible facilities as to make an abridgment of all the evils, sins, and iniquities committed by the wicked against the just since the world began. This God did to destroy utterly the current of sin which has flowed through humanity since the fall of the first man, Adam, so that he might show and prove the power of his Christ to destroy the power of that man of sin, in his most powerful existence in humanity. This was done that God's people might gain faith and trust in his Christ's supremacy and sympathy for the children of men, by seeing what has been done to destroy sin, and yet what mercy shown to save the flesh wherein sin and iniquity reigned in its predominant power.

The judgments of God through his Christ, while exploring the worlds of sin, show and prove what is sin and what is not sin. His judgments have destroyed the great errors which were sealed up in the kingdom of darkness, and were honored, worshipped, and magnified as being the holy and eternal God. The trials through which the holy saints have passed show that the Lord God created righteousness, and created sin to perfect righteousness, and to show the sempiternal endurance of righteousness, and its perpetuity; they show that the fulfilments of God's purposes in the mighty works of depravity during the perilous times of the saints were as holy as the fulfilments of his purposes in the works of righteousness. This does not justify sin; but it shows the righteousness of God, in each and every purpose, to give birth to the fulness of the perfect life, while using both sin and righteousness.

As the Lord God had a holy purpose in the erroneous works of the cherubims and flaming swords, through the troublous times, all that has been done which was conflicting with holiness has been fulfilled; and all their work during the perils of the saints is accounted unto them for righteousness. The powers of corruption, which were sealed in them, have been destroyed by fire and judgment, so that God may use the earth for the implanting of righteousness.

When the dark and tormenting powers of sin were unsealed in Isaac and John, they, from time to time, presented themselves to Samuel to be delivered through him of sin, so that they could serve righteousness as God would have them; but Samuel would tell them that the Holy Scriptures must be fulfilled concerning sin and iniquity, and that they would receive righteous rewards at the end of the trouble, because of the holy purpose of God in making them the full embodiment of sin. They had to be as I have described, that the second man and woman might amalgamate with the seed of men, so that the Holy Christ would destroy the kingdom of sin from the land which he aforetime promised to his people.

The natural family, which mingled with the holy family, was the earth, wherein was beautifully erected the bottomless pit, namely, "hell." The profound depth and the apex of the Devil's kingdom were substantial in the four foundations. John was the empire of the chief metropolis city of sin, both ancient and modern, and the capital revenue belonging thereto. The material bodies were the land, which was inhabited by the ancient Babylonian warriors, and was focalized in these tangible bodies aerially and substantially.

John and Isaac were chosen out of the Babylonian kingdom, because they were composed of prime substances and fertility for the growth and increase of divinity. Those who were destroyed materially were not composed of material, honorable substances for the implanting of divinity, and for this cause they were used as fuel for the fire, that the honorable might be delivered out of cruel hands that shed innocent blood. When John and Isaac finished up their worldly career, they committed all things concerning their lives, both earthly and heavenly, into Samuel's hands, for him to command the thing he determined to have done, and they would carry it into effect by the power of Samuel's speech.

When Samuel gave the command, saying what was to be done to accomplish the fulfilment of the Scriptures, the Holy Spirit used the one most suitable for the accomplishment of the work; and when the Spirit was using each instrument, they had no fear of what would come out of the work, nor any doubt of its being according as Samuel had given the commandment.

A short time before John was summoned from his earthly work, his whole desire was toward Caroline; and he increscently burned in his lust for her, and his desire was not going out for any other woman. John fought against that unnatural desire, and regarded it not, to satisfy the lust thereof, because he believed that in man's material existence after death that ravenous desire would not be cherished or admitted.

When his work in eternity began, the power of that desire worked by involuntary force, and increased rapidly until he confessed it to Samuel, saying that it was the sole cause of all his suffering, which came in griefs and burdens. The power of this desire ruled him through the seven seals, showing itself in many forms, with all kinds and ways of deceivableness, which continuated the hazardous trials and desolation of the genuine saints and Christ. Samuel made many attempts and changes concerning his trouble, to annihilate and exterminate the reigning power of lasciviousness, but to no avail, until the abomination of desolation went to the vertical point.

John, being the god of metaphysics, the transcendent glory and wisdom of the world, was endowed by inheritance with the extreme principles of arrogancy and self-esteem, and possessed great dexterity, craftiness, and subtlety to perform any work he was called upon to do for Samuel. John had great wisdom, acute and perspicuous understanding, and insight to see and understand any mystery that Samuel revealed concerning the dark sayings of the Holy Scriptures; and in many dark sayings he had searched them out and interpreted the meaning, and how it was to be fulfilled, before the Holy Spirit revealed them to Samuel.

The second plague, the vial of God's wrath, fell upon the mother city of Babylon, and destroyed the fluent power of her speech, which is symbolized in the prophecies as channels of waters. This plague destroyed the great force of her speech and then her simple speech, which was symbolized as small bodies of water and as material beings, which were the spiritual souls that appeared in Mary's mind after the resurrection. These mortal, abominable souls were plagued and perplexed until they were taken with loathsome disease, gave up all hope, and died from her mind, while some were cremated by the spirit of divine truth typified as fire.

This was done that the desperadoes which freakishly inhabited the temple Mary would be killed and burned by God's wrath and vengeance, which came out of the mouth of his Samuel. These desperadoes, in many instances, manifested themselves materially in dishonorable characteristics without godly reasons, which were at war with the daughter of Zion and the Son of Righteousness. At that time the daughter of Babylon opposed everything that was being accomplished; whether for her or against her, she worked to the contrary, but the greater portion of her combativeness was mental, and operated upon the pure soul of the revelator like canker.

Everything she did, and every thought she had, was to destroy and defeat the ordinations of the divine and holy physical God, and impede the movement of the covenant as God had determined it. All she did for the holy covenant was in the interest of her two sons; and all her suffering, endurance, and confession of Samuel's work to be of God, came out of a false heart, and was uttered by feigned lips, that she might remain with Samuel, where she could see what would befall her sons. This was the tap-root of her life.

The daughter of Babylon spoke in defence of Samuel's mission, but inwardly she used the spear and weapons of war. All her mental power and time was occupied in searching out the real science of craft, to acknowledge what was not in her, and to be what she was not. She possessed the science of mental witchcraft, and the science to foretell mysteries of divinations; she contained the embodiment of fallacious doctrines, and familiar prophetic fallacious divinations; her entire wisdom of science was to foretell approaching evils, and to deceive. She was the grandmother central point, which was the co-ordinating degrees of corruption of all the false prophets of the ancient days and those of the modern times. She contained by substance the profound depth and the vertex of the most ancient and modern corruption, which had been refined and wrought in the flesh through the power of mental science and art; and these principles of science were long-enduring, patient, kind, and faithful to abide in trouble to overcome falsely.

The daughter of Babylon was obedient to the commander of the new covenant, yet she was the focus of corruption, namely, lust of the flesh, the glory and pride of the world. Her material structure and outward appearance were entirely godlike, and in harmony with the so-called Christian life; but all was science and formality of godliness. This was the formal globe of the uttermost perdition, the scientific totalship of the bottomless pit. The real powers of this vast body of corruption were mental, but were outwardly transformed into an angel of light, which deceived the very elect, until the Holy Spirit uncovered her and showed her nakedness.

There was more wickedness besides what was manifested in her, in speaking of quantity; but she contained a small portion of all the essential powers of sin and iniquity, which was the creative germ of sin, the man and woman slayer. As she was the raging billows of abomination, John was the pre-eminent branch, who extracted her essential dexterous and subtle characteristics, because she was not materially organized to exhibit them after the scientific corruption of the latter age.

Isaac's science of deception was extracted from this vast body, because her principles were the vine planted in his blood, which compelled them to bend one toward the other ; and also made them of one mind for a time, to fulfil God's words. The rebellious branch extracted a portion of the real mental power, which empowered him to carry out his work with such warlike force without yielding to the right. When the Lord God smote this spiritual embodiment of corruption, the branches of abomination that fed from her vast body began to loathe and die.

These are the four great wicked beasts which arose out of the sea of corruption and divided one from the other; which definates that they were unlike and did not cleave one to the other in characteristics. On the right hand there came up out of the sea of trouble and great tribulations four holy persons, typified as holy beasts, which were the four winds, or spirits of heaven, that formed the cherubims and flaming sword, the four grand divisions around the spiritual land of Eden. The holy beasts were also divided one from the other, and did not harmonize nor mingle in principles ; which made them like unto the kingdom of darkness.

The Lord God organized and constructed these four material beings, and endowed them with such substantialities and firm principles that they were powerfully instrumental for the Holy Spirit to use to carry God's purposes into effect, so as to make the Bible the third, and a totally spiritual book, that through the refining, cohesion, and union of the three divisions, they would make an abridgment of the Holy Bible, called " the Lamb's Book of Life." The reality and essential parts of the apostolic Bible are recorded in the " Lamb's Book of Life," both in the mysterious powers of sin and righteousness, which is the unveiling of the face of the word of the Lord God.

The Lord God did not make manifest the science of perdition to stigmatize those who bore the image of corruption ; for this purpose he created and fashioned them, as narrated, to show and prove the supremacy of his Christ over sin. The power of darkness had to manifest itself in every degree of its mightiest and simplest existence, to separate the righteous from the ungodly ; for through trials cometh praises, and without the persecutions of the wicked there could be no glory for the righteous.

The righteous obtain praise and honor unto God by his delivering them from the cruel powers of the mighty enemy, when they reach the end of suffering and selfish choice and desires ; and that person, people, or nation who has not been downtrodden, punished, and persecuted for righteousness' sake has no part in the glory of the Lord God.

The Lord God spoke the word, and created the powers of utter darkness and death ; and he spoke the word and created the powers of the translunary light and life, the author and creator of righteousness. After the power of corruption performs its work, it is thenceforth good for nothing but to be cast into the fire and burned, just as men put fuel into the fire to give heat, which is made for their glory and that purpose.

Each human temple is created and organized to do a certain portion of work to carry out God's purposes in making his name an everlasting praise, even as the substances of the material universe are created for man's purposes, which they use to their glory. Cannot God do as he chooses with his own, when he is the Creator, Author, and Ruler over all ? Then why are ye double minded concerning the way God shall perform his work in establishing righteousness in the earth ?

The abomination that made the holy spiritual Jerusalem desolate was the image of the man of sin, the metropolis city of Babylon, namely, John. This embodied image of abomination was set up January 27, 1888, to worship man and his works and to deny the power of the infinite God, which rules mankind by the triniunity government of word, spirit, and truth. In this image of abomination were found the late supreme powers of the physical governments, and all the gold and silver belonging thereto ; and the people who exist in this finite kingdom were found worshipping and paying the highest reverence to the gods of gold and silver and precious things, glorying in the most renowned men, and those highly educated, physically and politically, but regarding not small and simple things. Neither was it found in their hearts to show mercy and benevolence to the poorer class of mankind ; they bestowed gifts and mercy upon the rich and renowned, whose needs were exuberantly supplied, and whose barns and storehouses were filled.

This coagulated orb of abominable humanity despised poor and simple people ; and his heart was lifted up and magnified and eulogized the simplicity and smallness among the great men of the earth. He wanted to see the poor and simple put to death, and the wise and pre-eminent men and women have full access to God's glory and kingdom, because of their greatness in the animal kingdom, which they labored to obtain merely for their own glory and fame, regardless of God's kingdom, which, through generations and generations, has slumbered in supine desolation while man attributed all glory to man and woman.

When the subordinate officers saw that their chief and ruling king was interested in Samuel's mission, they renewed their hope, confirmed their determination, and followed on after him. Isaac continued to follow on, and grew more and more interested in Samuel's mission, to follow the example of his great captain. When his great king joined in the work with Samuel, Isaac sacrificed his life and all he owned, to stand in defence of Samuel's mission, so that his mighty king would not fail in the step which he had taken. Then Mary followed on after Isaac, and sacrificed all she owned, to see that the step which her sons' had taken dangerously would be successful; but the rebellious brother did not continue to pursue, because he was inclined to exhibit the reality of Babylon. This was the raging, turbulent, and propelling current of abomination, which marred the beauty, tarnished the purity, and diluted the strength and power of the holy city and sanctuary.

When the chief king of Babylon covenanted with the king of Jerusalem mutely, and deserted his physical work, it was then rumored that the work Samuel was doing would soon result in something marvellous, and would give birth to something to agitate the whole world. They said, "There must be something brewing that is wonderful, to cause a man of his ability to sacrifice his prosperous business to go into such reproachful looking work as Samuel's vocation." But they did not remain firm on that idea and statement; they soon said that he was insane, and had been influenced by Samuel and Caroline to sacrifice his progressive business and be a member of their work. The revelator beheld their ignorance and blasphemous comments and evil surmising.

Isaac's suffering, submission, and obedience to the holy covenant were for the support of his king, who followed on; when the vengeance in judgment fell upon him, and he complied with the conditions, and became willing to be a servant in a low degree for the commander, Isaac did the same, and travelled all the way through the troublous time, following and supporting his king. Still, his king respected not a man of his organization; but this Isaac knew not, because he was Isaac's hope, trust, and safeguard.

When Isaac's mighty king became troubled, Isaac was troubled, also; when the king was glorified, Isaac was glorified, also; therefore Isaac's sacrifices and work, all the way through the troublous times, were to sustain and follow his safeguard and captain, John. If his great captain could have turned materially against the holy covenant, he could have done the same.

Mary endured and abode in trouble until death, to sustain her king and prince; and the Lord God overcame the Babylonian kingdom without further trouble and war, because the Babylonian king divided against his own kingdom and kind. Mary and Isaac were more of one mind than the rest; and this only worked, at a certain time, to fulfil the Scriptures on this matter; and then the harmony was destroyed, so that God could deliver his holy kingdom out of the power of the Babylonians.

John had no love nor sympathy for the members of his family who resisted Samuel and Caroline in any way whatever; it was firm in his heart to destroy all of those belonging to his family who opposed the covenant and conflicted with its course of work.

These are the modern names of the kings, princes, and queens who reigned over the land of those who contained the totalship of polluted mental science, which is Biblically typified by the desperate wickedness of the ancient Babylonians. Lust is the fertility of sin and the soil for its growth, increase, and continuity; lust is the formal globe of the nethermost region and the continuator of mortality.

The seven streams of corruption, which are symbolized as mountains and other visible objects, were spiritually manifested in the globe of lust, and they are, namely, deception, enmity, contempt, disobedience, disbelief, jealousy, and lustfulness. The ten horns out of the Devil's kingdom are the monarchs; namely, vainglorious pride, unthankfulness, self-esteem, prejudice against color, craving for beauty, self-will, filthiness, laziness, robbery, and murder. These are the warriors who reigned over the temple Mary, whose spiritual body was called "the daughter of Babylon;" and these rulers made the temple the full embodiment of sin and corruption. In that day, the revelation of these mysteries was the cause of the material destruction of the temple of sin.

During the severe times of these troublous mysteries, Samuel asked Mary if she was willing to continue in the trouble until the end of the seven seals; her reply was that that was her desire, and she had no other desire than to abide with the revelator and receive life of him. Samuel told her if she had rather live apart from him he would return to her all the things she had given him, take his family and move out from her, and let her have full control of the house; but she said if he left her she could not live, for she could not mingle with the people as she had done before. Samuel gave her the privilege of taking her choice, — to remain with him or to separate, — but she refused it, each and every time, and even became sorrowful when he mentioned it to her.

The Impartial Judgments; the Unloosing of the Third Seal, and Solitary Desolation; Sundry Fulfilments.

I. the Lord God, prophesy through the mouth of my instrument, Samuel, the vengeance which shall be executed upon those who are not materially organized to attain life eternal in the material body. I have therefore put on my second figurative body, to fulfil the promises I have made to mine elect people ever since the creation of the heavens and earth. The time has come for me to fulfil all Scriptures which were sent unto you of old by the prophets; and in order to do this thing, I must first choose seven instruments, and purify them to be subject to the spirits of the seven righteous Ethiopian branches. These seven instruments shall be the reapers, to go into the harvest-field and gather the vines of the clusters of the earth, for her grapes are fully ripe.

The third plague shall fall upon the rivers, seas, and oceans. The first symptoms of those who meet the fate of this plague will be an exceedingly high temperature of blood heat; the blood will become deadly poisoned, and will at last turn jet black, which will result in a disease called "the black death." This plague will first fall upon the smaller bodies of waters, and then upon the larger ones; and this plague will make straight my course, and prepare my way. It will begin to germinate September 27, 1889, at which time I will use my instrument, Samuel, to establish my free and independent organization where my prosperity shall spread its broad wings over my faithful and chosen people. I will then use my carpenters to build my celestial temple, which shall be built by my hand of wisdom. I, the Lord God, prophesy on the third vial of wrath, and behold, four others cometh quickly.

January 27, 1888, was the beginning of the first period of desolation of the New Jerusalem, after making its advent to earth. This period lasted until March 1, 1889; but the first period was not solitary desolation. September 1, 1889, was the beginning of the second period, and the beginning of the period of solitary desolation of the New Jerusalem. This lasted, uninterruptedly, until June 15, 1890, at which time the holy prince stood upon his feet and began to consume solitary desolation. During the time of the solitary desolation, all the work done by the people of the holy prince previous to this time was utterly suspended, and all means of support were cut off from Samuel and those who were with him. At this time there was great commotion among the people who were interested in the great failure of Isaac's fruit business, and great perplexity among the members of Babylon, because they looked ahead and beheld the approaching hazards which their feelings convinced them they were compelled to face.

After the attachments were made on all property belonging to the store, the creditors grew wroth, and raged at a fearful rate ; and it was published and circulated, among the adversaries of the genuine truth, that the reason there was no money in the bank to pay the indebtedness of the store was because Samuel and Caroline had become the possessors of it, and it had been used for their support. This manner of publication again stirred up the enemies of the new covenant, and the majority of the people believed this flying fiction. Many of those who did not believe the original lies were seduced to believe, at that time, and bowed down and worshipped the abominable beast and his ostentatious image.

Because the people did not understand the real causes of the great failure of Isaac's business, the fact that he was a disciple of Samuel was a strong delusion, to compel the false believers of the truth to decide that Samuel's vocation and work was not ordained by the Holy God. This was because their faith was fiction, and their thoughts created and issued false judgments against the holiest of holiest. When the creditors found that Samuel's brother Walter had bought the horses and running-gear belonging to the store, some among them declared it a fraud, and re-attached the property, and it was taken from Samuel, and held in bonds for many days. They were compelled to return the property, and it was again presented to Samuel by Walter to help forward the building of the holy kingdom ; and Samuel covenanted with Walter to sell the property, and refund the money, if the property could not be used materially in some kind of business to sustain the work. It was Samuel's agreement to do this, and not Walter's request ; he was more in favor of leaving the matter unconditional, and without stipulations, but hoped to secure work in connection with Samuel's mission when he again established himself in business.

Samuel made attempts to have John and Isaac acquitted of insolvency, so that they might go into some kind of business, to obtain an honorable support, being at that time ignorant of the desolation into which they were hurled, and of God's purposes in the desolation. No attempt proved successful, because the Lord God concealed the mystery of desolation from Samuel all the way through, so that he would not reveal it to the members of Babylon. This was to make them continue to hope falsely, according to the imaginations of their lascivious hearts, until his purposes were carried out; for as soon as the knowledge of a thing was made known to Samuel, he made it known to those who dwelt with him; therefore God did not reveal to him his deep purposes, until the time to divulge them.

God placed the mystery of the horses before them as a door of hope, which kept them hoping that they would be put to work and throw down the shame of their all sitting around and not making public anything as a means of support. These reproachful looking scenes did not change the determination of the Lord God. They all had work to do; but it was to stand before the judgment seat of Christ and answer to the names of the iniquities which transgressed the laws of the holy covenant. The Lord God did not specify any particular work to be done at that time, to show why they had no means of support, and that means of support that by chance came to them, came through those who had been standing afar off, waiting to see what would befall them, and to see some ndications of godliness in the work.

Those who did help the desolate thought it was preposterous to support so many, when some among them might earn something for their support; but they knew not the thoughts of God, which fulfil God's words, saying, "Therefore wait ye upon me, saith the Lord, until the day that I rise up to the prey: for my determination is to gather the nations, that I may assemble the kingdoms, to pour upon them mine indignation, even all my fierce anger: for all the earth shall be devoured with the fire of my jealousy. For then will I turn to the people a pure language, that they may all call upon the name of the Lord, to serve him with one consent." After the creditors made attachments on the store, they acquitted Winston and sold the stand to him; and Winston re-opened the fruit business in the same store, took one of his kind as partner, and tried to make it appear that the Holy God was with him, and Samuel and his followers were the false army. He did all in his power, through the force of the red-head dragon, to have Samuel and his followers prosecuted for fraudulency; and through the prevailing power of this red-tongued dragon he kept the creditors believing a lie, that there was fraud in the failure of the business, for the purpose of using the money to support Samuel's work.

To tell the plain truth, to wash away the deluge of lies and infamy which makes friendless the holy truth, I will declare that there was nothing substantial at the bottom of the business in the outset, — neither in business talent, capital, nor management; it was a total sham and delusion. God only started and upheld it for a time, to effect this purpose. The re-opening of the business made a progressive show for a short time, and Winston and his army rode the red-head dragon, and published the lie, verbally, until his time ended on earth; which fulfils God's words, saying, " And I saw by night, and behold a man riding upon a red horse." — Zech. 1: 8, 21.

The four horns that scattered Judah and Jerusalem define the four members of Babylon; and the horn that was lifted up over Judah defines the man of sin, who was the burning altar and sanctuary belonging to Babylon, — he who was exalted by the members of Babylon above the holy city and sanctuary, which is called Judah, Israel, Jerusalem, and many other holy names. The four carpenters were the four divisions of the Holy Spirit, which fell upon the four material beings to accomplish a certain work, and enable them to abide until the indignation was accomplished, and the Scriptures fulfilled. The triniunity power of Christ moved with a continual effux in the tabernacle Samuel to fray out of his people the principles of hell, and all abomination and corruption belonging thereto.

The four horns of the Gentile world are, namely, excessive love and partiality for blood-kin rather than for God, his people, and righteousness; desire for property, greed after gain in riches, love for money, trust in it, and sacrifice to obtain it through suffering and self-denial more than willingness to sacrifice in honor of God, to inherit his righteousness and live for his people; burning zeal, through lasciviousness, for sexual commerce, with magnanimous honor and reverence to both of the natural sexes rather than to God, merely to satisfy and nourish the lascivious unicorn king; commendation, honor, and trust in the educated, the judgment and wisdom of the world, rather than in the wisdom and judgment of God, and commendation, honor, and trust in his wisdom and righteousness, manifested in his chosen people.

The members of Babylon loved, sought, trusted, honored, magnified, and reverenced these four horns of mortality more than they did their Creator; and burned in their lust to excel and compete in the glory of these four kingdoms, when the power of life was offered freely unto them, if they would deny and turn from these kingdoms and receive life by being as faithful and loyal to the doctrines of the higher kingdoms as they were to the lower kingdoms. When they saw that these horns were being extracted from their spiritual systems, they lost all hope of the attainment of the higher kingdom, and sought death rather than life. This was because they suffered excruciating pains from extracting the members connected with those four chief horns; and these are the strange and false gods whom all the people living upon the earth worship and serve, unawares.

The powers of dense blackness, corruption, and abomination which were sealed up in Babylon benegroed the Son of Righteousness while fulfilling his mission therein, which is the express likeness of all nations now in existence upon the earth : for all that were sealed up in the members of Babylon are now ruling and reigning over all material people, nations, kindred, kings, and tongues inhabiting the terrestrial globe, who are not connected with the new covenant.

These horns of mortality, the kingdoms of the pre-adamites, were purged and refined of their corruption and abomination, the dense blackness, called "ignorance," was dispelled, and the perfect and eternal light was produced, and set to burning, which caused the consumption upon the natural body of the called and chosen members of Babylon, so that the spiritual saints would have the land for their inheritance and dwelling empires. This fulfils, as follows: " And I turned and lifted up mine eyes, and looked, and, behold, there came four chariots out from between two mountains : and the mountains were mountains of brass." — Zech. 6.

The four horns that preside over righteousness are, equity, judgment, mercy, and sincerity. These are the four great horns, or principles, which were wrought in the revelator and gave him power in every time of need, and overcame the abominable horns of Babylon.

Samuel had to wait forty days without the spirit of truth and judgment, after entering into solitary desolation ; which was to fulfil

God's words, saying, " Lie thou also upon thy left side, and lay the iniquity of the house of Israel upon it : according to the number of the days that thou shalt lie upon it thou shalt bear their iniquity. For I have laid upon thee the years of their iniquity, according to the number of the days, three hundred and ninety days : so shalt thou bear the iniquity of the house of Israel. And when thou hast accomplished them, lie again on thy right side, and thou shalt bear the iniquity of the house of Judah forty days : I have appointed thee each day for a year."

When this time expired, the revelator sought earnestly to find the cause of the trouble which had come upon him ; and the Lord God began to open to him the Scriptures, to make manifest the chief evil that had befallen him, which reads as follows : —

" And the word of the Lord came unto me, saying, Son of man, put forth a riddle, and speak a parable unto the house of Israel ; and say, Thus saith the Lord God ; A great eagle with great wings, longwinged, full of feathers, which had divers colors, came unto Lebanon, and took the highest branch of the cedar : he cropped off the top of his young twigs, and carried it into a land of traffic ; he set it in a city of merchants. He took also of the seed of the land, and planted it in a fruitful field : he placed it by great waters, and set it as a willow tree. And it grew, and became a spreading vine of low stature, whose branches turned toward him. and the roots thereof were under him : so it became a vine, and brought forth branches, and shot forth sprigs. There was also another great eagle with great wings and many feathers : and, behold, this vine did bend her roots toward him, and shot forth her branches toward him, that he might water it by the furrows of her plantation. It was planted in a good soil by great waters, that it might bring forth branches, and that it might bear fruit, that it might be a goodly vine. Say thou, Thus saith the Lord God ; Shall it prosper ? shall he not pull up the roots thereof, and cut off the fruit thereof, that it wither ? it shall wither in all the leaves of her spring, even without great power or many people to pluck it up by the roots thereof. Yea, behold, being planted, shall it prosper ? shall it not utterly wither, when the east wind toucheth it ? it shall wither in the furrows where it grew. Moreover the word of the Lord came unto me, saying, Say now to the rebellious house, Know ye not what these things mean ? tell them, Behold, the king of Babylon is come to Jerusalem, and hath taken the king thereof, and the princes thereof, and led them with him to Babylon ; and hath taken of the king's seed, and made a covenant with him, and hath taken an oath of him : he hath also taken the mighty of the land : that the kingdom might be base, that it might not lift itself up, but that by keeping of his covenant it might stand." — Ezek. 17 : 1-14.

The two eagles typified parabolically in these words of prophecy explanate the daughter of Babylon and the man upon whom the king of Jerusalem imputed the blessing of prosperity for the physical support of the covenant and its members during the perilous times. The divers colors and great wings full of long feathers were the many inclinations and ways of deception, great faith and long patience, the daughter of Babylon contained, to abide in suffering to achieve victory over the king of righteousness, to change the course of God's workings at that time.

The highest branch of the cedar of Lebanon was the rich blessing of divine and physical prosperity which the king of Jerusalem imputed upon the filthy and uncircumcised man Isaac, who, after receiving the blessing, repented in his heart — after seeing the straightness and purity of the covenant — that he had ever given his word voluntarily to speak in favor of it and work wholly for its support. The great eagle that did bend her wings toward him signifies the spirit of antichrist that carried his mother, Mary, whose mind was tormented and grieved to the uttermost for fear he would give all of his earnings for the support of the new covenant. She worked by the power of mental craft to win his entire love and sympathy from the daughter of Zion, so that he might agree with her and keep his earnings concealed between the two, and turn his interest and devotion away from Samuel's mission and retain it as she formerly had done. This she did for a time, and this was one of the great weapons that destroyed the blessing of prosperity when imputed upon the natural spiritual body of Isaac.

When this mystery was disclosed and conveyed to the minds of the Babylonians, the mental war increased, and the trouble became more and more grievous. At this time the love and devotion which were in the daughter of Jerusalem for Isaac were utterly destroyed, and great wrath was manifested in her against the natural bodies of Isaac and Mary ; which put it in the hearts of Isaac and Mary to agree on the mental powers of evil against the covenant, because of Caroline's arbitrary, strange, and unreasonable acts, which threw the holy covenant into the height and depth of jeopardy.

Then Samuel's knowledge became darkened as pertaining to this mystery; and the Lord God revealed the truthful workings of this mystery, which were concealed, in the following chapter and prophecy: "And there came unto me one of the seven angels which had the seven vials, and talked with me, saying unto me, Come hither; I will shew unto thee the judgment of the great whore that sitteth upon many waters." — Rev. 17.

Samuel did not bring the daughter of Babylon near to him to pronounce the judgments upon her until this mystery was searched into and seen; and then he appointed a time to adopt her into his family spiritually, so that, through adoption, she might become a daughter born into his family, legitimately, after the birth of the new covenant. Therefore, he appointed a time for the adoption; and he, and his people with him, went into a fast to bring her up out of the land of Egypt into the land flowing with milk and honey, that she might be recompensed for all the good that she had done with the object of aggrandizing the kingdom of Christ, which she acknowledged boldly, at first.

Samuel stipulated with her that he would be an husband and a father unto her, and she could be his daughter, look to him for all things, put all her trust in him, look steadfastly to him for all things she needed for support, give up to him all her cares, burdens, herself, property, sons, and kindred; and the Lord God would do with them as he had determined, and give her, in return, the attainment of eternal life, if she complied with the conditions.

The daughter of Babylon declared that she was willing to comply with every condition; for all she wanted was life eternal, and she asked Samuel to bring her to his will, because she could do nothing herself, and the powers of evil were too strong for her. Mary understood that leaving all her cares, griefs, and burdens with Samuel was leaving it with God; because she experienced that every word spoken by Samuel was apodeictical and deifical. This was because God was embodied in the revelator in his supreme power, and the words spoken were quickening, creative, and controlling in power, showing the ruling sceptre, the righteous government of the people.

When the revelator saw her straining and tormenting herself openly, as though she was struggling falsely in her own strength to do what he had said to her, he commanded her to be mentally still, and let his words work in her to do as he had said; for the Supreme Being would perform the work, after the words were spoken, according as it was determined, and God would use her to his will, and to accomplish his purposes in all things concerning her, as foreordained.

Samuel saw that she was not composed of the proper substance to pursue the way he had spoken, and that her god was trying to deceive him with an outward show and form of circumcision and righteousness, which purports the golden cup in her hand, as prophesied. When Samuel would see her in the clutches of despondency, and know that he was wreaking his vengeance upon her, and devouring her flesh unmercifully, he would take her alone and speak cheering words to bring comfort near. He was compelled to flatter her, that she might gain hope and faith to trust in his words, and turn her mind away from the stream of corruption and the world of darkness, misery, and woe. She continued to confess that all power was in Samuel to save her from sin; and all she wanted was to be delivered from the great powers of the Devil, and be made contented to live as he had said. When the judgments were pronounced upon her, showing the evil powers reigning within her, she confessed that the judgments were true, and said she knew Samuel was the true God, because he knew what was in her.

The powers of corruption had grown from the internal to the external, and there was no substance or soil for the word, or germ of life, to take root: the climate was too severely frigid to give birth to the new life, hence the flesh of Mary could not be saved to reign on earth materially with God's Christ. The embodiment of sin and the flesh were totally consolidated, which made the two bodies the express likeness, so that the members and nature of sin could not be eradicated to accomplish the redemption of the corporeal body to live upon the earth; so God saw fit to save by purging the essential part of her human spiritual body, and took it to himself to use in fertile soil to his glory, and caused the suffering of Mary's flesh to cease through semi-mutual separation of her spirit and body, whence came her just compensation.

This fulfils the parable spoken by Jesus, saying, "No man putteth a piece of new cloth unto an old garment, for that which is put in to fill it up taketh from the garment, and the rent is made worse. Neither do men put new wine into old bottles: else the bottles break, and the wine runneth out, and the bottles perish: but they put new wine into new bottles, and both are preserved."

And he put forth another parable touching on this mystery: "The kingdom of heaven is like unto a net, that was cast into the sea, and gathered of every kind : which, when it was full, they drew to shore, and sat down, and gathered the good into vessels, but cast the bad away. So shall it be at the end of the world : the angels shall come forth, and sever the wicked from among the just, and shall cast them into the furnace of fire : there shall be wailing and gnashing of teeth."

The gloom of darkness still overshadowed Samuel in the midst of the wonderful revelation, while unveiling the man of sin ; and he still sought for some means of support. for the responsibility of the family was heavily upon him, both physical and divine. The interest on Mary's property, which was placed in Samuel's hands to keep up, had to be paid, that they might have a home during the time of their trouble , all this had to be done, and there was no means of income to do it with. The Lord God quickened Samuel with the words of this chapter, saying, " Who is left among you that saw this house in her first glory? and how do you see it now? is it not in your eyes in comparison of it as nothing ? "—Hag. 2.

This prophecy revived great hope in the minds of the desolate, when it was read and simply explained by Samuel to his people with him ; and it lead them to believe that the horses would again be put to work, and the blessing of prosperity spring up and flourish. The explanation which the revelator gave on the exegesis of this prophecy located a great door of hope, by which the members of Babylon expected to gain access into the world, to retain the glory and honor of the holy kingdom under a pseudonymous name, and pseudomorphous forms.

An epidemic of La Grippe prevailed during the third seal, and Winston was captured by it, and died very suddenly near the close of the third seal, which was the destruction of one of the fortified walls of Babylon which had closed upon and besieged Jerusalem. This fulfils God's words, saying, " And the third angel sounded, and there fell a great star from heaven, burning as it were a lamp, and it fell upon the third part of the rivers, and upon the fountains of waters ; and the name of the star is called Wormwood : and many men died of the waters, because they were made bitter."

The third part of the Babylonian warriors, that authoritatively besieged Jerusalem, was destroyed at Winston's death : and the redhead dragon had to be transformed and transferred into another image and to another temple, to rule over the saints by sagacity and stratagem, to fulfil the time prophesied of concerning the number of days in which God would accomplish his work and fulfil his pleasure in the desolation of Jerusalem. This fulfils his words, saying, " I will utterly consume all things from off the land, saith the Lord. I will consume man and beast; I will consume the fowls of the heaven, and the fishes of the sea, and the stumblingblocks with the wicked; and I will cut off man from off the land, saith the Lord." — Zeph. 1.

Then came the word of the Lord by Haggai, the prophet, saying, " Thus speaketh the Lord of hosts, saying, This people say, The time is not come, the time that the Lord's house should be built. Is it not time for you, O ye, to dwell in your cieled houses, and this house lie waste ? " — Hag. 1.

Immediately after the solitary desolation began with God's elect people, their appetites became so ravenous that they were not satisfied nor filled with any quality or quantity of food set before them; neither were they thankful for their food and drink. When they got one kind of food and drink, they contemned it and lusted after another, and when they were blessed with that they wanted previously, they contemned it all the more, and so on; their greedy appetites lusted for all kinds of food, and were not pleased nor thankful with any that were given to them.

This was because God was discharging his wrath and vengeance upon the rapacious, lascivious, unthankful, begrudgful, and fastidious belly gods that rule the human appetites excessively and corruptly. The elect people had no means of support except through the mercy of those who believed that the work was determined of God; and they were few in number, and some among these were bound and cruelly persecuted, having husbands opposing the covenant desperately.

While the people of the holy prince were passing through the judgments, there was great pain and agony while dissecting the members of the man of sin. When the operation of anatomy reached the strong members of that man of sin, the Son of Perdition, it was so painful and agonizing that at times the patients lost full control of themselves, and at times the gas of unconsciousness was given by the Holy Spirit, to enable them to abide and endure unto the end of the reign of perdition.

When the judgments were pronounced on them, the piercing and consuming power of the trio-persons of divine truth symbolized a sword, a rod of iron, and fire; when these were cast into their earthly bodies by the extemporaneous sermons delivered by Samuel, it made war with the nefarious laws and doctrines of that man of sin, ignored and ostracized them, and plucked him out, one member at a time, and burned, in some cases, to destroy the root and fœtus where it was deeply rooted. When a member that gave very great pain was dissected, the Holy Spirit prescribed and conveyed to the physician a sarcotic, soothing, and healing remedy to exterminate the pain in a short time, and the patient was soon ready for another operation.

While the Lord God was working out the mysteries of the anatomy of the man of sin to graduate Samuel, and make him the divine physician of the human soul, his people at times made war with him, and blasphemed him because of the severity of the pain. But the revelator was gentle, kind, loving, patient, and sympathizing, while performing these painful operations, and told them that they were compelled to go through severe suffering to make manifest the prevailing power of that man of sin who is a mystery to all nations. While they were waiting to go into another operation, the healing balm issued from Samuel, through sympathy, so readily, to heal their wounds, that they laughed and talked freely with him concerning how much pain and suffering they had undergone in the last operation, and expressed their willingness to undergo the next, knowing that for this purpose they were fashioned and reserved.

Samuel knew that when they made war with him, and blasphemed the holy name of God, it was not they, but the involuntary powers of sin which God unsealed in the souls to resist his Holy Christ, to demonstrate his power and mission to mankind. This fulfils God's words by Isaiah, saying, "And there shall come forth a rod out of the stem of Jesse, and a branch shall grow out of his roots." — Isaiah 11. "And in that day thou shalt say, O Lord, I will praise thee: though thou wast angry with me, thine anger is turned away, and thou comfortedst me." — Isa. 12.

When Samuel adopted the daughter of Babylon into his family, illegitimately, and betrothed her to his life, irreverently to holiness, he — to establish peace between Caroline and Mary, so that strife would have an end between them — wrote a form of house ordinances concerning how the work should be done, as follows: "Mary shall keep clean the first court of the house; take charge of the dining-room, the kitchen and cooking utensils, and wash for Isaac and herself. Caroline shall be the mistress of the house, and Mary shall be her servant; and Caroline shall be kind, loving, sympathizing, and patient with her, and teach her what she does not know how to do, after the manner of the covenant. Caroline shall keep clean the second and last court of the house; do the vegetable cooking; make the drinks; wash for Samuel, John, Eva, and herself, and do the sewing. Samuel shall be the principal over the house, and do the catering. John and Isaac shall be his servants, to do according to all he commands them. When Mary needs anything she shall notify Caroline beforehand, and Caroline shall notify Samuel concerning the needs of the house. Caroline shall notify Mary when the baking shall be done, what she shall bake, and how much to bake; and economize in the use of the food, and be thankful for all that is given, whether it appear small or great. And the Lord God of this covenant will bless and supply your needs."

As soon as this commandment went forth, enmity and jealousy revived in the two women, and Caroline grew hasty in manner and impertinent to Samuel; and he chastened her severely to destroy her imperial power, and compelled her to make friendship with Mary, and carry out the commandment. And there was a speedy change from this time until God's purposes were fulfilled — friendship and unity, apparently. This was the time they lifted up the ephah between the heaven and earth: but it only lasted a short time before evil revived afresh and destroyed the feigned friendship between the two women. When the trouble reached this juncture, Mary was cut off from doing any housework save her own washing and room, until a few weeks before she died, which was in harmony with her desire.

During this time Samuel occasionally communed with Mary alone, sympathizingly, to cheer her up, and eject the mighty hopeless demoness. He allured her by making her concealed additional promises, conditionally; but found it inexpedient to make mention of the conditions at this time, as it would strengthen and retain the hopeless demoness. When the judgments fell grievously upon her two sons, and she could gaze upon their pitiful looking carcasses, the powers of evil vengeance raged in her against the holy truth despite their suffering. This was manifested in her acts and severe expression, and in the dense blackness upon her face.

This fulfils God's words, saying, "Plead with your mother, plead: for she is not my wife, neither am I her husband." — Hos. 2.

"Then saith the Lord unto me, Go yet, love a woman beloved of her friend, yet an adultress, according to the love of the Lord toward the children of Israel, who look to other gods, and love flagons of wine." — Hos. 3. "The burden of Babylon, which Isaiah the son of Amoz did see. Lift ye up a banner upon the high mountain, exalt the voice unto them, shake the hand, that they may go into the gates of the nobles." — Isa. 13.

From the day that the Lord God wrought the miracle in the supernatural commandment to Samuel to go and be a companion to Caroline, in whom he established the millennium doctrine, in the meantime, for the fulfilment of this commandment on Samuel's part as an embassador sent forth from God, to harmonize with the commandment given to him, and to realize the ordinances of the Lord God concerning the preternatural and transcendent glory, honor, and power of the animal kingdom in humanity, God wrought a miracle of the most essential love and jealousy in Caroline, the millennium kingdom, to attribute all glory and honor to Samuel, corporeally, in whom God established the perfect life and doctrines, the fulness of the holy life of both millennium and postliminy. This was to purge, purify, and refine the entire genuine doctrines, laws, styles, and customs of millennium, and to teach the same to the people who are spread abroad over this great millennium universe.

The involuntary and propelling power of love and jealousy which God suffered to reign in millennium involved the fulness of the animal kingdom. This was realized and produced by the resurrection and revivification of Caroline's natural and preternatural propensities, transformed into the same image as that of the divine doctrines of millennium, by occupying and flowing through the channels of her nature that were permeated and occupied by the divine doctrines, using the same language, authority, and penetrating power of speech, exercising the same power of faith in the Holy God, pseudonymously, to exercise craft and stratagem to rebel against and oppose the perfect doctrines of Christ's second coming to earth.

Caroline contained by nature, through the abalienation of the divine kingdom to Samuel, the mighty wrathful dragon which, it was prophetically declared in both ancient and modern prophecies, came among the saints with power, because he knew he had but a short time to reign in and over humanity.

To bring in and realize the masculine word "he," to prove this judgment pronounced upon the abominations of millennium, I do herein declare, firmly and substantially, that the Lord God did also work a miraculous power of love and jealousy in John for Caroline, when he entered into the mute covenant with the holy king. This was the realization of Caroline's helpmeet, then after her own image and likeness, which gave ventilative and procreative power to her nature to fulfil her mission with God's Holy Christ. It was accomplished by the spiritual sexual intercourse between the harmonious spirits and substances which were contained in John and Caroline to realize the fulness of the wrathful dragon, the mysterious and preternatural powers of sin, contained in the animal kingdom, and the essential powers of abominations which carried the desolation to the consummation, by working scientifically and mysteriously in the spiritual bodies of the two sexes.

This concealed mystery at first caused the mighty dragon, the monstrous leviathan and the subtle unicorn, the abominable science of the transcendent Lucifer, to be transformed into an angel of light, received, and honored as being the powers of the Holy Divine. This mystery empowered the men of millennium to heartily confer all honor upon women, and to reject the original and genuine God, which is the triniunity of word, spirit, and truth.

God would not suffer the women's love of millennium to continue toward the men of millennium, lest they would cleave to each other and defeat his determinations. Therefore the women of millennium conferred all honor upon Samuel, and idolized his material body, and rejected the genuine Holy Christ, who exists in the fulness of divine truth. All the atonements and intercessions that proceeded out of Samuel's mouth from Christ, in pleading with God, in defence of the holy kingdom, and in behalf of the people subject to these predominating sins, were to slay and consume the mighty powers of abomination, which brought desolation upon the holy city and sanctuary.

This, in its expression, spirit, and substance, is the express semblance of all nations, the power that rules and governs the human family in their present state; which fulfils God's words, saying, "Send ye the lamb to the ruler of the land from Sela to the wilderness, unto the mount of the daughter of Zion." — Isa. 16.

PART V.

NON-UNITY BETWEEN THE SON OF RIGHTEOUSNESS AND THE MILLENNIUM DAUGHTER OF ZION; GOD'S JUDGMENTS BECOME GENERAL IN THE FOURTH SEAL; THE BEGINNING OF THE SPIRITUAL WAR BETWEEN THE SON OF RIGHTEOUSNESS AND THE SON OF PERDITION.

It can be understood by the tone and expression of this revelation that the man of sin in the two genders in the annals of this doctrine conflicts to annihilate and exterminate the antagonizing constituents and molecules of sin and vice; that the solving of the great mysterious flight of the woman into the wilderness signifies and explanates the depth and height, width and length, of the aggregated mass of imperial abominable zeal and tendencies of life and pleasure contained in the millennium nature, which once was looked upon as being the queen of beauty, but now the lady of mortal kingdoms, the height of vainglorious pride.

The many millions of arbitrary and tyrannical freaks of animal propensities, which manifested themselves, repugnantly, in millennium against the characteristics of the second coming of Christ, were the vast wilderness where the small percentage of humanity and divinity of millennium were lost in gross darkness, and swallowed up by the rapid increase of animalism, so that they could not find the straight path of divine rectitude to find their way out. This compelled the small percentage of immortality to succumb to, and amalgamate with, animalism, to obtain food and drink, life and vigor, which were compelled to be distilled, and to issue from Lucifer, the nihilist, the pernicious scientist, the subtle unicorn, the monstrous leviathan, and the mighty dragon, which are the four sovereigns of mortality, the ruling sceptre of the animal kingdom transformed into another image, and raised to a higher government in humanity.

These four sovereigns embodied in human earth are the bottomless pit, the torment for the wicked who dwell among the just. The first king, which is Lucifer, is located in the brain lobe of humanity; the second king is the subtle unicorn and messenger to King Lucifer, and is situated in the pelvic region; the third king is the monstrous leviathan, and is situated in the epigastric region; the fourth king is the mighty dragon guided by the seventh demon and demoness. " Mephistopheles," better known as "jealousy," manifested in male and female. This last kingdom is situated in the umbilical region of humanity, and creates and fashions the members to populate and uphold the four kingdoms of mortality, which are united, but globular in shape, so that the pollutions that exist in one part of humanity may exist equally in all parts, but in different ways by using different laws to perform the same unjust acts.

This high and deep secret, when imparted in knowledge and understanding to the revelator, caused him to be filled with wrath and vengeance against the subtlety of sin and vice, which subsequently caused the vehemence of zeal to kindle and burn like fire, to find the true and modern language of sin and vice. Therefore God imparted to him the wisdom and understanding to give the proper names to sin and vice, not personally, but characteristically and universally. This led him, by the way he had not gone, to explore the human sphere, to learn the names of the rivers, oceans, seas, gulfs, lakes, cities; empires, and locations of all lawless people and tribes, kindred and nations, kings and tongues, carnified in the human sphere, to reveal the book of sin just as it is printed upon the pages of humanity.

In order to create light in the entire sphere of humanity, I must glance acutely into the language of the astronomy of divinity, and place, by language and utterance, in the dark firmament the true star lights, which, first in order, are the twelve constellations, containing in themselves the next brightest star lights. These twelve constellations are the twelve tribes of Israel; and in each one of these twelve tribes are twelve thousand godly inclinations which are eternal. Each one bears a different holy name and office, characteristically, to make up the perfect luminous human sphere in its laws and government. The laws and statutes which God has created to govern this vast and luminous human sphere are entirely adverse to the laws and statutes now reigning arbitrarily and tyrannically in the momentums of the human and animal sphere, which are distilled from the mortal being.

Leaving behind the antique names of the twelve tribes of Israel, and to avoid personification, I will add that God was creating the spiritual tribes while raising up the twelve material tribes; this was to put an end to the material tribes, as being the real people of God, and to put an end to the idolatry of flesh and matter.

The eternal godly races are spiritual, and, namely, thankfulness and peacefulness, trustfulness and repentance, unity and fidelity, humility and benevolence, endurance and sincerity, submission and mutuality. These are the constellations of heaven, which contain in themselves thousands of star lights; these are the third rank of the chief members of the immortal soul, the twelve jurymen, who sit in the judgment council of the Lord God. These are, also, the seed-bearers and the prime ministers of divine truth in the third rank.

When Samuel was made the leader and commander of the new covenant, the propelling powers of darkness revived in Caroline, and wrestled against him in all God's discrete and impartial judgments; and she opposed him in every important matter, to destroy the motor of equity, truth, and discretion while pronouncing the judgments of God upon the wicked motives, and showing mercy, love, and sympathy where it was required. Not only did she wrestle against the judgments of God, but the entire family who were with him at times rejected the judgments in their hearts, and did not believe, when they were pronounced upon them, that they were true; but the words that he spoke ignited in them spontaneously, which compelled them to yield to truth and judgment. This fulfils God's words, saying, "Who is this that cometh from Edom, with dyed garments from Bozrah? this that is glorious in his apparel, travelling in the greatness of his strength? I that speak in righteousness, mighty to save." — Isa. 63.

The Opening of the Fourth Seal.

I, the Lord God, prophesy on the general judgment days which will make desolate the abominate, and destroy wholly depraved men from the face of the earth, so that I may open the gate for my chosen people to come into my righteous judgments universally. The fourth plague shall be poured out upon the Son, and power shall be given unto him to scorch, wilt, and afflict with Son-strokes both man, herbs, cattle, beast of the forest, and fowl that fly in the firmament of heaven. The Son shall scorch these with fire, universally, and a vast number of these cases will result fatally. There will be a faint visible observation of this plague seen, commencing January 27, 1890; it will envelop five months from the above date.

The Son will send forth a hot, fiery stream, which will gradually increase in temperature each day, until it reaches its full dimension of heat; and when it reaches this point, in some parts of the globe, it will produce spontaneous combustion, and men will blaspheme my holy name because of the severity of the plague. On the twenty-seventh of June, the Son will return to the usual temperature, and the fifth plague will speedily succeed. I, the Lord God, prophesy on the sounding of the fourth trump, and woe, woe, woe, to the inhabiters of the earth, by reason of the other voices of the trump of the three angels, which are yet to sound.

When the time arrived for this plague to manifest itself, it was sought for earnestly by Samuel; and on the day prophesied for it to be seen, God's general judgments began on John, by revealing the powers of evil that had him disfranchised on this day. The evolution of the truth which the Holy Spirit revealed on that day, as touching on the cause of John's griefs, burdens, and hopelessness, was the beginning of the heat of the Son of Righteousness, to destroy the prevailing power of the Son of Perdition. The judgments were laid upon him heavier each day, and his griefs and torments increased all the more, until Samuel and the family began to wonder with amazement; so much so that all hearts grew faint, and minds became overwhelmed with cares, doubts, and unbeliefs.

Samuel entered into a fast to find out the cause of John's mysterious trouble; and the Holy Spirit evolved the cause of his trouble, which reads and fulfils as follows: " In the first year of Belshazzar king of Babylon Daniel had a dream and visions of his head upon his bed." — Dan. 7. This chapter revealed the predominant and preternatural power that the Son of Perdition possessed, through his scientific power of speech, which, like a severe peal of thunder, and lightning, ignited the solid and substantial substance that he was composed of, to prevail against the holy people in the righteous era.

The power of the Spirit that carried Caroline, to accomplish her work, so daring and vicious, was the first beast, symbolized as a lion, whose power was in her sharp and penetrating speech, to defend the man child when he was brought forth.

The second beast, having the appearance of a bear, and having three ribs between the teeth, was used to symbolize the three material instruments which were guided by the shark commandments of God, through the revelator, when he loosened the four angels to devour the flesh of all who invaded Jerusalem.

The third beast, typified as a leopard, having four wings, and given dominion, was the power of the Spirit that carried Isaac; who obtained dominion according to his desire to rule over righteousness through the holy blessing of prosperity that the prince of peace imputed upon him, when the four angels were loosened to destroy the desperadoes who then had the members of the sanctuary fortified against God's purposes.

The fourth beast, dreadful and terrible, was typified as the Spirit that carried John in the annals of these doctrines; which signifies the magnificent and adamantine substances of carnal truth of which John was substantially composed, so that when he spoke in wrath and vengeance against an antagonist, no unclean beast could stand in opposition of his vengeance and live. This power was the king of kings, clean beasts. At the roaring of this beast, the earth shook, the mountains were moved, and the inhabiters thereof fled from his presence; while the terribleness of his roaring pierced to the bone and marrow of his victims who made him rage.

The four horns that the fourth beast contained, before whom three fell, and the smaller, that came up last, were the three horns, namely, the desire and love for woman-kind, love for gold and silver, blood-kin and family circle; the prevailing power of these three horns was destroyed in John's nature before he became a member of the holy city and sanctuary. The smaller horn, that came up last, is the full and essential love and lascivious desire that all great and renowned men of this day possess, to compete with, and excel each other in educational science, dexterity, and beauty, ostentatiously.

The horn that came up last became the strongest, for it grew rapidly, through the increase of wisdom, and became great and honorable for a time. This was the horn that subdued the three kings, destroyed the power of the holy people, and prevailed against them until the ancient of days came. This horn stood up supremely in John, magnified the animal kingdom above the divine kingdom, and contemned and despised the simple words of wisdom revealed through the revelator; because this horn had such acute wisdom, searching insight, and understanding of dark sayings, that he had searched out points of wisdom that Samuel had not thought upon, and when Samuel brought forth his wisdom to give him light, he snuffed at it, and regarded it as nothing.

This is to show the power and might of irreverence, dishonor, and haughtiness that exist in this day in the normal sphere of educational science adversely to genuine divinity; yet it has power to assume this name. John was equipped with affluent and mellifluous language, superlative qualities, and pre-eminent tendencies in every plain of life, which came, through endowment, to realize and accomplish this purpose. Although he was unlearned, he was possessed of demons who had ravenous tastes and appetites for caligraphy and prosody, orthography and syntax, etymology and composition, sophistry and philosophy.

The revelator found, by searching carefully this venomous being, that he was the embodiment of metaphysics, who was bottomless and topless. This gave him knowledge that his rapacious desires and bombastic words were not natural among his kind ; he saw that it worked through mental action, like the breath, compulsorily. Samuel discovered that the foundation of John's practical learning was not equal to that of the revelator ; and for this cause he found John to be nothing but the bottomless pit, which was loosened in nature to fight against God's Christ, because John was organized and brilliantly constructed with the supreme substances of animalism to use for battle-field.

Samuel searched out this mystery, and found that he was no more than any natural, ignorant man when hewn down from his lofty throne ; so Samuel arose and used the weapons of war upon his spiritual being, until his body of death was slain and given to the burning flames of truth. The ten horns that stood up out of his four kingdoms are. vainglorious pride ; unthankfulness to God ; self-esteem above God ; hatred against his own color ; the scorn and prejudice against his own color, Ethiopia ; desire for excellent beauty ; self-will ; haughtiness ; stubbornness ; jealousy and craftiness. These are the monarchs who reigned in the animal kingdom by the government of the mighty horn.

There were ten horns reigning in the four wicked kingdoms that stood up out of the earthly body manifestedly ; but there were monarchs who reigned in one kingdom who could not reign in power in another, so another was appointed instead of the one who was not capable of enforcing laws for the sovereign. The book of Daniel was the focus of all the great warriors of old, including all the co-ordinating prophecies of the apostolic Bible concerning righteousness and unrighteousness ; the supreme powers of righteousness and unrighteousness concentrated in that book, consecutively, and made it the integrate focus of power that was manifested in the Son of Righteousness and the Son of Perdition.

During the times of these phenomena, the Son of Righteousness devoted himself to the science of philosophy and physiognomy, guided by the true soul of psychology, to obdurate the planets of metaphysics, the false brother of psychology. The revelator bore the memoir of all the essential powers of both good and evil ; and the words that the members of the sanctuary had spoken, antecedently to the judgments, re-echoed and mementoed in judgment as a testimony against their sinful nature. This fulfils God's words, saying, " But I say unto you, That every idle word that men shall speak, they shall give account thereof in the day of judgment. For by thy words thou shalt be justified, and by thy words thou shalt be condemned."

Even the words spoken by the members of the holy sanctuary while in the judgments reverberated and souvenired, and by the same they were judged and condemned. The involution of the mysteries concerning righteousness, desolation, and the man of sin did not cause the dynasty rebellion between the kingdom of darkness and the kingdom of light to cease. As soon as the officers of each prevailing and succeeding regiment were overpowered by the simplicity and discrete judgment of truth given through the revelator, another proceeded, and in a short time the demons and heresies gathered another kingdom together, and made ready the implements of war, selecting the most prudent men among them to officiate, govern, and command.

The artillery of truth, equity, and discretion was used on both sides as weapons to destroy the ungodly people. Wisdom performed its work on both sides ; wisdom was rebelling in perdition to obliterate the circumcision of the Jews, and to demonstrate the fact that the Jews' spiritual worship was contaminating and irreverent to purity. The Son of Righteousness was the battle-field whereupon the holy people fought, through wisdom, discretion, and equity, to destroy the adulterating powers and idolatry of the Nicolaitans' worship, which are extolled by all civilized nations existing upon the earth.

This judgment is not upon any individual tongue, people, nor race, but upon the entire civilized notoriety. All who are proselytized into the state of immortality shall pass through the same judgment, and stand before the Son of man. All who have not this doctrine are antichrists, and hold the doctrines of the Nicolaitans, which shall be a curse upon all who do not receive the pure divine truth and serve God according as he has spoken. These judgments destroyed from the members of this doctrine the modern and ancient idols that were worshipped by this people, and called "gods." These are set up in the empires or hearts of this generation, and are worshipped through using the name of Jehovah for a cloak.

All people who have existed since the human creation began are existing now and holding the land in bondage: and each race and kingdom is worshipping idolatry, which is the sensual love, lascivious desires, and concupiscent craves of each individual empire or mortal body. This judgment shows that the material existences of the world's inhabitants are spiritualized and embodied in the people, which is called "the land" or "earth," manifesting themselves in the godly and ungodly characteristics of the people of this day, and this generation, repeating their work incorporeally in both good and evil.

The world has reached such period of wisdom, in science and vanity, that the most advanced honored, and godlike races appear to be worshippers of the god of holy truth; but not so — they are magnifying, adoring, worshipping, and commending their lives unto the safe trusts and deposits of gold and silver, the riches and precious things of this day, as they did in ancient days. Consequently, the gods that are worshipped in this day by the antichristians are called "the gods of mortality," the root and germ of death, the degenerator of humanity.

When the judgments become sorely grievous to the Son of Perdition, Samuel sought to know the time and season when the veil of obscurity would be removed from over the Son; and he was empowered by wisdom to evolve the mysteries of the succeeding chapters, which read as follows: "In the third year of the reign of king Belshazzar a vision appeared unto me, even unto me Daniel, after that which appeared unto me at the first." — Dan. 8. "In the first year of Darius the son of Ahasuerus, of the seed of the Medes, which was made king of the realm of the Chaldeans." — Dan. 9.

When the four angels were loosed, the Son of Righteousness took an oblique course, moving on an indirect line; and he had no rule, time, system, nor regularity, while journeying around the world of mortality. The Son had no regular light nor method of doctrine to teach; sermons awoke in the revelator to eject the opposing host, — anything that revived in the members that did not agree with God's purposes.

There was no understanding of what manner of covenant was established in the soul of the revelator, to be established with others;

yet a few in number were enraptured over the wisdom, life, and understanding of the revelator, and felt compelled, for some cause, to follow him, after starting. They had the feeling that there was no way back, because the former love and pleasure which were in the world were destroyed. They felt that they would also be destroyed, if they revolted. The enchanting power revived in the revelator at each conflict, spoke enticingly, and encouraged them to follow on, for something wonderful would soon spring forth and convince the people that God was with the revelator.

This manner of speech adhered to the substances in the people God had fashioned with the principles to realize the fulfilments of the Holy Scriptures. The Lord God worked in the hearts of each one to come to the same city that he had prepared for the beginning of the new covenant. God had prepared just such members of the nethermost region to fight against divine truth, to bring his Christ out thoroughly purified and tried by the despotism of perdition.

These tyrannies that God had prepared had power to command fire to come down from heaven to prove the false rumors against the holy truth to be truism; and the fire which they called down was to feign themselves righteous, by composing lies and predicting what was going to befall the holy people. Their prediction came to pass, which was the fire that came down in the presence of those who worshipped the unclean beast and his image, and caused all to receive a mark of his name.

This thing those necromancers and abjects were empowered to do; and their composed lies were believed and received by men of sound natural discretion, when their statements against the holy people were preposterous and without bottom. Still, all nations bowed down and worshipped the curse execrated upon those abjects and desperadoes who blasphemed, ignored, and reproached, unreasonably, the holy name of God. Through the reception of the Lord to be evil at his second advent to earth, all nations existing upon the earth have taken upon themselves an unfathomed curse.

This conveyed the world through all the past dark ages, by spiritual degrees of wickedness, because the nations re-equipped themselves with weapons to fight against God's Christ throughout this generation, and for this cause one will turn to the doctrines of divine truth while another will fight to put it out of the earth. Henceforth, and for this cause, the third part of this generation will suffer verily in the worlds of perdition from the tormenting effects of the red-head dragon; which will be manifested in all manner of diseases, accidents, failures in business, disappointed aims in life, and all manner of ancient suffrages, which will awake in this generation, both spiritually and materially.

This is because the evils and curses that this evil generation pronounced upon the holy people were interwoven in the nature of the false judges; hence they must suffer for the very same sins, curses, and judgments that they laid upon the Lord while fulfilling his holy concealed course of work. Had they been free from the sins, curses, and accusations brought against the Lord and sustained by their law, they would not have sinned; hence the same judgments are poured out upon them without mixtures, so that they may be rewarded according as the Lord found them working, which must continue until these characters are consumed from the land. All who receive the holy truth in this generation shall be saved; and those who receive it not shall be consumed from off the earth, where they shall cease from troubling the just, and from corrupting the pure air with their poisonous breath.

Amid the great flow of revelation in solving the mysteries of the man of sin and the Son of Righteousness hung also the thick, black clouds of darkness and desolation, to destroy the lumination and the reflection of the Son light as soon as one mystery was revealed, and the members of the sanctuary made to see it. Inasmuch as the light was at times bright and clear, and shone out upon the desolate earth, the darkness at times was fully as great, which spread hastily over the skies, and the great light which had shortly been seen was soon forgotten, and all was soon in the sad, lamentable state of hopelessness and woe.

The flames of perdition had reached the holy skies, which brought piercing grief upon the Son of Righteousness; and other visions unfolding, the cause of the trouble was opened and looked into by the revelator, and then explained to his members, by which the transgressors of the holy covenant were judged. The visions read as follows: " In the third year of Cyrus king of Persia a thing was revealed unto Daniel, whose name was called Belteshazzar; and the thing was true, but the time appointed was long: and he understood the thing and had understanding of the vision." — Dan. 10. " Also I in the first year of Darius the Mede, even I, stood to confirm and to strengthen him." — Dan. 11.

These visions and revelations, given through the prophet Daniel, contain the origin and end of the mysterious perils of the saints. The germinater and function of the trouble were discovered in those words which were sackclothed from the view of the holy people until the purpose of the Lord God had fully gone into effect. The dark sayings of these chapters were the black veil that concealed the mysteries of the Son of Perdition, who occupied the temple John, and through peace, craftiness, and disguisation continued to prevail until the time appointed for him to be given to the burning flame. The temple who contained those mighty weapons of war was supposed by Samuel and his members to be his dearest companion. They were so closely allied in characteristics, both in motive and purity, that they slept in the same bed until this mystery began to unfold itself, and then it was condemned and caused to cease.

When Samuel and John entered into the mute covenant, Samuel did not esteem nor magnify himself above John, but looked upon John as being his equal in qualities and purity, which seemed to be centred in his motive ; but Samuel knew himself to be the covenant of the people according to inheritance, and those who connected themselves with his mission he considered one with him even as he was one with the Holy Father.

Those erroneous principles which manifested themselves at the first, Samuel did not stop to condemn with authority, because he said within his heart that God would right that which was abnormal to his life. He knew that his mission in the troublous times of the saints was to fulfil the Holy Scriptures; but he made no positive decision, neither openly nor in secret, concerning how the Scriptures would be fulfilled and the covenant established with the people. He knew he was raised up and endowed as he is, for a gift to the people ; but he could not think what steps to take to give himself and life to them. He knew that the people would not receive him when the power and works of the new covenant stood up in him extemporaneously, because he had no proof nor sufficient testimony that God's Christ had made his second advent to the earth in a disguised way. Hence he had no desire nor power to speak of the mysteries of the holy kingdom, except to those who voluntarily followed him by forsaking the world and its customs, with the object of obtaining life through him according as he had so plainly and simply shown the power in him to redeem mankind from sin.

When Samuel saw that the powers of evil began to increase in his people, he preached private and extemporaneous sermons touching on the powers of darkness which he saw in them; and as the evil increased the sermons increased, also; for when one regiment of evil seducers was destroyed another quickly revolved, which increased the trouble through the resurrection of depraved souls until his members began to think that he was preaching a false doctrine. These thoughts proceeded from the demons and heresies which were propelled mentally through them to make an acute manifestation of the different sinful tendencies in humanity, to give the revelator a practical knowledge of all the crafty powers of spiritual corruption in the antichristian world.

John's dissolution of friendship and interest in the antichristian world began through involuntary choice of the inner man, which forced him to make a sacrifice of perishable things and seek a better world, a happier life, before Christ made his post-millennium to the earth. John was a total voluntary member of the sanctuary; and the covenant between Samuel and him came through the same source, which forced him to follow Samuel; and it was in him to be the recording secretary when Samuel began to prophesy. The league of friendship revived in one for the other, because they agreed in conversation when John was journeying mentally from the antichristian's seat of customs; and this was the power that made them adhere in motives and determination. The total propensities and mutual agreement between them was the false league of friendship and verification that they were proximities in every plain of divinity. Through the proximities of John and Samuel being unanimous in characteristics and understanding, the man of sin obtained power and dominion to prevail against the holy people, because he was looked upon as being the Holy Christ in the temple John.

The daughter of Zion was the king's daughter of the North, with whom the king's daughter of the South came and entered into a covenant. This defines the daughter of Babylon, who was the devil that was unsealed and loosened out of hell, with mighty wrathful powers, and cut off the Messiah when the holy city and sanctuary lifted himself up among the nations. The two sons of the daughter of Babylon gave her up when they saw that she abjudicated in judgment; and the branch out of her roots who was finite in power extracted the essential pre-eminence of her kingdom, and became rich in wisdom, judgment, and renown in all laws and idolatry that ancient Babylon had in its province.

The devices which the king of Babylon forecast against the prince of the holy covenant was the godlike stratagem that the Son of Perdition contained to strive to excel and eclipse the Son of Righteousness in every art of science. This was the basis of the judgment upon the man of sin, which began to consume him and take away his weapons of war. He was judged and proven to have been seen striving to eclipse the Son of Righteousness in every way, which he did for a time. When he saw that he had the implements of war and all riches on his side, he then set his face to enter into the glorious land and obtain the dominion and the greatness of the holy kingdom through peaceful stratagem; but he made such mighty and bold attempts to accomplish the work that he was forced to act it openly, by acting contemptuously and disdainfully toward the revelator, and hasty steps were taken to hew him down from his lofty throne. His secret stratagem was to speak the better language, and excel on orthography, caligraphy, and every art of science.

This branch of Babylon was thoroughly equipped with acute facilities to carry out his time of indignation upon the saints, so that God's Christ would thereby obtain a plain and simple testimony of his power and office. While the enchanting and shammistic powers of darkness were working upon the satanic chosen battle-fields, the king of Babylon became overwhelmed with griefs, because he burned excessively in his lust for Caroline; and she utterly rejected the glory and honor which the Son of Perdition conferred upon her, and contemned his affections. Caroline's feelings of friendship, love, and honor turned involuntarily away from John immediately after he became a member of the covenant; and the image that carried him did all he could to win her love, devotion, and honor, through subtlety and secret sagacity.

After failing to carry out his devices on this point, he then demanded his rights by passing his own judgment upon how it should be with him in regard to Caroline and Samuel, by saying, "I am the son, and Samuel is the all-adorable, and Caroline, the mother." This was the time there was a raiser of taxes in the glory and honor of the wicked kingdom, which caused Samuel to give him the privilege of showing his excessive love and devotion toward Caroline; but she refused upon oath, saying that she had no desire nor friendly feeling toward him to receive the nearness of his person.

Through the daughter of Zion's rejecting his person in not saluting him, embracing him in her arms, and giving him equal honor to that of Samuel, his heart turned against the holy covenant until the selfish and tyrannical powers of sin were consumed by the spirit of truth and judgment. This fulfils God's words, saying, "And at that time shall Michael stand up, the great prince who standeth for the children of thy people: and there shall be a time of trouble, such as never was since there was a nation even to that same time: and at that time thy people shall be delivered, every one that shall be found written in the book." — Dan. 12.

The visions and revelations contained in this chapter testify to the legend of the historical annals of the saints: which limited the period of time it would take the Son of Righteousness to accomplish the fulfilments of the Scriptures, and make a total eclipse and everlasting obscuration of the universal orb of mortality, or the extinguishment of the transcendent lights of Lucifer in the disk of perdition. Hence John was raised up from among the people, and given to the covenant to contain the microcosm or epitome of the late sciences of mortality in its most substantial and essential degrees.

He, by nature and substance, was the king of mortal kings, who reigned over the mother city of abominations; he was the father of all mortality, the sinful Adam who revolved from the Adamite world through all the past ages, and was tried and refined to a solid and substantial subtance, so that the Lord God might use him a frictional and polishing stone for the refining and purgation of his Christ, all along through the eventful careers of the godly people even to the latter days. In him was found the powers of sin presiding over all renowned men, and common men; and the fatherhood of all mortality from the Adamite world even to the most modern branches of science, and great merchants of this advanced age of commerce governed by the spirits of mercenariness.

This was the reason why his sons, the great merchants of Springfield, were stirred up and became so wroth — because the kingdom of mortality, who was their forefather, was going to be destroyed and put out of the earth. Of this the merchants of that city knew not: but the nature and substances of mortality, and the spirits of the times, were exasperated and troubled about the rumors from the Lord, because they had heard the truth, and the root and fœtus of mortality was being extracted and expatriated from the fertile soil of humanity. The physical structure of this mortal microcosm was called "the son;" and the substantial power of mortality which was imbedded therein was the mortal image of man, called "the father of perdition."

Ethiopia was the first man created in the beginning of humanity; and Ethiopia degenerated the human family through amalgamating with the brute race. As through the first man, Adam, man lost his creative state, through the creation of the second holy Adam man shall be reclaimed, and retain his creative state and sovereignty. The name "Ethiopia" is a derivation of "earth," because the first man, Ethiopia, was taken from the earth, whence the name "Ethiopia." Ethiopia is an attribute of the earth, because he was the earth that was created when it was void of form, which earth the Lord God formed, shapened, and painted many colors for his mansions and footstools. The names "earth," "land," "ocean," "seas," "rivers," and many others recorded in the apostolic Bible. have reference to the human soul and body: and the words "spirit" and "truth" of the Lord God is that which he created to exist upon, and to flow through, the human sphere. This mystery is the basis upon which the whole apostolic Bible is founded.

The Bible is the word of God, and the word is God: and the fulness of the word of the Lord God, dwelling in the human family, will be the Lord God occupying his holy mansions, journeying gloriously over the earth, and glorified over the works of his hands in the saints.

The physique of the Son of Perdition contained the stratum of all fine and precious stones; and they were beautifully carved and fashioned after the most advanced cunning workmanship. His stratum was of such brilliant and adamantine substances that he contained the excelsior of all precious things that have ever come into the possession of the mortal man, and everything that has ever entered his mind. Because he was the epitome, the microcosm, of the mortal kingdom, his secular stratum was the science of the alphabets, the professor of nefarious scientific arts, the germinator, propelling power, and inventing tactics of all the leading wisdom, the science of modern corruption.

The luminous and adamantine stratum, with which he was ordinately and excellently erected in figures and the alphabets, made his suffering severe; because each letter, word, and figure of nefarious science which the revelator declared he contained and named, and which was placed into his hands to record, was the power which, by his own hand, was given to the burning flame, and consumed. The involution and evolution of the man of sin in these doctrines was to blast his solid stratum. In this corporeal and incorporeal microcosm was found all the essential principles of the antichristians, the Gentile world: which was manifested in irony, corpuscular excellency, which was the entire powers of the Gentiles harvested in him to reject the perfect truth until the time specified was fulfilled.

As this man was the epitome of modern Gentilism, when God's Christ, by truth and judgment, smote and consumed his noxious embodiment, by casting it into the lake which burneth with fire and brimstone, then the Son of Righteousness had judged the entire globe of mortality, and eclipsed the mortal worlds of science. The power of wisdom, truth, and judgment of the righteous is the flame of hell, and the punishment of the wicked. The anger and vengeance of the Lord God is the brimstone, and the consuming fire poured out upon the wicked, that did devour and expatriate them from the land. The divine truths were in its creative power in the temple Samuel, according to God's purposes, because in him God wrought the creation, the lumination, and the everlasting precious stones of immortality, the substances for the building of the kingdom of Christ in the hearts of his elect. This is conveyed to the human soul by the alphabets, whose brilliancy obscures all other luminations.

When the first man, Adam, lost his creative state, the creative word lost its creative power and dominion; for the holy, happy, and perfect man was the word of God. Now man has again reached his creative state, and the creative word holds its creative power and dominion. Therefore, when the word is spoken by the transhumanized spokesman, that that is spoken shall be done, according as the creative word declares it; for the man Samuel, in his spiritual being, is the word of God and the minister of the new covenant, and is the covenant, also, and the propitiator given to the people to burn up and abolish sin by the consuming fire of word, spirit, and truth, which the Lord God revealed through him in judgment.

The bright, affectionate, sweet, and smiling countenance of the Lord God has been veiled with sackcloth and ashes since Ethiopia lost his holy, happy, and perfect state. Why? Because Ethiopia, in his perfect state, is God's creative power, which reigns in his true language, both physical and divine. The term "English language" is a phraseology, a derivation of "Ethiopia," and has the same meaning; the Ethiopian language is the precious stones, the stratum to the building of God's spiritual and material temples.

The word is the firmament of the spiritual world, and the Holy Spirit is the light. The luminous rays of the felicitous Son light form the angelic host, which are manifested in the glorification of the saints. The word and the spirit are of the same substance and purity; but the word is visible, of a solid stratum, endless duration, and unchangeable substantialities. The light, or holy function, that flows through this sempiternal substance makes it in power and obsequious after waiting and abiding many years.

The word is productive and in power to generate, it matters not how long it waits for the light, and when the light makes its appearance, the truth is always ready to ignite the fuel and produce a burning flame. The word is perceptible, and the word is imperceptible; hence it can be used for fuel, and it can be used for substantial structures and those of an inconsumable nature. The word is sarcotic in power, and the word is sarcophagus in power; it can be used to do the same work in the spiritual world as that of material things in the temporal world.

The word is the seminal that produced all things which were uttered by the masculine being; and the Holy Spirit, which is feminate, and masculated and reciprocated, is the hand that formed and fashioned all formal substances in the matrix. The word, spirit, and truth is compliant, and is the holy sanctuary, and the peace and felicity of sempiternity. They are of total propensities in every sense of the word; but the word is the leading sovereign, the governor of all things existing, mental, material, and immaterial. There are two sempiternal existences of the word; one is material and the other mental. The mental is the transporting ecstasy of the material; and the material is the recluse for the service of the mental, acquiescently.

Man is made immortal through the attitude of submission to divine will; mortality opposes and wrests against the divine will, which increases from childhood until man becomes a total mass of mortality. The longer and stronger the powers of mortality grow and prevail in humanity, the weaker and more hopeless the horn of immortality is in defence of the flesh that continually succumbs to depravity. Mortality is the black veil of sackcloth and ashes that has hid the face of the Lord God from the human family, because they have never understood God's language and power to save them; for God has purposed and spoken for his work to be accomplished in a certain way, and the sagacity of mortality has inspired man with ideas to please himself, because the substance was not in man to understand God's language. Hence God has poured out his spirit upon them to rejoice in the hope of his glory according to their understanding and conception of the promised glory. Their language and understanding was mortal, and man has labored to perfect mortality, when mortality will not labor one day to destroy its existence.

Mortality is the prime motor of death, and non-submission to divine will and power is the continuator of death and hell. Mortality and divine will are at war against each other in the human race, from birth until divine will is wholly rejected by the person, and swallowed up and stamped under foot by the victory of mortality, which then is transmuted into an angel of light, uses the same language and doctrines as the just, and fails to live the life they proclaim in words.

This craft of sin keeps the human family ever dying and tormented in the fiery realms of hell. Hell is mental, and burns according to the quantity of depravity in the human flesh; and sempiternal ecstasy is mental, and its glory flows to the remotest parts of the human flesh, where righteousness abounds.

The mind which issues from the nature, the general make-up of a person, is the soul, whether mortal or immortal; when the mind is tormented and seeking rest, the body is conformed to the same powers. When the mind is filled with felicity, the body is enjoying the same blessing. Through this point of wisdom I have located and described the pit called "hell," which is within the corrupt earthly body of man. The powers of demonistic principles that take man into captivity are the science of the Devil and his angels, who strive mentally to make the body of man a full subject for corrupt service.

As long as man's type is set with the mortal letters of science, the demons and heresies, both material and mental, have power to minister to man through the letter, and doom his mind, deeper and deeper, in the state of misery and woe. Grief is the consuming and devouring flames of hell; doubts, hopelessness, and disbelief, in the immortal language, are the burning fuel that the wicked angels cast into the pit to produce a burning flame. There is no base nor summit to the language of the wicked angels who preside over the mental pit.

When a subject of perdition is led into solitary suffering of spiritual pain and misery, they make attempts to deliver themselves from the evil one; and when they find no power in themselves to redeem, they turn their eyes toward the divine power, and become faithful to its teachings, and conformed to its will until they are rescued from the hands of the spoilers. As soon as they are free from the cruel powers of the extortioner and tyrannical destiny, they no longer subdue themselves to divine will and power. Their hearts become inflexible to the divine will and power, stiff, haughty, and independent; and the powers of mortality are so bewitching and pleasing to the eye and adhering to the desire, that the former sufferings are forgotten, and the enchanting demons and heresies have the soul journeying into torment by a way which they had not gone, with the promise of obtaining felicity in the end thereof.

The prime embassadors of perdition are, doubts, hopelessness, and disbelief; these three demons administer the fuel of sophistry and theosophy, which dissimulate the divine will and the knowledge of the Lord God. Then the phalanx and judgment of hell emit and send forth a thick black smoke and hide the face of the holy truth and judgment through logical reasoning; then the adulterating thoughts and fallacious judgment make the being conformed to wicked devices; and the heart becomes contemptuous and disdainful toward the judgment of truth, and scorns the ministers of truth.

Free thinking facilities, sophisticating reasoning, and pseudo-opinions are the scientific powers of naturalism and preternaturalism that produce infidelity, continuate the black veil of mortality, and prepare the fuel for hell fire. The visible spectrums of perdition are the hideous phantoms of the corrupt mind, which are based upon calidity and pseudodoxy, ingulf the truth, and make inert the influx of the true light and life. For this cause, the punishment of the wicked from death to the second resurrection is inevitable.

There was a continual eclipse and occultation between mortality and immortality while passing through the immediate states from the mortal life to death, and from death to the resurrection of the dead seminals of immortality. The obduration and obscurity that prevailed in and over the holy orb came through the interreign of holy kings; which definates the intervention of time from the reign of one king to the ascension of the successor, which left the holy throne vacant and obumbrated. This then concealed mystery made obtuse the immortal wisdom, interrupted the inflowing of immortality to the time of the end, and brought to sight, by a microscopic view, the integration of the sins and iniquities prevalent in the mortal world, to reach the resurrection of the dead, wholly desert the nethermost region, extinguish and obumbrate the lights of Lucifer.

This was because the lights of the nether world occupied the stratum of immortality, and brought into the holy land the adulterating powers of theocrasy, which means that the orb of mortality, the so-called luminous body of perdition, ran in the solar system, and caused solar spots to appear on the Son of Righteousness, and darkened him in his going forth.

Worlds of mysteries and occultations reigned intermundane, which emitted the aspersion of stigma against God's Holy Christ; but the powers of immortal ingenuity which are imbedded in God's anthropomorphism shall consume the stigma of infamy cast upon him by the black acts of corrupt science. This is God's judgment on that man of sin when the purgative fountain was open to the inhabitants of Jerusalem.

The same judgments that were pronounced upon the members of the sanctuary were pronounced upon the daughter of Babylon, which was on this wise: when the revelator had put forth every effort that came in his reach to bring the daughter of Babylon in union with the characteristics of the true daughter of Zion, he saw no possible way of bringing the family under the honor and worship of one God except to deliver Mary, and all she owned in household and wearing apparel, fully into the hands of the daughter of Zion, to constrain her to live in harmony with the liberal and mutual characteristics of the daughter of Zion, which then issued from the commander in doctrines.

It happened on this wise: the bedroom which the daughter of Babylon had occupied prior to this occurrence was taken from her, as it was the largest room, and given to Caroline and her little girl, and Caroline's room was given to Mary; and all the mysteries and idols that the daughter of Babylon then had in her kingdom, and was worshipping, were found in the room which she occupied, laid away in different lots, according to value. She had reserved small and useless articles, of no value whatever, which would number a large amount, that would be too simple for a child to admire for play-toys: but she kept track of every one, and if any one could have broken into her room previous to this time of discovery, and kidnapped one of those minute gods, she would have felt the loss of it, become sorrowful over its departure, and seen its vacancy from the throne of idolatry. Her great idols had been destroyed from her heart, and these atoms were the remnants of the sacred things of the Babylonian's idolatry. All her hope at the time of this discovery was destroyed, because she hoped to retain them by thinking that they were concealed from the Lord God.

When these little trashy idols were destroyed, Mary had no more desire to work for the covenant, in reality or assimilation, and no hope in life ; for her last hope had been consumed, and her gods utterly destroyed. Again Samuel stretched out God's redeeming hands and drawing love to take her into the sheep-fold; but her very heart rejected the truth, the light, and life, and she did all she could to keep out of Samuel's presence, by confining herself to her bedroom.

All this was done to fulfil God's words, saying, " And after these things I saw another angel come down from heaven, having great power ; and the earth was lightened with his glory. And he cried mightily with a strong voice, saying, Babylon the great is fallen, is fallen, and is become the habitation of devils, and the hold of every foul spirit, and a cage of every unclean and hateful bird." — Rev. 18.

This fulfilment was read to the daughter of Babylon, and Samuel made a brief explanation of it, and then pronounced God's judgments upon her in strong and acute statements ; which made the earth shake and tremble at the sound of God's voice, and she sat astounded with wonderment as he so graphically expounded the secrets of her heart.

Samuel did not cease from sympathizing with the flesh, and expostulating with her after the utter depredation of the Babylonian's idolatry ; but he warned Isaac, who was her nearest and dearest friend in love and sympathy, to turn his heart against the natural love and sympathy which he had in store for her, lest he would be destroyed with her. This was one of the hardest trials that Isaac had to encounter during the epoch of the saints, because his blood flowed warm in his veins for her ; and if any one spoke a word against her previous to this time, his spirit and body would wilt and die as though she was his source of life.

This was the great horn, concealed by deception for a time between Isaac's eyes, that made the daughter of Babylon and him of one mind, and made war with the Lamb and his army, — love and sympathy for blood-kin more than for his creator and perpetuator is the name of the noxious horn. This horn was substantially rooted in Mary's blood, so that it could not be consumed nor eradicated at such age as that of hers, because her entire life was interwoven and grown into the roots of blood-kin and family circle. Mary thought in her heart, and remarked, also, that her sons should love and honor her more after they became members of the sanctuary than they did before; and she obtained judgment against the covenant to be evil in its doctrines and works, because she was not preferred by her sons.

This fulfilled the words spoken by Jesus, saying, "The queen of the south shall rise up in the judgment with this generation, and shall condemn it: for she came from the uttermost parts of the earth to hear the wisdom of Solomon; and, behold, a greater than Solomon is here." And also fulfils God's words, saying, "Moreover take thou up a lamentation for the princes of Israel, and say, What is thy mother? A lioness: she lay down among lions, she nourished her whelps among young lions." — Ezek. 19. "Come down, and sit in the dust, O virgin daughter of Babylon, sit on the ground: there is no throne, O daughter of the Chaldeans: for thou shalt no more be called tender and delicate." — Isa. 47.

As John was the embodiment of all mortal renownship, when he saw that Mary was abjudicating in judgment, and becoming silent and forlorn in action, in spite of all of his vengeance and rage, which previously had been manifested against her, he lamented over her condition, and sympathized over her precarious state, into which she had been doomed by the Spirit of judgment, although he execrated her time and again before he was summoned into judgment, to be judged according to the evil which was sealed in him in high powers. When he was compelled to acknowledge the truth concerning the principalities of sin and vice, which were disguised in him, he had great intelligence concerning Mary's spiritual trouble and suffering; which agglutinated and gave great strength to Mary's spiritual enemies to fulfil her time of crafty rage and indignation against the just.

John's desire kindled vehemently to bring in a separation between his mother, Mary, and Samuel's mission, so that she would not have to suffer to receive that to which she would not be able to attain; since his sufferings were so severe and yet he was not at home, it was utterly impossible for his mother to inherit eternal life in the material body at such great age. Still, he did not have the tender, kind, and loving feelings, for his mother and brothers, that he should have had in order to have the true amount of humanity, which made him very different from other people: yet he was the essential strength of the four wicked kingdoms whose characteristics were closely allied to the four-footed beast, more so than to humane facilities in parental love and honor.

He could not stir up any real sympathy for his kindred, so the sympathy that revived in him for them during the grievous rebellion came through intelligence, which was his knowledge of the suffering, pain, and woe one was compelled to pass through in order to inherit the promised life through the judgments which had been pronounced upon him. In the meantime the judgments of the Lord God were grievously upon the whole Babylonian kingdom, and Isaac was at the mouth of death, while the Lord God was antidoting that venomous serpent which was in many branches in his blood. This serpent spews up floods of deadly upas to flow through humanity.

The stream of blood-kin and family circle is the smallest division of mortality, yet it is one of the most turbulent, deleterious streams of mortality and he who crosses over this stream, after it swells to the highest tide, is near the fragrant and peaceful land of Canaan, which is reached by receiving the fulness of the seven doctrines. The Lord God used the temple Caroline, in the uncivilized rebellion against the tyrants and desperadoes of Babylon, to represent the characteristics of the daughter of Zion, the mother of Jerusalem, in the antique rebellion of righteousness and depravity in that day, while setting the type to print the spiritual book, the history of sin and vice.

Caroline rebelled against the new covenant's holy law of circumcision; which is full submission and consecration to the divine will in all things by having no selfish will nor desire, which continued from the time that Michael, the great prince, stood up until abominations went to the extreme. She was disobedient to God's commandments to her, given through Samuel, and she blasphemed God's judgment and doctrines in the most lewd way; and when the judgments were pronounced upon her lewd and imperious disposition, she utterly rejected the judgments at first, and contemned Samuel's exhortation. She was unfearful, unbelieving, and careless about what he predicted would befall her if she did not hearken unto his voice, and she boasted over the judgments which he pronounced upon the powers of evil that had her in captivity, until different plagues and afflictions came upon her, and then she was compelled to hear him, to be healed and delivered. This fulfils

God's words, saying, "Son of man, cause Jerusalem to know her abominations."— Ezek. 16.

This prophecy contains the abominations and excessive lewdness which the mother of Jerusalem committed, openly and partially concealed, from the time she was compelled to lay aside the idols of modern Egypt until the purgative fountain was opened to the members of the sanctuary. When the promised son was given, she exercised all the power of wisdom which she had in store to preside over him in excellency; and when she found that she could not be the commander, she turned and opposed everything Samuel spoke of doing for the promotion of the cause.

Jealousy continued to increase in Caroline until she became nefarious in her speech to Samuel. When any woman came to visit Samuel and her, and Samuel showed them the least respect, as though he loved them, she would become enraged with unconscious madness, which issued from the jealous tyrant. If Samuel spoke a word to exhort her to repent of such vile principles, she would exalt herself, and judge that she was pleasing the Lord God. She used abusive language in the most haughty and contemptible way, and strove to change things from what Samuel said they should be. She would disagree and hold a dispute with Samuel in the presence of those who visited him. Samuel would explain, and judge matters to be one way, and she another; and this would create an open dispute and strife between them, and she would never relent, but held fast to her sentiments.

Caroline did not want anything done the way Samuel wanted it done; she wanted it done to her fancy and liking. She did not care whether a thing was done justly or unjustly; if it was done to please her, she considered it to be righteousness. Then Samuel would become filled with wrath and vengeance and carry out the thing according as God had put it in him to do. He knew that she was not circumcised to his life, will, and way; and knew that the love and jealousy in which she was clothed for him was to bind her to him to fulfil all of these things.

Millennium was so abnormal to Samuel's way that at times it would bring such mighty trial, it seemed too much to withstand; but he would take a thought that it was only to try him, to make him pure white to the end. When he searched out the cause of her diabolical and despotic power, his anger removed, the trial subsided.

and he would look upon the flesh with a pitying eye and a sympathetic heart, knowing that she was ignorant of what she was doing, since she was not organized to be taught, nor to take correction. He saw that any power that came into her could use her to do according to its will, and that she had no reasonable thinking facilities. She was organized without sound discretion, intellect, and self-controlling power, to be the mother of the New Jerusalem, the Son of Righteousness, who was given in such marvellous way that any natural, reasonable, thinking person would have been confounded at its wonderment, if placed in her stead.

Samuel also discovered, by searching, that Caroline had been given an instrument in the hands of the eminent and essential arbitrary powers of mortality, some of which had formerly been cast out of her, so that she might fill the office in doing Christ's first work. He, at times, would reason with her, but always found her void of reason and sound discretion; he found that she was a total muse of theocrasy She had a vehement desire to have men to visit her and Samuel, but she did not want to see women visiting them; all her suffering and woe came through the jealous, fiery, flying serpent, who forced her to be disobedient to the commander.

Involuntary powers of dexterity worked in her acutely in the most majestic way, by the science of magianism, to keep all female kind away from Samuel. Her desire for Samuel to recline with her was excessively tormenting; but she declared that she did not desire for him to live with her after the fashion of male and female. She regarded not his wisdom and law of circumcision, yet she loved him beyond telling. She had no desire but for him, yet she did not obey him. She had no knowledge nor understanding of the covenant, and she resisted his purpose and determinations because they were conflicting with the desire of her ravenous lust. These many baneful qualities made her the sister of the daughters of Sodom, and other wicked empires, as prophesied, and far in excess of them.

She sought to please her ravenous desire with Samuel; but when she heard of any one else striving to gratify the desire of the flesh in any way, she was the first one to evoke a curse upon them without consultation or reason on the case. The most of her talk was against women, whom she abhorred; it was in her to destroy every one she could. It mattered not how clean and virtuous a woman was, she was filthy and abhorred by her. She was so filled with jealousy and scornfulness that she did not want any woman to come near her, because she exalted herself above all in nicety in every kind of work belonging to the feminine; and not only the feminine, but the masculine, also ; her pre-eminence had no base nor summit.

This mighty power working in her made her bone of the same bone, and flesh of the same flesh as that of John ; but she did not cleave to him in desire. She and he were helpmeets for each other all the way along through the troublous times. John cleaved to her in desire, but she did not cleave to him: they were coincident in characteristics and greatness of strength mentally and substantially. John's desire toward her was the exact likeness of hers toward Samuel, which kept John from attaining that which tormenteth not unto the end of the time spoken of.

John could not become reconciled to Samuel, because of his ravenous desire toward Caroline: and Caroline could adhere to truth and judgment, because it did not teach the doctrines to fill the bowels of hell, and sustain the science of the Nicolaitans. The non-unity and great rebellion between Samuel and Caroline was based on the lust of the woman's flesh, which created the murdering dragon, namely, jealousy. She did not lust as the heathen do : she lusted to exercise all power over both male and female.

The powers of scornfulness, disbelief, jealousy, lying, enmity, disobedience, begrudgfulness. and witchcraft took Caroline into captivity, and obtained full dominion over her, so that neither she nor God's Holy Christ had power over them to cause them to cease, until the time of the Gentiles was fulfilled. Her natural propensities, the stratum of her physique, were of a deleterious and tyrannical substance, and uncivilized nature. She was the queen reigning over the queens of abominations, because she contained the late and antique science of the natural and preternatural refined corruption, which made her the great feminine deceiver in the late science and arts of sin. She could not be united with the mother queen of Babylon, because she was too antique in science and arts. She could not cleave to John. because her love and jealousy for Samuel was the source of her life ; and when she turned from him, life would waste away. She could not love young women, because her very heart shed their blood, for fear they might win the love and affection of Samuel, her idol, who was a prey to her lust.

When Caroline was summoned of the Divine Spirit and forced by involuntary doctrine into the sphere of civilization, the sovereign powers of sin and idolatry, which had governed her from the early state of her life, were cast out, so that she might obtain the true civilization, to be instrumental in performing the work that God had determined to accomplish through her. God fashioned her, purposely, with the adamantine, modern, and feminine upas of mortality, which made her the epitome and the prime mover of the feminine woful corruption.

The primality, apexity, and substantiality of the mortal woman's influential predominance was seated in the pillory flesh and blood, bone and sinew, of the millennium queen, which is called " the man and woman layer," the deadly upas that surrounded the mortal globe and prevented any one from passing over into the fragrant and luminous land of Eden. This deadly upas is, namely, sensuality, jealousy, vanity enmity, scornfulness, deception, unbelief, necromancy, unfearfulness, disbelief, self-esteem, uncivilization, monomania, partiality shown to blood-kin, and niggardliness. Her material structure was the compound of the world-wide sovereignty of sin and vice. Those who had received thrones were cast out when she was chosen of the Lord God; but the essential stratum of sin and vice was left, which was the mattery substance, the motor of sin, reigning over the Adamite race now living upon the earth.

The language with which she was built is the excelsior, and most powerful of the finite kingdom. She was the feminine substance who gave birth to the occult planets to make up the fulness of the Adamite kingdom; still, she was the epitome, because she contained the generative power, and her mortal sanctuary, John, in whom she disguisedly trusted, was the germ and fœtus, the creative word and power, of the sinful kingdom.

John and Caroline were acquiescent in substantial qualities, so that John would be Adam, and she would be Eve: so that the Adamite generation would repeat their work in an abstract, spiritual light, to take therefrom a spiritual law, and show the man of sin in his spiritual predominance.

The judgments of the Lord God did not condemn marriage in the antichristian world, neither the love and honor due to money, education, blood-kin, and family circle; but the judgments condemned the entire antichristian customs, which are not called for to sustain and maintain life and truth among the people who forsake the world, and lay up their treasures in heaven, to be heirs of the righteous family, which is the attainment of the second resurrection of the dead, the sempiternal dominion over sin, death, and hell. Some of those who believed on Samuel while he was opening the seven seals were joined to husbands who were desperately opposed to Samuel's vocation; and some among them did not take pleasure in living submissive to their husbands, as they had done, by conceiving ideas concerning Samuel's calling and mission in regard to how male and female should live together in holiness unto God. The enthusiastic desire of some among them, to destroy the fashion of man and wife, set their husbands enraged against the perfect truth, and they created a Nicolaitan doctrine, opprobriously, which was based on one condition and sacrifice to constitute holiness, — to deny and condemn sexual desire and conjugality; and this heinous doctrine became prevalent among the antichristians, and it was emphatically declared by the Abyssinians that such was taught in the orthodox church.

This scurrilous doctrine was a deadly infection, and stigmatized mark of scorn, stamped upon the holy people by those living in Springfield; and not only in that city, but it was circulated abroad, and stirred up the people in other cities. These nefarious reproaches caused Samuel to see that he must cut off from visiting him, those women who had unbelieving husbands, and he issued a decree, for this purpose, during the fourth seal, which was accurately carried into effect. In a short time, the antagonizing power and evil devices of the Abyssinian race, which were plotted against the just, soon fled apace, and the turbulent billows of mortality were calmed thereby, for the material antagonists had attempted to abolish the work of the covenant, by reason of getting out a writ, through an assignment of neighboring despots.

At that time, there was only one married woman visiting the sanctuary who was, apparently, devoted; and this was Georgiana, Caroline's sister. Her love and devotion were strong. She and her husband were believers in Caroline's mission before the son was given. When Samuel was chosen, Georgiana and her husband visited Samuel and Caroline, and Georgiana gained faith and strength rapidly in the mighty doctrine which was prophesying on the judgments and the perilous times of the saints during the judgments; and her husband appeared to be the same.

As soon as Samuel prophesied, Georgiana's husband commenced to make frequent visits, and he commenced asking Samuel questions on different points pertaining to his mission. These Samuel explained to him, and gave him the primary basis of his mission,

He grew more and more interested in the work, having a quick understanding of the things explained to him; and he became vigorously spirited over what he heard, so much so that he devoted a part of his time to playing the violin for the sanctuary at nocturnal hours during the first seal.

Georgiana grew more fond and devoted to the sanctuary, and finally, the diabolical and imperious demoness of jealousy stood up blasphemously and malignantly in millennium, against Georgiana's love and devotion for the truth and the truth for her. And the wrath and vengeance of millennium were conferred upon Georgiana's husband according to millennium's ardent desire, which made him wroth; and he raged with murderous jealousy on account of Georgiana's devotion to the sanctuary. This caused him to turn against the sanctuary desperately and unreasonably; and when he turned from the sanctuary he was exceedingly strong to be the betrayer, because he had learned the title of the truth, which was personified at that time, and the basis of the covenant, — which was the "second coming of Christ."

Through the publication of his baneful reproaches, the city at large learned the cardinal principles of the holy truth's mission to humanity; and then the Messiah was betrayed into the hands of desperate men, to cut him off from obtaining work and support of the people when the sanctuary lifted himself up by having members of his own to work on both divine and temporal things. This antagonist started out in a dreadful rage during the latter part of the first seal, on the first day of March, 1889. This was the day that the holy city and sanctuary lifted himself up among the nations of the earth, and was laid waste through calumnious reproaches the first day of September in the same year.

As long as the wrathful, pernicious, and reproachful dragon reigned in millennium, by being looked upon, partially, as godliness, the powers of desolation reigned over postliminy; because the holy kingdom divided against itself when she chose the desperado — who was the second Judas, the betrayer — to defend her, because of jealousy and her rapacious desire for the flesh wherein the holy city and sanctuary was erected. She remarked, while in wrath of jealousy, that she would tell Georgiana's husband of her fondness for the sanctuary. This man was highly respected by Caroline, and she was also highly respected by him; and he took her for his physician. He had no respect for the sanctuary, though he had pretended to have, which millennium knew. He always blasphemed the sanctuary when he visited her house, with the cloak of a joke. He was brought — in Caroline's house, while strongly influenced by drink, through her invitation and loving enchantment — to curse and abuse the sanctuary in the worst form, so that she could express her sentimental vengeance through him.

This is the way that she polluted the purity in millennium, made to herself idols of men, and marred her comeliness, — by going after strange men, clothing herself in harlot's raiments, and forsaking the Lord, who brought her up out of the land of Egypt, set her in an eminent place, and made her famous among the nations. The jealous monster captured her and she was a total infidel while in his kingdom; and she did not believe that the man Samuel, who was placed a god before her, to lead and govern, and direct the straight and perfect way, was the same spirit and power that chose her, and made her eminent and famous among her kindred and nation. She bore the wrathful image of the Devil, who came among the holy saints in his entirety, both male and female, to bring forth Adam and Cain, through whom she hoped to be restored to fame and honorable eminence among her antichristian friends and relations, who stood afar off, in honor, respecting her mighty power.

The jealousy of millennium raged with fierce wrath as much against the honor shown toward the sanctuary instead of her as against womankind; but the betrayer showed all honor and respect to her, and made mention of her healing power among the nations, which thing she loved. All these abominations were in millennium to empower her chosen people to crucify her holy king, who came to redeem her, and make unto her a pre-eminent place, a famous name, a just recompense, and eternal praise, which could never be blemished.

Georgiana continued her love and devotion for the sanctuary, in spite of the jealous adversary under whom she had to suffer, until the covenant required her to make a complete sacrifice of her family, herself, and all she owned. This was that God might do his will, and fulfil his purposes concerning them; but she thought it was too hard, and refused to make such sacrifice.

This sacrifice was required of her during the third seal, which was before the decree went forth to cut off from visiting the sanctuary all married women having unbelieving husbands. The requirement of such sacrifice destroyed the greater portion of the love and devotion which she then had in store for the sanctuary, because the horn of blood-kin and family circle was stronger than the horn of salvation, which was love and devotion to the divine family; and from this time her enthusiastic desire to visit the sanctuary was quenched, and she was stirred exceedingly in awe of this sacrifice on both sides. She was closer to the sanctuary, before this time, than any other woman.

Until the third seal there had been no holy sacrifices placed upon the holy altar ; all sacrifices were totally corrupt, and unacceptable to the Lord God. The successor to Georgiana was Christina, an unmarried Swedish woman, who was shut out from visiting the sanctuary in the first seal owing to the unreasonable abusiveness of jealousy which the dragon exercised over her. The persecutions which she received from the jealous dragon forced her into the castle of doubts, where she remained imprisoned until the latter part of the third seal, at which time the sanctuary obtained a flame of love for her, a desire for her to return to the sanctuary, which she did. During her absence, the sanctuary wrote her a letter of sympathy, to cause an eternal flame of love and devotion to ignite in her for the sanctuary, to restore her strength, and revive the endless hope.

Christina returned to the sanctuary the latter part of the third seal ; but before returning, she was visited by Georgiana, who was perplexed and wandering about because of the sacrifice she was required to make to retain her office at the sanctuary. When Christina returned, her love and devotion for the sanctuary were ardent and sincere; and the sanctuary's love for her was a perpetual flame, because she had been purged of those torpid doubts and trepid agitations which led her into captivity.

A short time after Christina returned to the sanctuary, she was required to make a sacrifice of all earthly things; and it was a great pleasure for her to do so, but she felt herself unfit to present to the Lord, thinking that the Lord would not receive her. She made a total sacrifice of all she had in store, — herself, wearing apparel, money, occupation, relations, and what else exists in the millennium kingdoms. When she received her monthly payment, she came and placed it upon the golden altar which stood before the holy throne of God. Without being told, she would not spend one penny of her wages until it was brought to the sanctuary; and she would not change her attire until she consulted the sanctuary concerning it. She would say, " I will wear anything you say, and do anything you say, whether it seem right or wrong;" and she did not err one atom from the first system of the sacrifice she made. All this was volunary on her part; otherwise it would not have been acceptable to thet Lord God.

Most of Christina's sufferings were because she feared she was not pleasing the holy prince; and she wanted to earn more money than she was capable of demanding, for the advancement of the holy covenant. But the sanctuary would put down this strain and error, by telling her that she, without any money, was as acceptable as she would be if she had millions of dollars to present, because she had given herself, which was all, and more than silver and riches.

Christina was the first holy sacrifice that had been placed upon the holy altar, from the post-millennium of divine truth, up to this time, amidst the hopeless, solitary, desolate scenes of the fourth seal; and she was the mighty arms of temporal support that the Lord God stretched forth to deliver his kingdom out of hopelessness and solitary desolation. At the time that the Lord God raised her up to lend a helping hand to the desolate city, all arms that had helped, and hearts that had wept, had relaxed their hold.

Martha was the next most faithful sacrificer and devotee of the sanctuary in the time of solitary desolation. The rest of Samuel's parental relations stood in defence of the covenant to some extent. All, but Martha, stood in the renewed and quickened spirit, to befriend their blood with the cloak of godliness; and some among them stood wholly so. Martha extracted the most essential godly sacrificing inclinations of the natural family, and obtained the greatest propensities to devote herself to the divine will and purposes.

Martha devoted the greater portion of her time to conveying baskets of provisions to support the desolate family through the most troublous time of the solitary desolation, which was done voluntarily on her part. The provisions were furnished in part by the members of the family. The sanctuary always found her work free and easy, found her free from mental rebellion and opposition when she was in his presence, and did not observe the upas of partiality for bloodkin, as was observed in the rest of the family. She had no understanding of the covenant and its doctrines, yet she believed that God had a holy purpose in whatsoever befell the covenant.

There was also a youth, a brother to Martha, namely, George, who became a strong believer of Samuel when he began to prophesy;

and Samuel put him to work with Isaac in the fruit store when he imputed upon him the blessing of prosperity. George proclaimed unto the adversaries that the boils which were prophesied of in the first seal would make a material manifestation; and they failed to manifest themselves as he spoke, in defence of the prophecies. This caused him to be scoffed at, which caused him to fall a victim to disbelief and to be cast into its castle; and the power of belief which stood in defence of the prophecies, for the sake of blood-kin, was utterly destroyed, and was not restored.

Walter was the elder of the family, and was married. He was willing to do anything Samuel asked him to do, because he was his brother; but he was not willing to do anything for the sake of the kingdom of heaven, nor for the help of those who were with Samuel, which thing he acknowledged. The abominable horn of partiality for blood-kin and family circle made him strong in defiance of the cause; and the abominable horn of gold and silver withstood him from giving all he could spare for the support of the desolate family. Still, he bought the attached property which belonged to the blessing of prosperity, and presented them to Samuel; but he did not do this voluntarily; he was asked to buy them, so that business might be opened in his name, to support the falling Babylonian kingdom. Hence he gave the property to Samuel so that he might hew out a plan to put the horses to work in another fruit store, that he might obtain a share and earn much money from the power of the blessing.

Samuel searched into the matter pertaining to this step, and judged that if he opened business under the conditions of the holy sanctuary, it would only create a relapsation of trouble; so the property was sold, and the money refunded to Walter. He gave Samuel the privilege of taking what he needed at that time, and let him hold the balance in bank in his name; and he told Samuel to come to him and he would let him have the money at any time it was needed for other purposes than to pay on Mary's mortgaged property, upon which the sanctuary then lived.

Samuel accepted of a few dollars to pay a bill, but told Walter that he would not defile himself by coming to ask him for money. Samuel told Walter that if the horses were presented to God, a holy sacrifice, the money, which was the price of the horses and wagons, was his, also. But Walter stated there and then that he made the sacrifice with the hope of obtaining work when the horses were put to work; and as Samuel agreed to refund the money if the horses were sold, he expected it, according as Samuel had stipulated; and they made peace on these terms.

Samuel kept the two horses in the barn that he had built on Mary's property, and fed and cared for them, by using what little means he had given to him, from the latter part of the third seal until the same time of the fourth seal. He had to use most of the means he received charitably to buy suitable food for the horses; and all his family hoped that the horses would be put to work to support the desolate. All this was done that it might fulfil God's words, saying, "I will cut off the chariot from Ephraim, and the horse from Jerusalem, and the battle bow shall be cut off: and he shall speak peace unto the heathen: and his dominion shall be from sea even to sea, and from the river even to the ends of the earth."

It was peace to Walter for the sanctuary to renounce the sacrifice, upon oath, that he would not defile himself by coming to ask Walter for money, even if he stood in need of it; which fulfils God's words, saying, "If I were hungry, I would not tell thee: for the world is mine, and the fulness thereof."

There were others, whose faces were turned toward the holy sanctuary, who made charitable gifts; but they did not come nigh unto the sanctuary, and their names do not come in the exegetical adventures of the saints in the fulfilment of prophecies.

PART VI.

THE SOUNDING OF THE FIFTH TRUMP; CASUALTIES OF THE SAINTS; EXODUS OF THE HOLY SANCTUARY; SOLITARY DESOLATION ABOLISHED.

I, the Lord God, prophesy on the revelation of the fifth trump, which shall open the bottomless pit, and search out the profound depth of hell, and reveal the mysteries of sin and iniquity, and find the location and origination of the Devil's kingdom. The revelation of these mysteries shall awake the inhabitants of the bottomless pit; those who have been sleeping in the dust of the earth, powerless, all through the past dark ages of the world. They shall arise in the earth, and exercise great power and authority over the saints, such as has not been done before; therefore through the cunning craftiness of these occupants, they shall, if possible, deceive the very elect, by reason of the things they will be empowered to do.

When these inhabitants see that they cannot overcome the Lamb and his army, they shall seek death, but shall not find it; they shall desire to die but death shall flee away from them until God's words are fulfilled by them and then the Devil and his host shall be cast into a lake of fire, which is the second death, and a final dissolution of mortality. This plague shall make its appearance on the twenty-fourth of June, 1890, and disappear November 24, 1890, involving five months.

I, the Lord God, prophesy on the fifth plague, and behold, two others await to sound. This fulfils the vision shown unto the prophet John, saying, "And the fifth angel sounded, and I saw a star fall from heaven unto the earth: and to him was given the key of the bottomless pit." — Rev. 9. "And the fifth angel poured out his vial upon the seat of the beast; and his kingdom was full of darkness; and they gnawed their tongues for pain, and blasphemed the God of heaven because of their pains and their sores, and repented not of their deeds." "And I saw an angel come down from heaven, having the key of the bottomless pit and a great chain in his hand.' — Rev. 20.

Near the latter part of the fourth seal the adversaries of the sanctuary gathered all the reports and fictions they could obtain one from the other; and they had one of the most infamous and disgraceful advertisments, concerning the sanctuary and its members, put in a corrupt newspaper. In that publication they resurrected every false rumor and irrational lie that was previously created by the mighty dragon against the just; and they were refreshed in the minds of the enemies, which quickened them with wrath and vengeance to do injury to the holy covenant.

As Mary was a woman in years, many of the adversaries did not believe her to be staid nor sincere in the doctrine of the covenant; and signs had been seen by some of the neighboring adversaries that Mary was not in the best of health nor spirits. It was published that she was abused and treated in the most violent fashion by the younger members; and went so far as to say that it had been heard on the outside, by some of the neighboring antagonists, that the younger members were devising plans concerning how they might best make a speedy riddance of her.

When this publication rang in the ears of the people, they were moved with wrath and indignation; and the house was watched to see if such brutality was in action. When this flaming sword of fiction went out in circulation among the satanic race, Samuel felt confident that his name and power to accomplish any good thing in that city was destroyed, which caused him to take mighty and hasty steps to make a disposition of Mary's property to the owner of it, to secure means for himself and family to remove from the city.

In the meantime, Mary had a pulmonary cough, which had been quite harsh previous to this time, and no physician had been summoned because she refused to have one; and she died very suddenly, from the effects of the cough, with a slight hemorrhage. She had not been confined to bed, neither had she spoken of feeling any differently from what she felt all along. She died on the morning of the twenty-ninth of June, 1890; and then the flaming sword of reproachful fiction which went out before this casualty was the testimony for the red-head dragon to use to overcome the saints, because no one but the members of the family saw Mary for some time before she died.

As it had been published that death was determined in her case by the younger members, the way in which she died verified their statements, and mighty attempts were made by the Abyssinian race to prove the holy sanctuary and its members guilty of man-slaughter, by making their complaints to the law, to look after the matter concerning her death. The city authorized different parties to come to the camp of the saints, investigate the circumstances of the family, and make accurate inquiries as pertaining to Mary's death. The first search was made by the Board of Health and a news-reporter; and when they inquired of John something of the work of the covenant, the Holy Spirit used him with burning flames of truth, in power, to speak in defence of the covenant, which destroyed their false ideas and corrupt aim.

The second authorities who came wished to see the different parts of the house, — which they did, — and they went into Samuel's studio, where he did his work, and Samuel entered the room, was introduced to them, and gave a brief statement of his work, by showing some of the writings, and stated how he had gained admittance into Mary's house to do his work. This statement was made unto them in a tranquil spirit and tone, and was the fire that came down from God out of heaven and destroyed their power and aim.

The temple of the daughter of Babylon was buried on the thirtieth of June. All this was done to bring to pass the words of God, saying, " And when he had opened the fourth seal, I heard the voice of the fourth beast say, Come and see. And I looked, and behold, a pale horse : and his name that sat on him was Death, and Hell followed with him. And power was given unto them over the fourth part of the earth, to kill with sword, with hunger, and with death, and with the beasts of the earth."

As soon as Mary was buried, the severity of the trouble was transferred upon Isaac, which was manifested in extreme fear, and many other torments which were bottomless, signifying preposterous thinking facilities, false ideas, and obdurableness. His trouble was revealed by the sanctuary and pronounced upon the powers of darkness, which were controlling Isaac, as follows : —

"When you are alone, you are filled with all manner of demons and heresies, who come to torment, by bringing all manner of unreasonable things to the mind, and making them appear to be truth ; and as soon as the spirit of truth appears to find out the cause of the trouble, every antispirit departs ; and the sanctuary can find nothing in the temple to judge and condemn. When the antispirits depart, then you could make a holy sacrifice of yourself, because they have left the temple vacant ; and as soon as the spirit of truth disappears, the antispirits re-appear and set your heart against what you have sacrificed your body to do.

" When you are empty, any spirit passing by with power is free to come into the temple and make it miserable, or joyful : and when the spirit of joy and peace is with you, then you are willing to work for the sanctuary, and feel as though you could take pleasure in the work which God gave you to do. When the spirit of joy departs, the temple is again left vacant. By and by the antichristian spirits come along, and seeing the house vacant, they also find admittance and full access thereto, and change the meaning of the words of the spirit of truth in every true sense. These antispirits oppose the sacrifices which you make of yourself.

" You have no understanding of the covenant ; nor have you any power to retain truth, wisdom, and understanding ; for your natural culture is insusceptible of retaining knowledge. At times every way is right and holy with you; and your mind changes from this state, and doubts all things. Any one who appears friendly to you is perfect, and trustworthy in your understanding. Any one who appears friendly can influence you to believe the truth or falsity, if there is no one to guide you in the proper way. You have power to deceive, and are easy to be deceived. You have a kind, loving, and affectionate heart toward both male and female; and you do not wish to harm, nor bring harm upon any one. You are a friend to the holy covenant when the antispirits are not prophesying in the temple; but when they occupy the temple, it is then an enemy to the holy covenant, which makes you corrupt and bottomless."

Samuel saw that Isaac was composed of mutable and volatile propensities, which were subject to both pure and impure characteristics, because he was untaught in regularity and system. He could do mighty work if he had some true being to direct him; but Samuel found him incapable of supervision.

Isaac had been making sacrifices of himself and earthly glory, all through the time of solitary desolation; but he was not sincere in laying himself on the holy altar to work wholly for the upbuilding of the desolate. And as it had come a time for his sacrifices to be received of the Lord God, hell was stirred to oppose him, because the time for receiving the sacrifices was at hand. For this cause those demons and heresies were empowered to stricken him with torments and piercing griefs, which darkened the Son of Righteousness with hopelessness of Isaac's ever triumphiing over his trouble. This compelled Samuel to make a sacrifice of him to be slain or redeemed, whichever was to the promotion of the holy kingdom.

In a short time after this sacrifice was made by Samuel, he sent Isaac out from him, because he saw no hope of his redemption. This God did to purge and try Isaac, to make holy sacrifices unto the sanctuary, that he might lift himself up from waste and desolation. Samuel told Isaac that if he remained with him he would be destroyed materially; and leaving him and going off to work was the only hope of life.

The sanctuary made Isaac ready, and sent him to Boston, Mass., in the month of July, 1890; and instructed him to seek friends among the people, and he would be blessed and prosper. Samuel told him that he did not expect him to earn money to send to him; he told him to use his money to dress himself, and conform himself to the customs of the people. But Isaac said, when he secured work, he was going to send Samuel money to help him along with his work.

The mighty power of the pale horse destroyed all hope and possibilities of the holy city and sanctuary being lifted up among the inhabitants of Springfield, where the sanctuary was laid waste. The power of reproaches which came from Mary's sudden death deprived the sanctuary of a home in that city; for the abjects' preposterous aspersion locked every door against the Divine Christ in that city.

The property that the sanctuary and his members were then living on was alienated to Mary's heirs at her death, and the heirs were members of the sanctuary; but they had not been acquitted of the insolvent claim held against them for the non-payment of debts which stood against them at the failure of the fruit business, — at the destruction of the city and sanctuary, the overthrow of the blessing of prosperity. Therefore, after Isaac left, the creditors took immediate steps and had Mary's houshold goods inventoried; and in a short time the property on which the sanctuary was residing was sold, and a notice to vacate the premises sent by a sheriff. The vendee of the property appeared to be moved revengefully by the spirit of indignation, so that he re-notified the sanctuary and his members to vacate the house and premises in forty-eight hours' time, or they would be put into the street by law; and this notice was given by a lawyer.

During this casualty Isaac wrote Samuel a letter, saying that he would rent him a tenement in Boston, and he could come on there to live if he thought it best. Samuel had not informed Isaac of what had befallen him. Samuel then wrote him word to rent him a tenement, and also notified him of the perils which he was forced to face in a short time. Samuel did not have means to defray his expenses to Boston, still he commenced to pack up what few things were in the house, which belonged to John, Caroline, Isaac, and himself, that the vendee of the property might set their goods in the street, as the notice to desert the premises was too short.

When the adversaries found that they were making ready to leave, they were contented to wait, and give them time; they only wanted to force them from the city, because they were troubled about them all the time. They made ready for the exodus with scarcely enough money to defray their expenses; and they left Springfield, for Boston, at midday on the eighteenth of August, 1890. This was done that it might fulfil God's words by the prophet, saying, "Awake, awake; put on thy strength, O Zion; put on thy beautiful garments, O Jerusalem, the holy city: for henceforth there shall no more come into thee the uncircumcised and the unclean." — Isa. 52.

The sanctuary arrived in Boston on the eighteenth of August, 1890, at late eve, and lodged in the Sherman House until the twentieth day of the month, at which time a tenement was rented on Northampton Street, into which the sanctuary moved, thereby ending the desolation and lifting himself up from waste and perdition.

The sanctuary moved into his house, which was rented for twenty dollars per month, on the twentieth day of August, 1890; and on the same day he wrote an epistle to Christina, who was left at work in Springfield until a tenement was secured for the family. The epistle was for her to know that the sanctuary had gotten a tenement, and to cheer her, because she was filled with zeal to be in the city of Boston where she could visit the sanctuary. The epistle also contained the command for her to give her notice and come on to Boston; and she gave her notice to her employer, but he failed to recognize such, because he did not want her to leave, as her occupation was pastry cookery, and it was the busy season.

Christina wrote the sanctuary that she was compelled to stay until a certain time, and could not be released; and she also stated that she would do anything the sanctuary commanded concerning it — she would remain if the sanctuary said so, or leave, anyway, if the sanctuary said so. She said it was her desire to be near him.

The sanctuary wrote another epistle in haste, and gave her the proper word to speak to her employer, and limited the time she should work there; and when that time expired, she must come on to Boston. And Christina gave her employer her notice, — that she would finish up at the time which the sanctuary set, — but her employer refused to consent to it, and offered her more pay if she would stay; but she said, "I would not stay if you gave me the whole house."

The employer refused to let her go willingly; and when the time came for her to leave, she made ready, and left without her pay. They refused to pay her, in order to compel her to stay. She left the money, and obeyed the sanctuary. She was obedient to her Creator, which gave her the power and authority to stamp under foot the kingdoms of the world when they conflicted with God's command and purpose. Still, she used the world as not abusing it. Obedience was in her heart to do all the covenant commanded her; she did not strive to please herself, because it was peace, pleasure, and her glory to please the sanctuary in all things; and she suffered many things because she feared that the sanctuary was not pleased with her.

As soon as she arrived in Boston and reached the loving and sympathizing bosom of peace, and arms of power, the inhabitants of hell were loosened in Caroline, and they quickened those abominable principles which were solidly imbedded in her nature, and made unreasonable, brutal war against the sanctuary and the holy sacrificer. This was caused by the sanctuary's saluting the holy sacrificer with salubrious osculation, and embracing her in his arms of love in the most tender and affectionate way.

Christina devoted herself at one time to a continual osculating of the feet of the sanctuary; which stirred up the inhabitants of hell in the battle-field of jealousy, which fulfil God's words, saying, "Kiss the Son, lest he be angry, and ye perish from the way, when his wrath is kindled but a little. Blessed are all they that put their trust in him."

In a short time from this phenomena manifested in the brilliant star, Christina, the mighty wrath and vengeance of the jealous serpent began to find fault with Christina in different things irrationally; and the sanctuary spoke in vengeance against the satanic host in favor of the true soul; and they stood up in wrath and blasphemy, mingled with curses, to overpower the lamb and his army.

The venomous serpent of jealousy opened Caroline's mouth in a state of unconsciousness, with a loud cry of "Murder! murder!" which could be heard afar off; but owing to the locality, and the time that this casualty took place, no one on the outside discovered the sound, for she was rushed into a close room to deaden it. And the sanctuary spoke words to cause the inhabitants of hell to rage, and cast them out from mingling with the truth; and they were cast into a lake of fire, signifying divine truth. Then Christina became unhappy, thinking that she was making trouble for Caroline, and she was willing to leave the house and go straight to work, so that Caroline would not be punished on her account, as she thought. But hell had stood up against God's Christ to defeat and abolish every step he took to redeem the holy kingdom out of desolation; and those abominable principles which manifested themselves in millennium were the continuity of desolation, and the troublous conflicts of the saints.

After the great massacre of the antichristian race, the sanctuary secured a situation for Christina and she went about her work, continuing her sacrifices. Isaac was the next most obedient and faithful sacrificer, whose sacrifices began on the eighteenth of August, 1890. He fully consecrated himself, time, and labor to the support of the sanctuary, while he was annihilating the principal abominations from the temples of John and Caroline, in order to utterly abolish desolation. This was the second time that the Lord God stretched forth his mighty arm to redeem his holy kingdom out of desolation ; and Isaac's work was mighty in power in behalf of the covenant from this time until desolation was abolished.

At this time there were four of the family who did not earn anything for support, owing to the privacy that prevailed on account of the judgments which were then rapidly approaching. Samuel searched diligently into this matter, and the sanctuary determined to put John to work ; but the sanctuary knew that he would oppose such determination. Then the fierce wrath and vengeance of the sanctuary was hastily stirred up, to declare unto John that it was determined for him to secure work in the outside world, to earn something for a support, owing to the condition of the covenant. Samuel gave him the command effecting this determination ; but he snuffed at it, and regarded it as nothing and beneath his notice. The sanctuary then came to an absolute decision, on seeing that he was uncircumcised in heart, and gave him the command in a pointed way, with power and authority, and explained to him why such actions should be taken ; but the inhabitants of perdition stood up combatively in him, an innumerable number.

The sanctuary mustered his army together and made war with John, and in a few days he partially surrendered and went in search of work ; and the army that surrendered smote his intellect, and he became stupid, and dormant in his thinking facilities, and at times he was unconscious of what he was aiming to do. This power, exercised over his brain lobe, was the strategy of the dextrous warriors of perdition, to defeat and overcome the army of the living God in battle.

The sanctuary detected this point and defeated them by going with John in search of work ; and failing to obtain work at this step, he put an advertisment in the papers by which he obtained work in the month of September. The firm for whom he worked seemed to be unable to pay him when he put in the first week; and John undertook to force them to pay him, by using abusive language in a vile way, but to no avail. He then voluntarily employed a lawyer to collect the money for him, but to no avail. John only worked in this place one week, which fulfils God's words, saying, "These words spake Jesus and lifted up his eyes to heaven, and said, Father, the hour is come; glorify thy Son, that thy Son also may glorify thee." — John 17.

When this chapter was read to the members of the sanctuary, Samuel then made ready to enter into judgment with John afresh, to destroy the ruling sceptre of the Son of Perdition, so that John might be made one with him in the triniunity of divine truth even as he was in one consent with the Holy Father. This carried into effect the following words: "And when he had opened the fifth seal, I saw under the altar the souls of them that were slain for the word of God, and for the testimony which they held: and they cried with a loud voice, saying, How long, O Lord, holy and true, dost thou not judge and avenge our blood on them that dwell on the earth? And white robes were given unto every one of them; and it was said unto them, that they should rest yet for a little season, until their fellowservants also and their brethren, that should be killed as they were, should be fulfilled."

THE SOUNDING OF THE SIXTH TRUMP; THE GREAT REBELLION BETWEEN THE SON OF RIGHTEOUSNESS AND THE SON OF PERDITION; ECLIPTIC PHENOMENA.

I, the Lord God, prophesy on the wrath and vengeance which shall be executed to destroy the kings of the earth, the great men, the rich men, the chief captains, the mighty men, and every bondman and freeman, to make a way for the redemption of my kingdom which now lieth in bondage to men of renown. These I have reserved through the past epochs of the prophetic ages as fuel for the fire during the time of this prophecy. I shall appear to my temple with unquenchable fire, October 15, 1890, and shall begin to sound the mysteries of sin and iniquity as I have declared unto my servants the prophets should be done at the latter end of the indignation. I shall execute wrath and vengeance on sin, as I have not done before. The earth shall quake, and the rocks rend asunder;

fire and vapor of smoke shall be seen in all parts of the globe. The sun shall be darkened; the moon shall withdraw her shining; and the kingdoms of the nations shall surrender to attribute all glory, honor, and blessings unto me henceforth and forever.

This prophecy shall make its full manifestation on the fifteenth of October, and make a short fulfilment of its work, ending November 15, 1890. I, the Lord God, prophesy on the latter end of the indignation. and, behold, the seventh angel is now at hand. This seal accomplished the words spoken by the prophet, saying, " And I beheld when he had opened the sixth seal, and, lo, there was a great earthquake; and the sun became black as sackcloth of hair, and the moon became as blood; and the stars of heaven fell unto the earth, even as a fig-tree casteth her untimely figs when she is shaken of a mighty wind. And the heaven departed as a scroll when it is rolled together; and every mountain and island were moved out of their places. And the kings of the earth, and the great men, and the rich men, and the chief captains, and the mighty men, and every bondman, and every freeman, hid themselves in the dens, and in the rocks of the mountains; and said to the mountains and rocks, "Fall on us, and hide us from the face of him that sitteth on the throne, and from the wrath of the Lamb: for the great day of his wrath is come; and who shall be able to stand?"

"And the sixth angel poured out his vial upon the great River Euphrates; and the water thereof was dried up, that the way of the kings of the east might be prepared. And I saw three unclean spirits like frogs come out of the mouth of the dragon, and out of the mouth of the beast, and out of the mouth of the false prophet. For they are the spirits of devils, working miracles, which go forth unto the kings of the earth and of the whole world, to gather them to the battle of that great day of God Almighty. Behold, I come as a thief. Blessed is he that watcheth, and keepeth his garments, lest he walk naked, and they see his shame. And he gathered them together into a place called in the Hebrew tongue Armageddon."

During this seal the magnetic powers of the luminating stratum which constructed the mansion John congregated and agglutinated to all the renownship and pre-eminence of perdition in its fulness. And the tabernacle Samuel congregated and agglutinated to all the pre-eminence and renownship of divine righteousness; which gathered all the most precious and luminous stratum which was created therein to shine silently in the presence of the mortal stratum, and obdurated the Lucifer lights to cast them down from heaven, which was exalted, and magnified above the holy constellations.

The sanctuary refrained from judgment, almost if not entirely through the sixth seal; he only made his appearance before John, the embodiment of perdition, the contents of the Lucifer lights, in a serene, calm, and silent manner, which surpassed, obtused, and made miserable the lights of Lucifer, so that they forsook their offices in the firmament of John's wisdom and understanding, and cast themselves down to the earth. The pre-eminence which was solidly imbedded in the firmament of the mortal world ignited during this time, and burned, in spite of all John could do, by involuntary action; but the excellency of the immortal, brilliant stratum shone over and around them with such power of light and heat that they were forced down to the earth, namely, John, so that he might be empowered to overcome them by the blood of the Lamb at the time appointed.

This fulfils God's words, saying, "How art thou fallen from heaven, O Lucifer, son of the morning! how art thou cut down to the ground, which didst weaken the nations!" "The word of the Lord came again unto me, saying, Son of man, say unto the prince of Tyrus, Thus saith the Lord God; Because thine heart is lifted up, and thou hast said, I am a God, I sit in the seat of God, in the midst of the seas; yet thou art a man, and not God." — Ezek. 28.

While the man of sin was passing through these different intermediate states of punishment, misery, and woe, it worked with much power in John to seek death at his own hands, and end his suffering; which thing John confessed to Samuel at each time he reached the verge of being tempted to commit the deed. When the sanctuary saw the aim of the desperate man, he would restrain the pressure which he had turned loose on those warriors until John rallied, and overpowered the great wrath and strain of perdition; and then the Almighty God loosened again the superiority of his anthropomorphistic being to destroy and utterly make away with his renownship.

At the close of the sixth seal the waters of the great River Euphrates were united; and those abominably pre-eminent and renowned principles in John were judged in a brief and pointed way, — all that had been manifested while the word, truth, and spirit waited for the time and season to accomplish the work.

The Sounding of the Seventh Trump; Meteoric Phenomena of Divine Aerial Region; Caliginous Observations.

I, the Lord God, prophesy on the seventh trump which shall sound to bind up the broken-hearted; to proclaim liberty to the captives of sin, and the opening of the prison to them that are bound; to proclaim the acceptable year of the Lord, and the day of vengeance of the Lord God; and to comfort all that mourn. This prophecy shall finish the transgression, make reconciliation for iniquity, bring in everlasting righteousness, seal up the vision and prophecy, and anoint the most holy. This prophecy will be manifested November 15, 1890, and make acute fulfilment of its work with a limitation of nine days, bringing the transgressors to a final end November 24, 1890.

I, the Lord God, prophesy on the sounding of the last trump; and I declare it is done. I am Alpha and Omega, the beginning and the end of sin, the last days, the end of the world, in the holy city and sanctuary. This prophecy finished the visions and words spoken by the prophet, saying, "And the seventh angel poured out his vial into the air; and there came a great voice out of the temple of heaven, from the throne, saying, It is done. And there were voices, and thunders, and lightnings; and there was a great earthquake, such as was not since men were upon the earth, so mighty an earthquake, and so great. And the great city was divided into three parts, and the cities of the nations fell: and great Babylon came in remembrance before God, to give unto her the cup of the wine of the fierceness of his wrath. And every island fled away, and the mountains were not found. And there fell upon men a great hail out of heaven, every stone about the weight of a talent: and men blasphemed God because of the plague of hail; for the plague thereof was exceeding great."

The meteors seen by the prophet in these visions and revelations are a metaphor of the fierce anger, wrath, and indignation of the Lord God against those disreputable and sovereign characteristics which manifest themselves in the two genders of millennium in the annals of this doctrine. The winking of the eyes of righteous wisdom is lightning when the anger of righteousness kindles against abomination: and the sound of God's anthropomorphistic voice is thunder, comparatively, and the language which is discharged from his mouth, expressing his indignation, is hailstones, figuratively.

Before these phenomena occurred in the Son of Righteousness in their entire power, the Son of Righteousness felt the power of the Son of Perdition when he induced the continent John to deliver him unto the will of those renowned and sovereign powers which rule over the human sphere tyrannically. Samuel felt the piercing pains of the spears, bayonets, javelins, staves, lances, battle-axes. the rugged whip, the thorny crown, and the hammering of the spike-nails, pinioning him to the cross. He felt the trickling of blood pouring freely from the gashes and bruises of his flesh; and he heard the voice crying, "It is done; Father, I have finished the work that thou hast given me to do." He felt himself passing through an acute metamorphosic state, conveyed by lightning velocity.

While the Son of Righteousness was passing through this change, he felt dead, helpless, lifeless, and powerless until this phenomenon produced another change, and then he felt that he had overcome the regiment that had gathered in the earth to battle against the great day of God Almighty. This was the time that the Lord God took to himself his almighty power to reign over abominations through the agencies contained in his holy kingdom, which is substantially in his Christ. But the army of the wicked did not desert the battle-field; they re-equipped themselves for battle, which was God's purpose, that he might slay them by the power of his omniverous and creative words, which passed through the changes, and had been transmuted into the power to destroy any prey that fell in its reach.

The Son of Righteousness, in passing through the metamorphosic state in an acute way, was to oxidize the mattery body into an incorporeal body. This produced the full doctrine of metempsychosis, which is man's progenerative state, after passing from death to life. This oxiodic phenomenon transmuted the Son of Righteousness from the mattery temple to an incorporeal temple, so that he would be a totally spiritual body, that God's people may put on his spiritual image, the quickening power of the corporeal body, the state of regeneration This state of the Son of Righteousness is man's primary state, and the apexity of humanity in the highest plains of godly development, which is divine, involuntary science of word, truth, and spirit governing God's people. This establishes the true doctrine of polytheism. Why? Because when man puts on God's spiritual body, he has put on God's person in the fulness in every degree. In this state man is omniscious, as pertaining to God's will, glory, and honor; and he is omniscient in all things that God created to glorify man in his first estate.

How can man obtain omnipotent power, omnipresent existence, and omniscious wisdom, when the material body of man is so minute to this infinite doctrine? In man's holy, happy, and perfect state, he is omnicorporeal, because he contains all substances created in the beginning, whether material or immaterial. Then all substances that were created in the beginning are in the fluid and stratum of the Son of Righteousness. The substances, both material and immaterial in every degree, that were created in the beginning and govern the material world, are the same substances that are contained in the construction of the God-man, and are his omnipotence, omnipresence,, omniscience, and omnispectiveness.

The anthropomorphistic God comprises all the essential substances, both corporeal and incorporeal; and each one of these agents is performing an opuscule work to procreate man, who is fashioned for this purpose. This, when realized, produces the endless change, and establishes the doctrine of polytheism, and the construction of the anthropomorphism in a pleomorphous light and in a trimorphous existence. These scientific doctrines unfold, and show the Origenism of God's Christ, and the integration of the sempiternal doctrine of pneumatology in the government of all the blessed and wonderful make of his hand formed in the creation of all things.

When the agents whom God has fashioned and clothed in his image and likeness attribute all glory, honor, and majesty unto the two genders in the transhumanized existence of mankind, then they will be honoring and glorifying the Lord God; and God will honor and glorify them. Then God's pure substances will be in them, which will be them in him, and he in them; and they shall glorify him, and he will be glorified in them; and they will behold his glory, which was before the world was.

The abrupt changes of the Son of Righteousness during the phenomena which took place in the fifth seal, evolving the sixth and seventh seals, made a synopsis of the two seals of righteousness, namely, Elijah and Jesus, whose descension and ascension took place in the Mosaic dispensation, who was the fifth seal. And the time spoken of had to be fulfilled from the eighth person, the embodiment of the seven righteous seals, who was oxidized into the seventh, and finished up the time prophesied of in preaching the fulness of his life unto the members of the sanctuary. This preaching, done by the Son of Righteousness after the ending of the seven seals, was to exhibit his life in the fulness, so that his members would see him as he is, through the proclamation of purity, which was to convert the members of the sanctuary to receive and live at ease the pure life of Christ. The same doctrine that was used to publish the truth among the members of the sanctuary is recorded to convert to divine, spiritual circumcision all mankind who are fashioned for God's glory.

The seven seals, comprising the exegetical, historical adventures of the godly and ungodly characteristics of humanity, have evolved the deep mysteries of psychomachy, and discovered the apathy of psychology; but this the God-man obtained through resipiscence. The work of the God-man, through the seven seals, has given him a practical knowledge of psychomachy, and made him the god and professor of divine psychology; which made him to be omniscious and omnispective in the estate of sempiternity.

The seven seals contain the full power to abolish the mortal life of man; and each contains the doctrine, proportionately, to convey man from death to the resurrection. Each seal contains in itself a mighty power and separate state for the mortal man to pass through to overcome the natural life, by the doctrines divulged in the opening of the seals and the legend of the saints. Man had to pass through these seven states of solitary punishment, to destroy the substances of mortality, before he could become fully circumcised in heart, and conformed to divine will and purposes, in spite of his zeal and courage to attain thereunto in the first seal. In each one of these seals through which man had to pass from the mortal life to death, his strength diminished, his trials grew more grievous, and his condition grew more hopeless; but he travelled on, step by step, until he reached the seventh, which was the end of mortality, and the last state, which was death. When he reached this state, the man of sin yielded up the ghost. There was no hope nor strength to be given to man to lift him up from this state, because it was the lowest degree of mortality, and the region wherein all mortality are utterly abolished.

The seventh region is man's last stage; still man was forced to linger in that deplorable region until the wrothful Son of Perdition yielded up the ghost, and died a gradual death. The suffering of the flesh is the consumption of mortality, which is the climax of punishment. By the Son of Perdition being zealous to reach the estate of felicity did not mitigate his suffering, because mortality was his life, and his pleasure was in mortal things; and if he was alleviated, the life, which was mortal, was strengthened, and he had to retrogress to inanimate and repel the animation and influx of sin.

After reaching the region of death, man had to pass through seven stages to attain the resurrection of the dead, which is the climax of life; and this stage of life can only be reached step by step, because the flesh itself must be oxidized, and pass through the metamorphosic changes in each successive stage. The powers of transporting scenes revive the hope, and increase the zeal, courage, and peace, until the blissful stage is attained, and then the fulness of life is inhaled.

In the seventh degree of mortality the soul and body unite in the nethermost region; and the body then is a total mass of corruption, namely, the burning pit of hell, which is the fulness of misery and woe. This is called the transformation of the animal propensities of the material body into a totally corrupt spiritual body, called "leviathan," who is the animating king, the perpetrator, the origin, and the strength of hell. This great king, who united with matter and transmuted the substance of the flesh into fluid substances, is aerially called "word, spirit, and truth," which comprises the totalship of metaphysics. Metaphysics is the glory and honor, riches and blessings, power and wisdom and strength of the physical world; and this science is based on physical things, but mortal judgment, equity, love, and integrity, and executed by the most honorable, according to men's understanding.

Leviathan is the pre-eternal god of temporal wisdom, created and scientifically indued in the beginning to govern and preside, through wisdom and the powers of language, over the physical world, so that he might be used as a metaphor for the building of the eternal human world. Leviathan was refined and oxidized, by purging out of his being all base and combustible substances; was reduced to a substantial and solid stratum; and obtained the eternal existence with humanity, because he was purged of his disgraceful characteristics, which made him more lofty than was due to him. His superciliousness that exalted him above the Lord God, omnipotent, and creator of his power, was judged and condemned.

This was done that it might fulfil God's words, saying, " In that day the Lord with his sore and great and strong sword shall punish leviathan the piercing serpent, even leviathan that crooked serpent; and he shall slay the dragon that is in the sea." — Isa. 27. " Canst thou draw out leviathan with an hook? or his tongue with a cord which thou lettest down? Canst thou put an hook into his nose? or bore his jaw through with a thorn?" — Job 41.

The exegetical powers of these substantialities were the firm and, durable stratum discovered in the golden sanctuary of metaphysics whose essential power, and modern science, made its advent to the temple John, in the fulness thereof, to be purged and purified, to make the chief ruler, according to divine will and power, over the holy age of temporal things.

The judgments of the Lord God fulminated and swallowed up the corrupt son of metaphysics, to bring the physical world and government into the laws and doctrines of divine circumcision; which subdued the supercilious sovereign of the physical world to divine will, so that the physical and divine laws may unite, acquiescently, by the holy physical laws' being distilled from the divine laws and doctrines. Through this system, determination, and discrete judgment, I have made plain the doctrine of polytheism; because God has fashioned his Christ to be ruler both in divine and physical worlds, by his agents' practising purity in all their works, each and every one who shall be progenerated through the powers of these doctrines.

There shall come a time when none shall exist upon the land of Eden but those who are governed, created, and fashioned after the glory, honor, and majesty of these endless doctrines. The holy truth, who is omnipotent, omnipresent, omniscient, and omnispective, shall govern all things existing, and convey all things that God has created for his glory under the luminous light and incessant blissfulness of these doctrines. At the end of the world the God-man sought for the troubles to end, because the sanctuary was still in a waste and pitiful condition; and the hope of lifting himself up seemed impossible, for the kingdom stood divided against itself.

John and Caroline were then in a state of apathy; the soul and body had united and formed an aggregated mass of corruption; neither one desired to live, nor had they any hope of obtaining life, as had been promised to God's elect. They preferred death rather than life, because their first hope was destroyed by judgment. The body had united with the mental pit, and their entire frames were cast into hell to burn up the wicked by the fulmination of judgment and the burning flames of truth that held the land in bondage.

All reptiles that maintain a material existence on earth awoke in nature from the fulmination of the judgments and the burning flames of truth, and were observed clearly in the different deleterious characteristics of John and Caroline; and the sanctuary bore the memoir of each deadly effect that those reptile principles had upon the human family, so that he could testify of it Biblically, and obtain a practical knowledge thereby. Those reptiles raged in the flames of hell ordinately, and successively, just as they grew in the flesh and blood, bone and sinew; and as soon as the burning flames of truth touched each one, Samuel knew what manner of reptile he had captured. The deadly effects were manifested in Samuel's flesh in feelings of deadly griefs and heaviness; and the names of the reptiles appeared upon the face of the firmament, which means the word of God. When the name appeared upon the firmament, he then sought for a witness to make up the power to produce proof; and he found the names of the reptiles in the prophecies testifying to what he felt and beheld, which was the fire that devoured them hastily.

All manner of animals and reptile races were gathered in the epitome of the world, who was an entire forest and vast wilderness, where all manner of unclean beasts, fowl, fish of the sea, and creeping things found places, under the cliffs of mountains and in hollows of the earth, to secrete themselves. The fowls soared high in the firmament of the son of metaphysics, where mortal eyesight could not reach and behold, because of his wisdom and great understanding. Unclean water creatures found refuge in his immense bodies of waters, which were his deep speech and mellifluous language, which flowed as the waters of the ocean. But the influx of the tide of mortality came seldom, with a loud turbulent sound; which made the inhabiters of the waters of immortality to quake for fear by reason of his thundering and deep uninterpreted sound.

As millennium had fled for refuge into this vast wilderness, she was the open plains, shallow waters, and the bright parts of the firmament, where the different animals ran, and challenged the God-man for war, when they could no longer cover and secrete themselves in their former homes. There were parts of the mortal globe where the light of the Son had never shone: and there were mountains and empires, watercoasts and wildernesses, frigid regions, obscure horizons, and shady landscapes, where the son of man had not trod, nor had the light of day ruled the great darkness.

There were also uncivilized nations inhabiting the foreign empires of this mortal globe, where the son of man had not gone, because of those brutish and hostile tribes. Many attempts had been previously made to enter into those uncivilized countries of humanity, to trade with the nations, so that holiness might be established with them; but signs of hostility had been plainly seen, and the God-man was warned not to go in too hastily. So the Son of Righteousness went in gradually, through allurement, until he snared them all; and then he opened his mouth in wrath and vengeance against them, saying, " Knowest thou the time when the wild goats of the rock bring forth? or canst thou mark when the hinds do calve? Canst thou number the months that they fulfil? or knowest thou the time when they bring forth?" — Job. 39.

In this phenomenon, millennium was the phylogenetic blastemas, impregnating from the fertilities of those great waters, luminous light, vast wilderness, and grassy plains which were perpetrated and continuated throughout the time by the influx of leviathan unicorn. She scorned and bruised the young that she had conceived in the matrix, to bring them forth before they reached maturity, because of the great shameful abominations that she was subject to for the re-opening of the womb.

Leviathan unicorn, or leviathan lust, was continually planting the seeds of mortality in the matrix of the feminine leviathan lust; but still she despised the children she brought forth, and had no pleasure in them, because she sought a greater increase of young, and the mouth of hell was gaping wide, and the bowels of damnation were unlimited, and could not be filled nor satisfied in drinking the gaseous fuel of perdition, which ignited in the earth and produced a volcanic, technical eruption, by emitting a pernicious, volatile lava. The leviathan unicorn sent out a pseudo-volcanic phenomenon, because his strata was so closely compact that it could not produce a burning flame, hence the gaseous fuel was absorbed by the feminine and by the harmony which exists between the feminine and masculine leviathan unicorn, which formed another substance when they compounded. This substance was jealousy, which prevailed over Samuel for many days in the millennium customs, in the most noxious and suppressive degree; and in the meantime she had no tenderness, love, nor sympathy for the members of the holy sanctuary.

The judgments upon metaphysics purged out of him all noxious substances, discordant governments, and nefarious laws, which were forced by the animal medium of life affluent in the human animal kingdom. The judgments of the Lord God upon metaphysics purged out of his being the animal spirit which is mortiferous to humanity, and the impure substances that have no liking for the Divine Spirit, so that philosophical power and the holy science of metaphysics would unite and form a pure compound substance; for each minute substance that is in this compound union is perfectly harmonious, performing an opuscule, whose laws and governments are in itself, and each minute substance is accomplishing its opuscule from every standpoint that is favorable to his minute brother.

The union and compounding of the tenacious substances of divine philosophy and holy metaphysics make the Lord God corporeal and incorporeal in his existences in the government of the world. Leviathan is the animal life in the integrate degree; the father of mortality and the god and ruler of mortal gods; and the covenant and lawgiver reigning over the higher animal kingdom.

Leviathan's unicorn power is the animal nature; and leviathan, who is the animal spirit of power and might, is the second higher rank of the animal kingdom endowed with human facilities and characteristics. This is the spirit of knowledge that God has purged and refined in mankind to use the cattle that he created for man's glory and pleasure, so that when man puts on the holy, happy, and perfect spirit, his servants will put on their natural image and power, so that they will be wise and harmless, having a knowledge of the divine seed, and obedience to their God.

The savage and ravenous beasts shall put on the spirit of the cattle, which spirit has been subdued and polished by man's cruel spirit; then there will be no more destruction upon humanity, for all powers shall hold their creative offices. The great power of leviathan's unicorn was the mighty power that ruled and prevailed over the woman who brought forth the man child. This jealous sovereign prevailed in millennium with such mighty power that it smote her rational intellect and made her devoid of wisdom, so that she had no power nor substance in her to overcome, because she was organized with the substances to be overcome by the powers of animal nature. There was no other power in her but what was called and chosen by the millennium sovereign to serve and obey the customs and commandments of jealousy. The power in her was monstrous, and ruled with great dominion, because she held a legal claim over the Christ; and he had been commanded to go and be her companion to fulfil this purpose as touching on the monstrosity of mortality in the two sexes.

The commandment that God gave his Christ, to go and be an helpmeet for millennium, bound him to her to carry out his predestination in the holy exegesis of the Scriptures concerning righteousness and unrighteousness. And through the righteousness and faithfulness of one man in the annals of this doctrine's mission, all whom God has called and fashioned for this purpose may be made righteous through being faithful and obedient to the holiness and perfection of God, manifested in the one man. And the wickedness which was sealed, and prevailed against the righteous, found in the first-fruits of righteousness, have given all who seek the way of life the knowledge of sin and the knowledge of righteousness.

Again, I shall declare the mighty and essential powers of the unclean beast that made war against God's Christ by the natural claim held over him by the woman to whom the temple Samuel was wedded physically. When the Lamb overcame this animal power which governed, through jealousy, the woman to whom he was wedded physically, the essential predominance of jealousy used the temple Caroline, who exercised all the power of the first beast, who held the first claim over Samuel, and whose claim was broken by the blood of the Lamb.

The triumphing victory that Samuel obtained over the first beast was through meekness and patience, serenity and endurance, which was to be still, and wait until the appointed time. And his victory over the second beast, or animal spirit, came through the power of wisdom and understanding in the interpretation and utterance of divine truth in solving the mystery of the woman fleeing into the wilderness, which fulfils God's words, saying, "The burden of Tyre. Howl, ye ships of Tarshish; for it is laid waste, so that there is no house, no entering in: from the land of Chittim it is revealed to them. Be still, ye inhabitants of the Isle; thou whom the merchants of Zidon, that pass over the sea, have replenished. And by great waters the seed of Sihor, the harvest of the river, is her revenue; and she is a mart of nations." — Isa. 23.

The mighty powers of the animal kingdom, which ruled and governed the queen of millennium, made her a pseudo-prophetess : and this animal power destroyed her divine wisdom, and all understanding of holiness unto God, so that she had no substance reigning in her during these phenomena to overpower the great errors of sin. Therefore her holy king suffered her to be punished and cast down to humility, to redeem her from the will of error, by the time appointed for all of these things to be fulfilled.

Near the latter part of the desolate and hopeless adventures of the seventh seal, the sanctuary was informed that Martha, who was left in Springfield, cherished a desire to come to Boston, and work to help support the desolate family. The sanctuary wrote an epistle to her, saying that she could come, providing she came before the termination of the seventh seal, which offer Martha gladly accepted; and she consecrated herself to the will and purposes of the sanctuary from the time of her arrival in Boston, which was November 18, 1890. The sanctuary tried and purged her, by different changes, to see whether she was sincere in her request and in the desire which she had shown. This was based wholly upon signs and actions, and was also to see whether she was circumcised in heart to carry out any purpose that the Lord God saw fit to perform through her.

Martha subdued herself to divine will and purposes in every command, which qualified her to make holy offerings unto the Lord God, to support the desolate family. The first holy sacrifice offered by Martha was placed by her upon the golden altar of divinity, and accepted on the first day of April, 1891. In the time that intervened from the eighteenth of November, 1890, the sanctuary was preparing her to make holy sacrifices unto the Lord God. He gave Martha her preference in working for the two families, the natural and divine, which was that if she desired to become a full member of the divine family, she could not entertain the former claim which she held over the natural family ; and she had to deny and forsake them, and work wholly for the kingdom of Christ.

The sanctuary also made Martha to know that if the natural family wanted to hear from her, or to know anything pertaining to the divine family, they must write to the sanctuary, for he was always ready to sympathize rationally. He instructed Martha that she should not look back, and feel sorrowful over the loss of them ; if she did this, she would perish. Hence Martha was tried sufficiently concerning her devotion toward blood-kin, so that she would live disconnected with them, to consecrate her body to the will of the Supreme.

The sanctuary became zealous to abolish desolation, and after the termination of the seven seals, he determined to put John to work out among the people, which he finally did ; and John made a vow that he would work for the sanctuary, but not according to his own desire and pleasure ; "for," said he, " I will do any kind of work that thou givest me to do, for the advancement of thy cause and kingdom." The sanctuary obtained a few hours of job-work for him to do, which he did ; and this was the first step he made during the time of desolation, in the method of offering sacrifices, and when the sanctuary saw that he committed his way unto the Lord God, he then sought other work for him. The sanctuary put an advertisement in the newspapers to secure regular work for John, but no work was obtained. He then began to make atonements, to lift up the desolate city, which read as follows : —

ATONEMENT OF THE LAMB, JANUARY 31, 1891.

I, Samuel, the messenger of this covenant, solemnly and zealously make this most ardent appellation unto thee, thou adorable and almighty Prince of this covenant, for thou to work through me one of thy supreme attractions, to lift us up from this abominable state. The yoke of bondage lay heavily upon us, because the deluge of abominations prevails as though it has no end. Carry us to the mountain of Ararat, where we may rest the soles of our feet ; for this flood has prevailed long enough against us. Father, command it to subside, and it shall be done.

We declare that thou hast, by the flood of thy supreme words, swallowed up the old worlds, which are now overflowed with waters. Command the mortal breath which is penetrating the systems of these victims to desert the temples, and abominations will surely end. We are placed in such a cursed state and hopeless condition that only thy tenderest mercy and greatest care are able to redeem us from where we have been driven. Watch over us ; and be thou zealous minded concerning our desolation. Has desolation an end ? Rise up and place thine eyes on the end, and enable us to proclaim it in truth and reality.

Give thy luminous light to the woman who was forced into the wilderness, or darkness, because of the persecutions she received from the red-head dragon. Rise up and show thyself to her, and drive him away from her. Cause every lie to be swallowed up by the victory of the truth; and show thyself to this people. Father, let this atonement go into a sure and hasty effect; for how can I longer forbear on this point? Awake to the redemption of this covenant; and through thy material eyes, wisdom, strength, and power, search out a more prosperous city for Israel's material camp-ground; for the burden of expense is laid heavily upon us; so take it away, and point us out a favorable place. Let this atonement be speedily received into thy courts above, and answered by a visible manifestation of it in the metropolis of immortality; and through thy power, carry this thing into effect, and speedily elevate this covenant.

When this atonement was made, the sanctuary put John to work recording the writings; and at this time the sanctuary began lifting himself up from desolation. This was the crepuscule of the eternal light of divine truth, and the time the saints possessed the holy kingdom, and began to consume the beasts of mortality that continuated the powers of desolation.

ATONEMENT OF THE LAMB FOR THE REMODELLING OF THE HOLY CHARIOT.

I, Samuel, the friendless, desolate, forlorn, and forsaken messenger of this covenant, make the most vehement petition unto thee, thou dreadful and terrible Majesty who reigns over and establishes the laws of the divine and physical worlds, and maketh whom thou wilt the ruler over the works of thy hands. Thou hast created the substance, ordered and fashioned the entire rig and chariot of divinity; thou wast the smith and wheelwright who built and set it in running motion; thou, also, when thou couldst no longer forbear to see thy holy name blasphemed among the profane nations, suffered it to collide with the chariot of hell, and dashed it to shivers. Thou didst this in a short period of time; and I know that thou canst repair the same chariot in the same time, restore it to its perfect state, put the four wheels where they will fit, and start it in motion as thou hast declared should be done at the end of the deluge of abominations.

Father, here we lay the four broken wheels, which are the running-gear to the holy chariot; and thou canst repair at once these which thou hast broken. We will show forth thy marvellous works unto all nations of the earth whom thou hast made to be instrumental according to thy ordained purposes. Bring it about by raising up thy chosen people, and make them peculiar and zealous in performing the things that thou hast purposed for them to do. Cause the light of thy countenance to cast its reflection upon this people; and make them what thou hast declared they should be after encountering the seven great trials of the world. It wast thou who laid us waste; thou didst it to carry thy determination into effect, in fulfilment of all righteousness; and this was to bring thy words, spoken by the holy prophets, of what should be in the latter days, to pass.

All that would befall thy people, to try them and wear them out — all this has come upon us, and we have not denied thy name, neither lifted up our hands and cried unto a strange God, by departing from thy precepts. And now we cry unto thee for the fulfilment of thy blessed promises, which is victory over all mortal science, false and perishable ways, and a full access into thy glory and kingdom; this is the reward of the saints. We shall wait here to achieve victory over all mortal things, and receive that great prize which thou hast promised to this people. Let the judgments of the saints on the inheritance of this great recompense be received into thy council above; and when thou art ready to gratify the saints on this petition, let it be manifested upon the ensign, and it shall be promulgated among thine elect; and thou shalt receive the glory, honor, and blessing perpetually. January 31, 1893.

THANKSGIVING OF THE SAINTS; THEY CONFESS THE MARVELLOUS WORKS OF GOD, AND THE SAFETY OF HIS WORK WHEN ACCOMPLISHED.

Father, we give thanks unto thee, because thou hast removed from us those abominable and desolating reproaches, under which no flesh can ever rise to a free, friendly state. We thank and honor thy name, because when thou hast once removed a stroke from us, it can never return. We praise thy name forever; for when thou exaltest us but a little, there is no power able to abase us, nor to turn us back, for the former trials passeth away, just as thou leadest us along this journey. We can say that we are founded on that substance that cannot waste away and wear down like other substances; though it appeareth small, it abideth forever. We are heartily thankful unto thee, because thou hast removed the great curse from our store-houses, barns, and provision baskets, which have, these many days, perpetuated desolation.

We thank and applaud thy name, because thou hast fulfilled the time of desolation, hast enabled us to see it, and write it upon paper in words of pure gold, which have been tried and purified seven times by fire, so that all may read it, eyes be opened to see it, hearts be opened to believe and receive it, and ears to hear it and be converted to thy way before it springs forth. We thank thee, because thou hast given us eyes to see, but not as others see. Thou hast given us eyes to see, and hearts to understand, that the work thou hast purposed to do is accomplished when the word is spoken by thee, saying, "What shall be done?" Whether others can see it or not, it is finished when the creative source of power declares it so; therefore I declare that our friendless, forlorn, and solitary desolation here ends, and the great curse is removed from the holy city. Let thy name be lauded and exalted above the gods of the earth; for thou only art worthy to be exalted in the earth.

Now we shall ask thee to open the barren womb that dost not bear, which definates the opening of the gates of Jerusalem; for without are all manner of abominable things which time and space will not allow us to narrate. Inasmuch as our suffering has gone to the full extreme to fulfil the prophecies concerning the abominations of desolation, we require, from this time henceforth, thy extreme, tenderest mercy, power and riches, glory and honor, strength and wisdom and blessing, to redeem us from where we have been driven. Thou hast used the seven great powers of abomination to overthrow us and abase us: so we beseech thee to make use of the same number of divinity to lift up thy sanctuary among the nations. Make us to harmonize with perfect divinity; and establish us among honorable beings, among whom we are now travelling in a disguised way, and as thieves that cometh by night when the watchman sleepeth. When he awaketh, he findeth his goods are broken into and stolen. We have searched diligently into this matter, and are more than sure that where there is non-unity there is no prosperity nor power.

We ask thee, with solemnity of heart, to bring us together in perfect union, under one command, one love, one God, one knowledge, one understanding, one aim, one desire, one intention, one spirit, one baptism. Cast out of the members of the sanctuary those abominable heretics who oppose thy truth, and wrest against thy anointed sayings, counsel, and judgment. We have found it to be truth and surety that thy supreme regenerating power exists in thy word when proclaimed by thy chosen spokesman, who is thy scientific word of flesh.

We have borne the memoir of this truth, that the unity of word, spirit, and truth is the science of salvation wrought in thy material body. We have also borne the memoir of this truth, that we cannot compound eternal science with mortal science; neither can man obtain this life by searching for it with earthly wisdom and understanding. All whom thou hast chosen and ordained can have full access into this life; the wise and prudent of the world cannot see life.

Father, thou hast enabled us to see that thy plain and simple hand created and fashioned this character of mankind; and the same hand which is grasped upon these pages can abolish the wise and prudent characteristics, so that the material may be fashioned to come into thy rest. We implore thee to abolish the haughty and high lookers, and fashion them to inhale the full science of life. Give them eyes to see, and understanding to see and understand the fulness of thy power, just as it is revealed in a simple way; bring them to love and magnify thy simple ways and works, which are as great as thy supremacy in the highest.

The only way to make this people acquiescent is to make simple the great, and make wise the simple; this will bring in the combinations of godliness and the harmony of spirits. Let this thing come about at once, and we will have a material manifestation that we have made a dissolution of friendship with the mighty agents of desolation forever.

THE SAINTS PRAYETH FOR THE REVELATION OF THE SON OF RIGHTEOUSNESS IN THE FULNESS.

I, Samuel, the called and chosen messenger of this covenant, accompanied by the incorporeal saints, make known our compulsive needs unto thee, thou all-wise King of kings and Lord of lords. Our request is great and notable; and thou art more than worthy of adoration when it is complied with. It reads as follows: —

Quicken the elements of word, spirit, and truth, and force them into one great head; and reveal the science of sempiternity, which is wrought in thy material body. Reveal it in all of its many changes and branches, and its wonderful phenomena. Continue to rough-hew out wisdom's seven great pillars, and thereby the son of man will be revealed. Place thine eyes on the seven great fundamental principles of thy kingdom, and I will begin to blast out, and then polish, the stones, the chief stones to the building of thy house.

We have determined to throw out of the members of thy sanctuary all damnable doctrines, and heretics who will not adhere to the doctrines of holy truth. This matter will be accomplished by the power of thy judgments, which have already been passed on the wicked. We find that these heretics are willing to take thee in part and reject the fulness, which keeps thy kingdom divided against itself. We will now rise up and blot out these heretics, and raise up a people that will take thee in the fulness through a speedy refraction of light. We acknowledge that the fulness of thy holy kingdom is contained in both divine and physical things; and we acknowledge that thou hast used both divine and physical agents to accomplish thy purposes in this thy fulness; so let us go in and possess them, and be glorified therewith.

Let us come into thy glorious presence, where we can see the wonderful make of thine hand, both physical and divine. Blot out all forms of godliness, so that thou mayest be glorified in thine elect over the artistical and skilful works of thine hands. Let this atonement spring forth at once, and thou wilt reveal thy goodness to us in its perfection. Let the affluent and mellifluous tide of thy words flow full and free, and in just such simple way as thou hast declared should be done. Let purity exist in this people while I am in thy simple course of writing, searching, and digging for the seven pillars of wisdom.

Let not thy simplicity be longer contemned by this people; and make them to glory in thy words, to attain unto that for which they have so long and ardently hoped.

When this is given to us, we will flow into the seven streams of wisdom, and what will be the result? A miracle will fall, and thy fulness will come to sight.

THE SAINTS TURNETH HEARTY THANKFULNESS UNTO THEIR KING FOR REDEMPTION AFTER A SERIES OF PRAYER.

We thank and adore thy name forever, thou Most High, because thou hast fulfilled our desire through the attainment of the thing we have so long hoped for. Thou hast brought it to pass, in accordance with thy promises, through thy marvellous power ; and hast redeemed Jerusalem, and we are safe in thee. The storms of the wicked have fully passed over, and we have landed safely in the ark of life. The violent ones are destroyed, the flood of abominations has subsided, and we have landed on Canaan's side, where thou art undisguised, and hast shown thyself to us, and where we can stand before thy face in peace, and make perfect peace with thee for the evil we have committed in sinning against thy holy sanctuary.

We have settled the bills that we created upon thy holy hills, and are free from any claim that can be brought against us, through the marvellous power which has already been wrought in us. The hazards and perils have all passed by, and we are at home with thee in the word, spirit, and truth. The yoke of bondage was laid heavily upon us; but thou hast consumed it by the blast of thy nostrils, and we are embraced in thy arms of love. Now let thy name be extolled, and exalted above the heathen dwelling in the earth ; for our very hearts sing praises unto thee for thy marvellous works. The personal presence of the Lord and Saviour Jesus Christ is with you now, henceforth, and forever.

The revealing and recording of these mysteries, in those days when the complete book of divine psychology was outlined, was the spiritual building of the waste places and desolate walls of Jerusalem. Divine word, spirit, and truth are the stone walls, the temple, the building, the waters, the builders, the inhabitants, the implements of war, and the translunary light of the New Jerusalem ; also the king reigning over the New Jerusalem, and comprises the totalship of the holy city, the New Jerusalem that is herein revealed from God, through man, unto the sons of men, that they may eventually become sons of God through receiving the fulness of his power, which is contained in the life of the New Jerusalem.

As soon as the building of the walls of the New Jerusalem began, the host of perdition awoke afresh, and stood in arms within the recording secretary, in combat against the New Jerusalem, to hinder the building of the walls. When the regiments of perdition did not use the recording secretary, they used the house keeper of the sanctuary to cause the work to cease; but the sanctuary made atonements each time that those tyrants stood in arms within the earthly bodies, to hinder the building. Nothing the God-man said or did was able to destroy their power, except through atonements; and when each atonement was made, that rebellious regiment that stood in arms against the saints was slain by the fierce wrath and vengeance of the sanctuary, which manifested itself in the language and expression of each atonement.

The historical parts of the apostolic Bible made acute repetitions of its work in a spiritual light, in all the different parts where it had not been done, which made the building of the walls of Jerusalem severely troublous and hopeless, and made the relapsation of solitary desolation imminent. The powers of desolation fought desperately against the New Jerusalem, to overcome, so that the holy saints would not possess the divine kingdom, but to no avail; the powers of perdition were overcome by the blood of the Lamb, propelled by the great testimonies of prophecies.

The nefarious and tyrannical powers of corruption were so prevalent in Caroline and John that these implacable powers stood up in the earth, and held mental rebellions against the New Jerusalem when he acted kindly toward those who had consecrated themselves to offer sacrifices upon the holy altar. These tyrannies opposed everything which the sanctuary said and did in compassion of the sacrificers ; and they scorned them in the worst way, actively, and would not so much as rise and offer them a seat when they visited the sanctuary with their holy offerings. They scorned them, and respected them not; and they partially thought the New Jerusalem to be such as they were, because of his long time of silence on this truth. They also magnified themselves above the oblations, and used blasphemous remarks concerning them, as though the sanctuary erred through receiving them ; but the sanctuary had no other means of support. These heretics consecrated and devoted themselves to unreasonable, corrupt, and pseudodox doctrines, in every sense of the word, and accepted no truth of any weight.

These two empires (John and Caroline) were received and honored by the members of the New Jerusalem as equal to the sanctuary, until they were uncovered and revealed ; and then their nakedness was seen as it was. The sanctuary did not cover their corrupt embodiments, when he discovered the truism of the mysteries concerning them, because he found them to be the fulness of the spiritual devils who came among the saints scientifically and disguisedly, — by being transformed into angels of light, — deceived the holy people, and prevailed against them until all these things were fulfilled.

The pseudo-prophetic powers of divination were so strongly seated in these two empires that John did not wish to do the recording, when the building of the walls of the New Jerusalem commenced, and Caroline was above doing any work for the sacrificers, and magnified herself above doing her own housework. Nothing could be done to satisfy these two subjects of perdition. They were above working in the outside world, because they were opposed to all things, and were above all things which heretofore existed, now exist, or shall exist henceforth; and for this cause they were devoid of foundation and summit, which shows that they were by nature and inheritance the bottomless pit, called "hell," and by the doctrine of metempsychosis, they were the embodiment of the animal kings and queens, being first in order and predominance, Lucifer, leviathan, the subtle unicorn, and the great dragon. The judgments of the Lord God, harmonizing with the prophecies, and bearing testimony that they were the cycle of hell, the power and strength of the Devil s kingdom, were the burning flames that destroyed their cities and towns, revenue and implements of war; slaughtered their cattle; detonated their ships; overthrew their governments, the ruling sceptre, and gradually consumed the inhabitants of these empires out of the land.

In spite of all John and Caroline could do or say, in struggling to overpower and triumph over the heretics' despotic dominion, they had power to govern the land, and do according to their own will. And they revived in the earth and partially equalled and obumbrated the bright Son light of the New Jerusalem in every branch of divine scientific wisdom, while the Holy Son solved the deep mysteries of righteousness and unrighteousness, and wielded the weapons of truth to disannul sin, and obliterate the heretics' principles.

THE SAINTS PRAYETH UNTO THE LORD GOD FOR DELIVERANCE FROM THE LUSTFUL POWERS OF THE FEMININE AND MASCULINE LEVIATHAN'S UNICORN; UTTERANCE ON ANIMALISM.

We commend thee, thou all-wise Prince of peace, and wonderful Counsellor, to deliver us from the cursed, lustful, and damning desires of the feminine and masculine unicorn, whose powers of lasciviousness continuate adultery in the sanctuary. We commend thee to cast out of the members of thy sanctuary the science of necromancy. Wilt thou let this scientific adulterating power defile our lives continually? We declare that this lustful abomination has reached the ultimate limits: so let it from this time be cast into the nethermost region. Let these words of science wash and cleanse our garments from the stains of this venomous reptile; and he will speedily desert thy holy sanctuary, and cease from diluting its strength and power. This will open the gates of the New Jerusalem for all honorable people among all nations to gain entrance into the holy city, where they will be exempt from this slavish curse.

We have searched this matter diligently in judgment, and have come to a final decision that the ravenous lust of the woman's flesh is the fœtus of sin, and is called "the flesh of swine." For this cause we acknowledge that it is abhorring unto all human flesh, and we also confess that it is the scientific ruling influence of the unicorn, the ravenous desire for sexual intercourse. We thank thee for thy power of triumph, because thou hast by the omniscience of thy wisdom fully destroyed the ruling power of the subtle unicorn, which has prevailed over thy sanctuary of life, light, and righteousness; and we are still at home with thee in thy holy temple.

When this atonement was made, the sovereign power of the subtle unicorn was prevailing in the temples of perdition: and these two had no other desire than to please the ravenous appetite of the subtle unicorn, the great lascivious king, who inflames nature with the desire of pairing, and seduces male and female to live in the state of prostitution. John wanted to live with Caroline connubially; and Caroline held the nuptial claim over Samuel, and demanded her nuptial rights and privileges. She forced her personal and lascivious desires upon Samuel to live with her connubially; and at times, when her unicorn became ravenous to approach the nearness of Samuel's body, the sanctuary partially yielded up his body to a certain extent to gratify the wishes of the feminine unicorn. From these tests he gained a sufficient proof that she was not devoted to him in unreasonable love for the inheritance of his pure life; but her executive desires were the craftiness of the Devil's kingdom, to continuate adultery in the holy sanctuary, and amalgamate with divinity.

By the sanctuary's yielding up his body to a certain extent to the desire of the monstrous unicorn, he took upon himself the loathsome effects, to rise up in vengeance and destroy the power of the unicorn from the members of the sanctuary. He bore the manifestation of the flagrant desires and loathsome effects it has upon humanity;

and also obtained a knowledge of its prevalence and strength in human nature while in its rage. The essential power of the subtle unicorn was seated in the Levite or colored race ; which power is called the "leviathan unicorn."

The subtle unicorn, which is the propensity to nourish sexua desire, is the deleterious current of mortality, which is seated in the Ethiopian race in its greatest power, and inflames their desire to gratify it. This flaming desire subdues and consecrates the Ethiopians, and compels them to serve, glorify, honor, and obey their unicorn king ; this power compels them to make the glory of the unicorn a specialty, and their chief object in life. This brutal power has always made void the intellectual facilities of Ethiopia in general, so that there could be no natural progression toward the higher plains of life to compete with the other godly races. All races in existence have fed from this current of animal nature, which has revolved from generation to generation, and increased in strength in each generation until it reached the fulness of art and enchantment, to win its prey.

Ethiopia is the root and fœtus, and the perpetuator of animalism in humanity ; and comprises in characteristics the fulness of the animal race. Through the amalgamation of human races, all have put on, through inheritance, the animal image, whose attributes are peculiar to those of Ethiopia. Still, the Lord God put it in the hearts of the other godly races to reject their fellow-men, Ethiopia. This was to keep the Ethiopian race from fully mingling with those races which had not the root and sovereignty of the Abyssinian race planted in them. The spiritual weapons of cruelty have always existed in Ethiopia ; and this spiritual sovereign has used the other races according to will to make manifest animalism, materially.

The prejudice and scornfulness which God has suffered to reign in the other races, to look upon Ethiopia as an inferior race, have kept the predominance of the root and fœtus of the animal race at home in Ethiopia. This was that God might make his postmillennium to the earth, Ethiopia, and abolish death and hell, the stings and dominion of sin, by destroying animalism from the land of Eden, where the Lord God was glorified in the beginning.

The cycle of Ethiopia has been redeemed from animalism ; and the Lord God is now glorified in the fragrant and luminous land of Eden, as it was in the beginning. Inasmuch as all nations have shared with Ethiopia's abominable principles, all nations shall share with their honorable characteristics, in God's glory, so that Lord the God will be polytheistic and anthropomorphistic in the glory, honor, and confession of his supreme power in the government of the worlds.

All abominable powers and agents which are controlling humanity were created out of lust, called by its existing name, "human nature;" but its proper name is "animal nature." The ravenous powers of animalism created in mankind all dishonorable characteristics that have ever wielded the weapons of cruelty over humanity; and for this cause animal nature comprises all powers of corruption and abject abominations affluent in the human family.

PART VII.

ATONEMENT OF THE LAMB FOR THE REDEMPTION OF JERUSALEM, AND TO NULLIFY HER SUPPRESSIVE POWERS OF SIN.

My dear Father, arise at once, and in haste, and return unto Zion, the mother Jerusalem, with joy, peace, and singing. Cause her mourning, restlessness, reproaches, and torments to cease immediately, and suffer them to be no more. Visit upon her the days of youth, when she came up out of the land of Egypt. Cause her marrow to wake from slumber and disgustfulness, that her bones may flourish and sing praises unto thee. Loosen the bands of Pleiades, and Orion will give his perfect light; Mazaroth will put off obscurity, and become the sons of Arcturus. Cause the constellations to give their glorious and luminous lights, and darkness will flee away, and the wilderness will be turned into a green plain.

Array Caroline in a robe of righteousness, and adorn her with the ornaments of fine rubies and pearls, diamonds and fine gold. Sprinkle her with the superfluous perfumes of frankincense, myrrh, and aloes. Plunge the tabernacle into the seven streams of thy supremacy, return unto her with love, glory, honor, and majesty, and suffer the earth no longer to be desolate; let her go at once, so that the tabernacle may be at rest. Come quickly unto thy masculine tabernacle with the flaming sword and the fire of truth, disintegrate abominaticns, and discipline her to cohere to the fulness of the perfect doctrines, and I will solicit thy full promises. This will raise up the former desolation, and build the waste and desolate city; this is the thing we greatly need.

I implore thee, defer not, but come speedily to Jerusalem's redemption; and she will walk in thy way, and keep thy statutes forever. I have searched her out, and have found the mysteries of her disobedience: she was clothed in filthy garments, to carry out the time of thy terrible judgments, and finish up the time of thy great calamities upon sin and iniquity. I have condemned this garment, and cast it into the pit; she has labored, and paid the price to procure the promised life; she is worthy to attain unto thy supreme feminine love, glory, honor, and majesty. She has paid the price to obtain a crown of life, and the office which thou hast promised her; and she is fully worthy of thy entire feminine glory: to reign with me, and live forever,— to reign with me on earth, and enjoy the fulness of the wonderful things which thou hast created, fashioned, and prepared for thy people's glory, that thou mayest be glorified in them over thine artistic patents invented through the agency of the natural man.

Father, according to my judgment in pointed and brief remarks, come now into thy holy temple and make full manifestation of this atonement made by the Son, and fashion her after the image and likeness of thy spiritual feminine person. Hear, and consider my judgment, and let it be received, and recorded upon the book of truth; and she shall enter into my rest, and cease from torments and suffering, to which she has been subject these many days. Make haste, dear Father, and come with thy redeeming love, and I will lift her above the swellings of Jordan. Suffer thy feminine tabernacle to be no longer contemned by this people. Come hastily, with the request of this atonement, and I will snatch her from the will of the arbitrary powers now holding her in bondage, and lift her up so that she may be thy glory through generations to come, and praise thee for thy wonderful victory and thy mighty power wrought in her to compass mankind to his creative state.

This atonement was made November 21, 1890, and recorded when the building of the walls of Jerusalem began; and these words fortified the walls of Jerusalem so that other oppressors and spoilers of the land could not enter to continuate desolation.

These words made inert the influx of corruption, and every pseudodox opinion which had formerly flowed through the land with irresistible power; after which, when an enemy who was besieged in the land stood up, this flaming sword turned every way to abolish evil seducers from the glorious land, and prevented others from reinhabiting the tabernacle. The mighty weapons of the Lord God were drawn without warning when an enemy was spied in the land; and the battles were severe and acute each time, until every mortal soul was consumed out of the land, the paradise of the Lord God, from the two empires contiguous to Eden.

The Sincere Petition of the Saints, that God May Make a Complete End of Warriors in Israel.

I, Samuel, the full, focalized embodiment of thy holy kingdom and its angelic musical hosts, herewith bring our needs to thee, our Father, knowing that thou wilt come speedily to our redemption, after hearing our cries and complaints. The land whereinto thou hast commanded us to go and to possess is inhabited by warriors and men of valor; they have gathered in all of their valiant men of different cities and countries, and have arrayed themselves in battle against us. They have fully fortified the land which thou hast given unto us, saying we should go in at once and possess it. We know that the land is ours; and we also know that we shall possess the land as thou hast declared; not by our own power and might, but through thy terribleness, and by thy strong arm of war, we shall destroy and drive out of the land these many hostile nations, from the beautiful and fertile plains of Jordan, and have the land for an everlasting blessing.

Father, allow us to entreat thee, inserting the facts, that those nations are gigantic warriors; and they are as the sand by the seashore, innumerable. They are men of renown; they are men of great skill, and exceedingly dextrous; and only thine instruments and weapons of war are qualified to subdue them, bring them under our subjection, free the land from their laws and governments, and give us full access thereinto, make the land blessed, build and inhabit the cities, and make them cities of praises unto thee forever. We have looked upon their cities, and find that they are totally corrupt; so let fire and brimstone rain down from thee out of heaven, and destroy them utterly from the land. Then the request of our petition will go hastily into effect; and the builders will return to the building of the walls of Jerusalem, and join them together; and the work will prosper in our hands, because we have seen the aim of our enemies, and will not make peace with them.

We bring not this petition unto thee for the satisfying of flesh, but for the express purpose of redeeming thy kingdom; and this thing no flesh is striving to accomplish as thou hast determined it shall be. Any way but the way thou hast determined is by far the better way, and most pleasant way, to all flesh, because thy way seemeth hard to them. We have meditated on this mystery with great care; and we have decided, unanimously, that thou hast taken the historical parts of the apostolic Bible for us to publish by; and also as eye-glasses, for us to look through into thy spiritual book. We can see clearly that all evil spirits who fought against thee of old in different material bodies, when thou wast setting the type, are here today in an individual body, — he whom thou prepared through the past ages to reach the fulness of wickedness. These opposing despots have the same power to destroy thy people as they had in ancient days, when they dwelt each one in a separate temple.

We also confess that we have the same number of ancient holy people working through thy mighty power to destroy wickedness from the earth as thou hadst in days of old. Unless thou wilt fight our battle for us, as thou didst fight for us in ancient days, we cannot say that we shall conquer; because we cannot trust in our own arm to save, for thou hast taught us that he who trusteth in the arm of flesh shall perish, because he shall not be able to deliver himself. For this cause we care not do any, for all attempts but thine have failed, and for this cause we present the accomplishment of this petition into thine hands, knowing that thou performest the things which thou doest in righteousness, and judgest all things rightly.

We present this great battle into thy hands, knowing that through thee we can be made men of valor, men of renown, and men of skill and sound discretion; and know how to judge the good from the evil, and know who are worthy of thy love and mercy. All this we acknowledge through thy power and spirit of acknowledgment, and without thee we can do no good thing.

At the time of this atonement, the builders were forced to leave the walls because an innumerable number of ancient kings and princes had wakened in the land of rebellion to hinder the work of revealing and recording, which was then going on. When the sanctuary made this atonement, he saw it was the aim of the warriors to defeat his plan in building the walls of Jerusalem; for they had taken the recording secretary into captivity, to cause the work to cease. The waters of Jerusalem froze thickly over, when the sanctuary was compelled to make this atonement; and in the meantime no stone could be laid upon the walls of Jerusalem securely, and if the builders attempted to put the stones upon the walls they did not fit. At this time the builders could not join the walls together; many compartitions had been built, but the builders could not get them to connect substantially; one part of the writing disagreed with the other.

The sanctuary was compelled to make many researches, with the most exquisite care, assiduous discretion, judicious wisdom and understanding, to overpower the Lucifer competitor. The Lucifer race revived in the recording secretary, through whom they brought in a mixture of impure stones, by disagreeing with the wonderful revelation, which came through the pseudo-wisdom and self-conception which Lucifer propelled through his agent, John. This pseudodox medium made inert the warm influx of the holy waters of the New Jerusalem; and brought on a cold wave over the holy and fruitful land.

The sanctuary searched with the fulness of diligence, and he saw no way to join the walls together, for every attempt had failed. He had much written ahead of the recorder, and one part was discordant with the other; and the recorder had refused to do the writing, when called upon by the sanctuary. The collateral atonement ignited in the sanctuary, and burning flames of fiery vengeance leaped out of his mouth, in wrath against the warriors, in pointed and brief remarks, which fell upon John, declaring that he must surrender to the truth, or there would be a separation. This utterance was the fire and brimstone which the Lord God rained down upon the ancient, wicked cities of Sodom and Gomorrah, and different kingdoms and races that fought against the righteous seed during the Mosaic dispensation and at other times and periods, who declared war in the temple John, in the strongest way, to cause the building of the walls of Jerusalem to cease. Those tyrannies were prevalent in John in the most diabolical way; and each tyrannical principle in the Gentile epitome represented a wicked tribe; and each tribe had a king over them to command, govern, and point out the course to pursue through the mighty power of his strategy.

The following names are the kings and princes who rule the corpuscules of abominations; and the meaning of each name represents the subordinate officers and common members who are involved in each kingdom, and are the tribes of the wicked who have revolved from the antediluvian world through the doctrine of metempsychosis, and made war with righteousness through all the past ages of the world. Lustfulness and enmity, hopelessness and carelessness, haughtiness and uncivilization, stubbornness and greediness, unthankfulness and unfearfulness, laziness and stupidity, jealousy and disbelief, scornfulness and vainglory, self-esteem and deceivableness, craftiness and hypocrisy, hypercriticism and self-conceitedness, scepticism and egotism, niggardliness and whimsicality, contemptibleness and independence, selfishness and superstition, sensuality and blasphemy, idolatry and disobedience, thieving and adultery, opposition and sagement, strife and brutality, insanity and lying — these powers have ruled over humanity and rebelled against righteousness since righteousness was driven by them from the glorious paradise and Eden of the Lord God.

When the sanctuary had pealed the utterance of thunder against those sovereign powers of depravity, he gave John warning to flee hastily from those principles metaphored as Sodom and Gomorrah, lest he should be consumed by God's vengeance, which fought against those principles, endeavoring to devour them at once. These pernicious and tyrannical principles made the time troublous, and continued the curse; which diluted the strength and power of the holy sanctuary of truth unto the end of the three years and nine months of prophecy against this black embodiment of death and hell's bitumen.

THE SAINTS PRAYETH FOR THE LORD GOD TO DESTROY UTTERLY THE ENTIRE WICKED WORLD OF KINGSHIP, NULLIFY ALL WICKEDNESS, AND ESTABLISH THE SON OF RIGHTEOUSNESS, WHO SHALL REIGN IN LOVE, HONOR, AND MAJESTY.

Father, we beseech thee to be attentive unto our prayer; hear and consider our cry. We are greatly suppressed by those ancient kings who now rebel against us, and impede the course that thou hast commanded us to pursue. They have taken some of thy chosen people into captivity, and they are greatly in bondage; there is no way for redemption but through thee. Let the words of thy power, and the fire of thy wrath and vengeance awake, as a man of war, and sever the wicked from among the good.

When thou utterly destroyest all of the immaterial ancient warriors and false hearts that fought against us of old, and are now resurrected in the earth to obstruct thy course of work and pre-ordination, we will sing the free song. They have been resurrected in this day to obliterate righteousness; and they are working more in unity in this day than they did in the past ages of the epochs of righteousness and unrighteousness. We find that they are in this day warring in their supreme skill and unity, manifested in the chief principles of abominations. We know that these cursed warriors of hell will never reach the point to agree with thee in thy way, and it is good for it to be so. When thou puttest on thy humble acts they are supercilious; and when thou art lofty they are humble and meek. Thine eyes have seen that these sagacious Abyssinians can imitate thee in all thy righteous ways, can show themselves more righteous than thee, while I am in this delusive course of work. Why dost thou allow them to mock thee continually? Why dost thou not say conclusively that thou wilt no longer be blasphemed by these bloody-hearted dogs, and destroy them from among us? They are no friends to us, nor ever will be; then why dost thou try us continually concerning them? I will answer that it is to show thy supreme power through a compendium spiritual repetition of the dark-aged literal type, which was set for us to show forth the hidden secrets and realities of thee. For this cause we do not demand an unfinished ceasing of trouble, but for thou to hasten the accomplishment of its repetition through an acute manifestation of the same work.

We do herein acknowledge that our many courses of work are to make a full completement of the Bible, so that thou canst take the literal type and thereby publish the spiritual book. We do herein confess that the spiritual light of the typical Bible history and prophecies is the luminous light of thy sweet, smiling face; and when the spiritual book is taken therefrom, it will be the unveiling of thy blissful, affectionate, and luminous countenance, and thy quickening, bewitching, and blessed face. We also acknowledge, and increase with glory, that a brief exegetical legend of the perils and hardships, which we had to encounter during the time of the great tribulations of the saints, will make an abridged spiritual repetition of prophetic fulfilments, and fulfil literally those prophecies concerning the latter days of sin. This has made our trouble long and severe, and exceedingly troublous and overbearing; and has made our conditions hopeless, which has fully destroyed the power of the holy people, as thou hast declared should be.

How do we know that our power is fully destroyed? Because we have put every enemy under foot, and the trouble still abideth with us. We have committed all things into thy hands to do with as thou thinkest best; and the trouble still abideth at our house. After doing all this, and to no avail, the hope of coming into a better state, in friendship, peace, and unity, and of obtaining the promises made by thee unto this people, is lost in this people. Father, let hope revive in this people by continuating thy supreme attraction in the building of the walls of Jerusalem. Come hastily, and enable us to hope in thy words, which are not of the future, but blesseth today him who trusteth in them. Revive thy work in this people, so that they may live today, and leave off looking into the future days, for there is no life for him who doeth the like.

THE SAINTS PRAYETH FOR PERFECT FRIENDSHIP TO EXIST BETWEEN THEM AND THE RECORDING SECRETARY.

Father, we appeal unto thee, through this petition, in behalf of John, that he may no more be taken into captivity by desperate warriors. Build about him a safe fortification against that wicked man, so that he may no longer suffer by his cruel regiment, with piercing weapons which they have wielded in him by the force of animal propensities. Let perfect harmony exist between him and us, and we will no longer be foes dwelling together in the same house, and fighting to achieve the same victory. Open his heart so that love may come into him for thee and thy holy work. Quicken his heart with pure godly love, and deliver him no more unto the will of cruel men, for we declare there is enough done. Wilt thou reject him any longer? We will answer, No; thou wilt now clothe him with the garments of salvation, and set his feet upon the sure rock, which is these thy words of power.

Father, open the gates of the New Jerusalem unto him and bid him come in, and have a full access into the things which thou hast prepared for thy people; and then the earth will be no more desolate. Father, be merciful unto him, and let not sin any longer have dominion over him. Wilt thou impute upon him this blessing, which is to give him full dominion over all abominations henceforth and forever? These are the promises to thy chosen and faithful people; this is the recompense of the just; and we declare him to be one of thy faithful and chosen people, because he has not denied thy name, although the profound depth and the apex of hell compassed him about. The land still remaineth firm for our inheritance.

He hath continued to suffer and endure unto the end of the prevalence of abominations, which had power to keep the land overwhelmed with griefs, misery, woe, and dense blackness. After enduring unto the end of these mighty powers, thou hast declared that such shall be saved. We declare that he is a fit vessel, and a qualified subject to accomplish any work that thou hast purposed to perform through him. From this time revive thy work in him; and give him the spirit of joy and peace for the spirit of heaviness, griefs, and burdens, so that he may be a tree of righteousness. Suffer him no longer to be made a stigma, a taunt, and a by-word in this assembly, because of impiety. Father, be merciful unto him at once, and build him in love, glory, honor, and majesty of thy kingdom: for after thou gavest him a prelibation of thy blissfulness, thou hast cast him down to darkness and woe. Convey to him the fulness of ecstasy and the holy exegesis of this doctrine, and we know that thou canst be glorified in him most marvellously. Let thy wrath cease from him, for he cannot reach thee in love when thou art angry with him; but thy anger must burn toward the temple until the wicked perish and are consumed out of the land.

Be merciful unto the flesh, let the wicked be hastily exiled from it, and thou canst use the temple with a greater power to establish righteousness than the original powers of sin fought to annihilate thy kingdom. Father, let these words bring this petition to pass very speedily; for the earth now athirsts for mercy and blessedness. Languor and loathing have deprived the temple of strength, which unables the temple to build as he should. Create and fashion him after the style of thine late architecture, and thou canst be glorified in him. Thou hast overthrown the original structure, and now he is but as a dead man. When the mass of ruins is utterly consumed from the land, thine anger will cease, and love and sympathy will abide in thine heart for him, spread abroad over the land, and make it fertile for the growth of immortality.

Cause the beams of thy radiating smiles to cover the land, and eject the creators of darkness, and the voice of the temple will be humble, soft, loving, and affectionate toward thee, and obduration will be no more. Impute upon him thy blessing of prosperity, and this will give him the power of triumph over all abominations ; thy everlasting blessing is to give thy people an integral knowledge of thee. Breathe into him the atmosphere of peace, and he will be at peace with thee ; let thy zephyrus breath breathe within him the fragance of trust, and he will trust in thee ; for he cannot have any of these, unless thou bestowest them upon him a precious gift. Father, give him the precious coins to purchase thy blessings, which are faith and hope, love and trust, stamped upon his heart for thy Christ. This is the means he must have to purchase knowledge, which is immortality reigning in the material body. These precious coins will give a thorough knowledge of thee, which is the knowledge of thy words which, in the past, has been utterly rejected and contemned by him.

Put these bands of iron on him, and make his heart, which is now inflexible to divine will and its pressure, malleable. Make his heart adhere to the holy exegesis, which will stay those black and disgraceful occupants of perdition from him, and redeem him from the power of their pit. Let not the fierceness of thy wrath, which fell upon the cities of Sodom and Gomorrah, which came in fire and blood, mingled with brimstone, abide with him, and compel him to hate thee. Drive away from him those damning thoughts that are harassing him to hate thee ; turn his heart against them, and make him their enemy, and the temple will soon be enfranchised. Open his eyes that he may see ; give hearing to his ears that he may hear ; place thy understanding in his heart, that he may speak of thy mighty power with much pleasure ; and give him a tongue to utter thy truth as it is in thy holy book. He cannot get to thee while he is endued with the wisdom of the earthly, which god his heart is adapted to extoll and commend with much pleasure. Make him to know that the wisdom of the world is envious against thee, and is the striking serpent which is destructive to the progression of one sojourning into thy rest. Break the implacable hold of this finite monster, so that he may vanish away. Put it into his heart to dissolve friendship with his enemies, against whom I now fight, to expel them from the face of the earth. Make him to know that if he continues to sorrow and lament over the loss of them, he must undoubtedly perish and be damned by the power of thy Christ ; for thy immortal soul sorroweth not, and lamenteth not, over the downfall and destruction of the wicked.

Thy Christ was raised up to utterly destroy that wicked being from the material bodies of thine elect, and to give the land unto the saints for their eternal inheritance, which thou aforetime promised unto Abraham's seed. Father, we know that righteousness is Abraham's seed; and the bodies of thy peculiar people that are in all parts of the terrestrial kingdom, among all nations, kings, and tongues, are the land that the righteous seed shall inherit and possess, after ejecting the wicked, who now are using them to their will, glory, and honor. Father, let this prayer of the saints, or atonement of the Lamb, be received at once into thy judgment council; and let its manifest power rest upon the members of the sanctuary.

The Saints Prayeth for the Lord God to Give Perfect Health to the Members of the Sanctuary, and to Give Them Power over the Afflicting and Death Dragon.

Thou gracious and all-wise God of this covenant, who has wrought marvellous things for Israel's salvation, thy strong arm has performed mighty things which are now concealed, but we shall soon proclaim them. Father, this is what we shall present into thine hands; and thou wilt perform it immediately. It reads as follows:—

We have been given a prey partially unto the will and revenge of that venomous serpent death and afflictions, these many days of trouble. We know that according to thy will he has been admitted into our flock, and empowered to smite and devour, as hath been done. We know that thou hast determined and purposed to fulfil it, to compel them to turn to thee, and to make a way for thy kingdom. Father, his time has expired, the gate is shut against him, and he shall no more enter into thy sheepfold to smite and devour, as he has done. The time has come for us to attain full dominion over him; give him a prey into our teeth, and we will make an utter end of him. Give us the full understanding to search out his original and late supreme, ruling power; let us find the entire history of his craftiness and artistical work, through which he has reigned since the fall of man. Let him be bound with the strongest bands of thy creative power, and put him out of the land. We have determined to put him out of the earth, and achieve the victory over him, as it is declared through the mouth of the prophets.

We will not suffer this ravenous beast to reign any longer among us: we will now rise up and burn him with the fire of thy wrath, and pass over. His afflicting power hath very often been manifested in Isaac ; so let him be redeemed and our work will advance rapidly. Let the dominion and ruling power over death be wrought in each member of the sanctuary ; and let healing power, and the continuity of health, awake at once, which thou hast in thy sanctuary of purity. Father, place our eyes on thy creative and healing powers, and the continuity of health, and we will give it freely unto all who have not denied the faith, but have continued in severe suffering unto the end of the reign of sin. Father, let this prayer of the saints and atonement of the Lamb be received into thy judgment court, and lift up the compliance of this petition upon the ensign.

At the time of this atonement Isaac was taken into captivity by the afflicting dragon, which power ruled over Isaac all through the seven seals. At the time of this atonement death was imminent, because his natural, spiritual body rebelled against the sacrifices which he went unto the New Jerusalem to offer unto the Lord God for the support of his sanctuary. Isaac was zealous to offer free offerings unto the Lord God, with incense when it was offered ; but the powers of darkness overshadowed the altar when he came forth with his offerings, which was somewhat defiling to the sanctuary. It was a burden to Isaac to make the offerings, and polluting to the New Jerusalem to receive them ; and for this cause the sanctuary endeavored not to receive the oblations from Isaac, but he commanded it to be made unto Caroline, and she placed Isaac's sacrifices upon the holy altar, which continued through the time of jeopardy. When the sanctuary took this step there was much incense burned upon the golden altar after the oblations were received from Isaac through Caroline ; and from this time Isaac received health to overcome the smiting enemy.

The sanctuary also refused to receive Christina's offerings when this change was made, because it had a similar effect as had Isaac's oblations upon him, though not so great. It defiled the sanctuary, and afflicted Christina when she made her offering to Caroline ; and for this cause it was again placed upon the holy altar by Christina, with much incense.

THE SAINTS REJOICETH OVER THE DESTRUCTION OF THE DEATH DRAGON: THE ANNIHILATION OF LEVIATHAN'S POWER.

Father, we sing praises unto thee upon the divine stringed instruments, and upon the harps of gold, because of thy great triumphant victory. We glory not in our power, for we know that it is null and void ; we glory in the fulness of thy Christ. We glorify thy name, because thou hast consumed the false judges of Israel, and hath brought their council to naught; and thou hast also brought to naught the profane priest and priestess, for they have polluted thy holy altar whereon we burn incense unto thee. We thank thee, and adore thy name because thou hast consumed Baal's prognosticators from the earth; and by the blast of thy nostrils they are cast into the nethermost region, burned, and are no more.

We thank thee because Elijah hath ascended in the chariot of fire, and Elisha received the mantle that he has waited for these many days. He fulfilled his time with the widow, and the days of his prophecies are gone by; yea, and the care of him, which was upon her, has departed, and she is delivered from the will of his enemies, who sought his hurt at her hands. Little David hast, with his sling stone, slain Goliath, the chief in strength among all nations. His arts and moves were unexcelled by man, and superior to other champions, the gladiators of this day; for when they strike men their lives are maintained, but when a blow was made by this spiritual gladiator, the days of his victims were no more, and the years they had spent were soon forgotten. Let the rain descend from heaven in torrents, and water the thirsty ground, that there may be grain in the springing up of the latter growth, and that thy chosen people may live, and reign with thee on earth.

The words of this atonement were revealed to slay the second advent of Goliath, and deliver the woman out of the woful care and misery that cleaved to her through the agency of jealousy during the years of Samuel's prophecies. This was to make a faint repetition of Elijah's stay with the widow, and David's work in war in slaying the king of human power and strength, whose power of science and art was embodied in the son of burden, in wisdom and understanding, to shun the edge of the sword.

The temple John was so well shielded and fortified with weapons and arts of science that when he was dealt a blow, it very seldom took effect. All manner of implements of war had been used by the Israelites to conquer him, but none proved successful until the determined, faithful, and truthful David challenged him for battle in a simple way by standing upon the free and righteous land, Samuel, without mercy to slay the warrior, that the saints might have the land.

ATONEMENT OF THE LAMB TO ESTABLISH THE CREATIVE HEALING POWER, AND DESTROY THE DESTROYER OF THE BODY.

Thou Almighty, Infinite, and sympathizing God of humanity, hear and consider this atonement; and defer not, for I have a case of affliction, determined and purposed of thee, and performed by the anger of the dragon. I do herein acknowledge that it is a just and holy purpose; for it is thy compulsory weapon to bring the human race home to thee. Through this system thou canst make the first step to establish and exalt thy supreme healing power above the physical science, eclipse the world of physical science, and be the leader, the commander, and the supreme ruler of diseases.

Hast thou forethought over this point of wisdom, and hast thou made thy thoughts manifest in thy Samuel? I will answer that thou hast breathed into thy temple thy holy purpose in this thing before it springs forth. This thou hast done to execute the fierceness of thy wrath and vengeance against human suffering through thy burning thoughts of wisdom, and the sharp and lightning sight that shall proceed out of thine eyes. The man who is inventing human suffering is, namely, death; and he is destroying the mansions which thou hast prepared to do the masonry of the holy kingdom, and those who shall glorify thee therein. For this purpose thou hast raised me up, and chosen me from among the brethren, — to destroy the destroyer of thy people.

The mighty dragon is loosened to exercise his power over the saints through afflictions; and through thy healing power thy people will know that thou art with us, which is thy supreme attraction. There is no other power, in thy kingdom that is prepared for thy people, more attractive and sympathizing than the power to extirpate diseases and mitigate pains. Come hastily, and let it begin in the fulness; and the great and mighty work which thou hast declared to be accomplished shall be verified by works. Let thy supreme and entire power of healing be manifested in thy Samuel; and place thy material eyes on the fulness of healing, and how it shall be performed.

Let thy eternal, divine, medical science spring forth in its many branches : and let thy wisdom search out the anatomy of the human soul, so that wisdom may perform its perfect work, and operate on each case of affliction, whether physical or spiritual. Place both material and spiritual eyes on the fulness of thy wisdom, on the hidden realities concerning how life ebbs and flows through the system of the mortal man. Dear Father, lift up the signature that points out, locates, and describes the severity of diseases, and I will show the slender thread of the mortal life. It is the office and power of thy Holy Christ to blot out and erase from the body of man all diseases, and abolish death.

I care not under what name disease comes, its origin is sin. I have searched diligently into this matter, and found the lust of man's flesh to be the origin of sin, and the creative seminal of sin. I have found, by searching, that lust created sin, and sin created all ailments now prevalent in the human family, both physical and mental. Man's natural state is lust; and the Devil, his angels, and kingdoms, were created and fashioned ornamentally out of lust. The globe of perdition, which is the exact measurement of man, is upheld and floats upon the mighty, rapid current of lust.

"Mortality" and "lust" are the same word, and have the same meaning ; for if a man is mortal, he is lustful ; and if he is lustful, he is mortal: for lust is the name of the first man, Adam, and is the soil for the implanting of all sins. "Animal nature" is the name of the first women, Eve, and is the controlling, sovereign power that has perpetuated sin and corruption. The burning desires that issue from animal nature are the seminals of sin, which have continuated abominations and woful desolation. The flaming desires are the germs of sin, centred in the soil of lust ; and animal nature feeds and nourishes them, and continuates the image and likeness of the foreparents.

Animal nature is the spirit or fluid substance that moves over the surface of lust, and keeps it alive, and the visible liquid nature that flows over the surface, and, through the channels of lust, is made mortal by the spirit of animal nature, which power sends this fluid to all parts of the body, and forms the members of the mortal seed. The spirit of animal nature is the compositor of all vanity, and the skilled artificer. Through the explanation and the decision of thy judgment, man is the footstool of mortality, and woman the goddess, and crown of glory; which is the glory and honor of the mortal world, accompanied by the other three kingdoms, — gold and silver, and dainty things ; educational science ; and the god of royal blood-kin, and family circle. Man serves, honors, and confers all glory unto these kingdoms; and man's chief object in life — and his desires to live a long life — is to glorify and honor these four kingdoms. According to this judgment, man cannot glorify and honor thee in his Adamite state.

ATONEMENT OF THE LAMB, TO DESTROY AND BURN UTTERLY THE RED-HEAD DRAGON.

Thou Almighty God, possessor of omnipotent power, wisdom, and scientifical medical power, hear this atonement, and let it be received into thy judgment court of equity. Father, I have found the seat and throne of the red-head dragon ; he has been cast down from his first throne, which was to invent lies publicly, to overcome the saints. He has been transformed from one degree of power into another, which is manifested in diseases : this he has done to deceive thy people, and destroy them from the face of the earth. He is wroth with those who have not taken counsel against thee and thy anointed sayings.

Father, thou hast said that thy people should overcome him by the blood of the Lamb, which defines the fire of thy words that proceedeth out of thy mouth. I have firmly decided, through the power of thy judgment, that his power is destroyed ; and those whom he hath smitten by craftiness are delivered from his cruel hands. I thank thee because thou hast destroyed his two great powers, which were inventing and composing lies, and creating diseases. As soon as thy material eyes are placed on his next seat, he shall take to rule over thy people, and prevail against them ; he shall not retain it, but he shall be driven into unquenchable fire.

Father, I shall from this time, by the power of thy judgment on his craftiness, deliver George's case of affliction into thy healing hands, to exterminate the power of the diseased dragon from his system. Father, let the fire concerning this case range from thy head to thy feet, so that there may be a reflux of nature from this time. Change the tide of the medium of life into its proper place and activity, so that he may obtain life and vigor, to be a full subject to perform the thing that thou hast determined to accomplish through him. I shall remain here, and wait for thy redeeming love, consuming fire, and shining light, to move on this case ; but let it make a speedy manifestation, with much power. Strengthen the hearts of the members of the sanctuary, so that they doubt not thy power to save thy mansions from the cruel hands of the angry dragon.

Father, it wast through the power of this strickening and wrathful dragon that thy power of healing was destroyed, — by his coming into thy fold, overpowering the truth, and killed with death and hunger. I held my peace, knowing that thou hast suffered it to be so to fulfil thy righteous words ; now I have him in my hands, and will destroy his power, which overcame thy people. Through death he overcame thy people, and through the abolishment of death I shall gain dominion over him through the victory I shall achieve in this case. This shall be the proof of the restoration of thy healing power, which was overcome by the wrathful dragon.

Father, I do herein confess that every material substance that thou hast commanded to create in the beginning has obeyed thy voice, made a visible manifestation, and is here today for man's glory and purposes. All material substances, of every degree and kind, are in the spiritual worlds in invisible fluids, in both corrupt and incorrupt existences, and are busy at work acting in their proper offices, just as the material substances, which are brought under man's command and control in every degree and purpose, do in the temporal world. All these different pure material substances are spiritually and aerially manifested in the elements of divine truth.

Holy truth, word, and spirit, are the food, raiment, and life of the soul, by receiving it for different needs and purposes, just as the material are used for the sustenance of the physical body, to maintain life. The different corrupt and deleterious substances that are manifested in the characteristics of man are the diseases of different degrees and strength seated in the human family, that drop the germs to create the numerous names of modern diseases now prevailing over the human race. It was the holy and creative truth, uttered by the Holy God, that spoke to warn man of these different ancient and modern diseases ; which declared that these things should come upon them in the latter days, if they failed to hearken unto the commandments of divine truth. Man did not take warning, to hearken unto the commandments of the Holy God ; and the words that went out of the mouth of the Holy God created these plagues and evils to rule and govern them instead of truth.

The good promised to the just, the subjection and obedience of this class, in hearkening unto the commandments of God, the correction of divine truth, the words of truth, created the elements of the pure substances to rule over them in glory, honor, and righteousness. When the word is spoken by the holy spokesman, if the temple has not the true inclination to receive the words of truth, the truth that is spoken revives the substances of corruption, and makes war against it as long as there is any corruption therein. If the earth is totally corrupt, the incorruption destroys the corruption materially; this stops the suffering of lingering troubles, and delivers the flesh out of pain in a short time.

I find, by searching thy being, that there is no creature, herb, tree, nor substance of any material sort, whatever kind it may be, but what is in the corrupt and incorrupt state, and able to perform its work spiritually when the holy command is given. Then the holy truth, word, and spirit is thy pre-eternal and sempiternal existence, out of which thou hast created every material thing. Every material thing thou hast made wast created holy, and if used in its proper place, it will not defile man; but man became vain in the imaginations of his heart, and changed the meaning in the use of the things thou hast created for his glory. Through man's changing the meaning of thy commandments in the use of these things, thy vengeance kindled against him; and it burned in the different depraved desires, and created in each lust a disease.

Those things that man lusts after are the things that thou hast commanded him not to strive to obtain; then the ancient and modern diseases are in the styles and fashions of the modern age of vainglorious pride and improvements of this day. Those things thou hast commanded man not to use, except in certain ways, and he disobeyed thy commandments. The substances of that unclean thing took root in the human family, and grew up in deleterious principles; and from that it corrupted the flesh, and turned to diseases. The old commandments that thou gavest the holy seed to keep strictly were only to set the type to print the holy spiritual commandments, and gave man a godly system of work to convey them on into the perfect state of life, and show by knowledge the different substances in them to create their sufferings. All substances, corrupt and incorrupt, material and immaterial, are thy many agents, through whom thou performest thy marvellous work.

When man is captured by physical diseases, he puts all his depraved trust in the physical for life; although the holy and perfect life of man is in thee, aerially, where there are all grades, and sorts of remedies to erase and extirpate all diseases. Men are so depraved and lustful, that thou changest the pure state they would enjoy through obedience into a corrupt state; and in many cases thou hast determined not to show mercy. When it reaches this juncture, nothing created has power to heal. In this case, all attempts, with whatever substance may be used, will prove ineffective, consume the sleazy threads of life, and shorten the days of the victim; for thou commandest the substances to lose their effects, and they obey thee, which commandments were issued in days of old to destroy the disobedient and the corrupt seed in the last days of the dominion of sin.

Thou commandest all things in the beginning of the divine creation; and they all moved, and still move at thy command, and perform things ordered, obediently. But when thou commandest the human family, they doubt thy power, and turn away from thy commandments, and then thou turnest away thy mercy from them; and as soon as thy mercy departs from sympathising with man, his flesh is delivered into the cruel hands of corruption, to consume away and die. Of all creatures and substances, man is the only kind that doubts thy power, and disobeys thy commands; all other substances and creatures are holy and perfect, acting at thy command, in their proper places.

Thy holiness, happiness, and perfection begin in the sacred chambers of man's soul, when he becomes heartily humble, submissive, and obedient to thy commands, and lets them be his chief love, desire, pleasure, motive, guide, and companion, and learns to serve, honor, and obey them. Man is fearful, and shrinks from performing the work that thou demandest of him, for fear of losing the mortal life, its fame and honor among men, trough thou art able to restore double for all that is lost for thy sake. In the meantime, the fearful are losing their mortal treasures, which are never restored in the world, and have no hope of this being done in this life, owing to non-trust in thy power.

When thou commandest mankind to do certain things, in order that thy plans may go into effect, and thy determinations be accomplished, he looks ahead of thy purposes, imagines that there is danger ahead, and invents plans for himself, that he may best shun the way which thou hast set before him. Because man imagines such things, and doubts thy power, thou turnest away thy love and pity, and brings upon him the evil imaginations of his heart. If man will put all his trust in thy holy words, and take pleasure in them, and magnify thy power, and teach his fellowmen the same, the evil pest shall not come nigh unto his path. Thou art the power that corrupts, and the power that incorrupts; thou art the power that saves, and the power that destroys.

Lust and animal nature make the blood of man mortal; and the blood conveys the nature to all parts of the body, and corrupts the flesh through the coagulation of poisonous pus. Nature is carried by the blood, by involuntary power and activity; and, like the nature that wheels the food to the passage, flows to the outlet, through which it should be emitted; and if there is not a regular expulsion of it, there is an increase of rapidity, and afflux and reflux to all parts of the body. This speed continues until the blood reaches a high temperature of heat from the rapid motion, and this burning temperature and hasty speed churns the blood, and it becomes emulsive, inspissated, and stagnant.

The stagnated blood, which is churned and poisoned by nature's rapaciousness, is then another mongrel mixture, namely, corrupt pus; this pus decays the flesh, until it finds its way to the external part of the body in a running sore, or some protuberance of the flesh, and the appetite begins to fail, and decrease, the organs become weak and exhausted, and the food does not pass off regularly. If the appetite is poor, and the digestion irregular, this is the assistant creator of diseases, although the blood is the motor of the involuntary organs, and keeps the food in motion, calling for it regularly, and wheeling it off the same; but when the blood becomes thick and stagnant, the vigorating and motor speed of life stands still and wastes away. The food and water are the drainage of the body, and are the mighty medicinal agents that drain the earth and prevent a collection of matter and poisonous feces in the blood, if the appetite is natural, and the food wheels off regularly. If the spirited animal nature emits regularly, the blood flows gently and easily, keeping all of the organs in the same motion and speed, and the food passing off under the same time and motion.

The organs of man are a perfect motor machinery, which is kept in running motion by the afflux and reflux of the blood. Divine nature — which manifests itself in holy characteristics, through being obedient to the holy truth involved in the spiritual commandments of the Divine God, the divine creation — begins in the blood, ejecting every atom of animal nature from the blood. This is done by human nature's receiving the elements of divine truth by gradual degrees ordinately. The two natures begin war against each other as soon as they meet; and when divine nature drives out and cremates animal nature, the electric light of divine truth spreads abroad over the earth, which then is the electric motor of the blood, and keeps it in eternal motion, carrying off all concrete matter. Then I shall stand up materially before the world and fulminate thy divine medical power, and show the mortiferous diseases that are seated in the human family through the current of animal nature, which medium regards not the holy doctrines of truth.

I do eulogise, and shall fulminate thy medical power from the basis of thy kingdom to the extreme culmination of thy glory, that thou hath made me the catholicon of diseases, and all ailments prevalent in the higher animal kingdom. Thou hast made me the pandect of divine science; and thou hast made me the pantologist of thy fine arts in the use of the alphabets in whatever way thou wilt have them used to perform thy marvellous work in any degree, simple or great.

Pure blood, divinely cleansed and kept pure and luminated by God's electric breath wafting softly, peacefully, and lovingly upon its tide, is the fulness of the higher life in the material body. Blood is the life of man; and divine nature in its perfection, unmixed with any other substances, is the quickening power, the shield and buckler, of the pure blood, to keep back the poisonous substances which are destructive to transhumanized bodies. There are two mighty existences of diseases; one is physical and the other mental, and the origin of the two is sin, otherwise neither of these could exist and rule mankind.

When man disobeys the commandments of the Lord God, and rejects, and turns aside from the doctrines of truth, he throws down the fortified walls of truth, and the life lieth in jeopardy. Then the spirited animal nature streams into the earth, and makes war against divine nature, which is unfortified by the walls of truth through disobedience. In a short time divine truth is ejected, and divine nature swallowed up by the propelling upas of animal nature; and then the whole frame of humanity becomes surrounded and fortified by the ravenous serpent of lust, and this makes the last state worse than the first; it would be better by far had this person never been in existence, nor never received any truth. This brings in the apathy of psychomachy, and realizes the doctrine of psychopannychism, because animal nature and divine partly mingle, which deadens divine nature, and it falls asleep, and slumbers in the earth until the quickening power of word, spirit, and truth appears to the rescue of the immortal soul, smites animal nature, and exterminates it from the soul, " whence the resurrection of the dead."

Before the immortal soul is reclaimed, and power restored to it, animal nature takes control of the body, wroth and greedy, and flows through the soil of lust, using it for its agents to direct the course to steer the frame; then lust stands as an ensign and commander, to direct the course that lust will have it go for pleasure. As soon as the commander of animal nature begins, mental disorders begin to issue, and the body is soon a congregated chamber of demons arising from the dead and working in the mind preposterously. In such case the soul is at war against lust, because it is excessively greedy; and when it reaches this state, the soul and body disagree and disunite, and war begins between them: "here comes the apathy," which consumes depravity from the corporeal body.

The body wants the pleasure of lust, and the soul hungers and thirsts after word, spirit, and truth; this is called "mental disease," and the word, spirit, and truth are the proper remedies to prescribe. In this case divine remedies will heal both soul and body; but in some cases of disease the material remedies must also be used; and such will be done if it is left to the will and decision of the Divine Physician, because in some cases, the disease has changed from mental disorder to physical disorder.

When the flesh, blood, and nature have turned to, or partly mingled with, poisonous pus, such diseases, at this stage, cannot be healed by either physical or divine remedies; for the soul and body are deadly poisoned, hence there is no pure soil, nor fertility for the seeds of life to take root and grow to produce a new life; "hence cometh the end of the body." Such diseases came through inheritance of nature, just as superfine qualities inherit divine nature; this fulfils thy holy words as follows: "Thou shalt not bow down thyself to them, nor serve them: for I the Lord thy God am a jealous God, visiting the iniquities of the fathers upon the children unto the third and fourth generation of them that hate me."

This is the unfathomed curse that thou hast imputed upon the forefathers, for they obeyed not thy commandments, neither walked they in thy precepts; therefore they provoked thee to anger, and thy wrath and vengeance burneth against their seed who inherited their disobedient propensities. This is the reward of the forefathers' disobedience, according to thy promises to the wicked.

THE SAINTS GIVE THANKS FOR VICTORY OVER THE IMAGE OF THE TRANSFORMED DRAGON.

We thank and adore thy name, dear Heavenly Father, for the victory we have achieved through the power of thy wisdom over the first case of affliction, which thou hast given a prey to our teeth, and meat for our hunger. This thou didst to frame the patent of thy healing power, and to invent the stamper in the fulness. We have subsisted on the flesh of the transformed dragon; and our souls have been filled through the abundance of delicacies which we found in his carcass. Father, we thank thee because thou hast enabled us to see into the hidden realities of divine medical science; thou hast made us to see and understand that all diseases were not created and imputed upon the victims who are in bondage by diseases, because of their disobedience alone. We thank thee, because thou hast made us to see that all things, both corporeal and incorporeal, are the many agents to make up and complete the integration of eternal life in all its many branches.

We see that thy perfect salvation could not be offered to perform its perpetual work, if pure corporeal and incorporeal substances did not have perfect harmony and affinity for each other, so as to maintain cohesion; and that is corruption to corruption, and purity to purity. We confess, and increase with glory, that corporeal medical science and its courses of workings harmonize with the workings of divine medical science, which treat on the diseases of the soul, and those of the flesh originating therefrom, by turning aside from the path of divine rectitude. We confess, and increase with honor, that thy salvation could not be given to the effects of its integral and perfect word, if physical medical science did not have perfect harmony with divine medical science. We acknowledge that mattery medical science must harmonize with divine medical science to complete the fulness of healing, and perpetuate life eternal; and he who receiveth the power of eternal life must trust in the union of the two, but the divine shall lead, govern, and command.

We thank thee, because thou hast inspired man to discover and perfect through wisdom the mattery healing elements; and thou hast endued man with wisdom to search into thy mysterious being, and ferret out the divine healing elements that are contained in word, spirit, and truth, which is composed of all the different pure gases and substances to heal the soul divinely stamped, and to work in the corporeal remedies to heal the body physically, and to maintain life therein. We thank thee, because we have seen that all things that love and obey thee are holy and perfect, when used in the proper way, and received with thanksgiving unto thee. And when man returns home to thee, all things that thou hast created to honor and glorify thee, and to benefit man, will awake from slumber, banish solitude, unite with its companions, and realize the work that thou hast said it should do.

ATONEMENT OF THE LAMB FOR THE ALMIGHTY GOD TO DESTROY LEVIATHAN'S GREAT POWERS THAT SCORNETH THE SICK, AND DELIVER THOSE BOUND BY DISEASES.

Father, we make this petition and atonement unto thee for thou to see and consider leviathan's wrothful powers against thy people who are in bondage by the diseases that he has been empowered to maintain. Leviathan is no friend to thy people who are in the castles of diseases; let him be consumed from the thrones of scornfulness, contemptibleness, and excessive nicety. Through patience, love, and sympathy, thou wilt abolish death, and erase every germ of disease; for thou hast imprecated diseases upon the human family, and thou wilt hastily abolish and erase them, but not by scorning the afflicted.

Father, destroy the great power of leviathan manifested in the recording secretary; put love and sympathy, faithfulness and patience, within his heart, to help share the burdens of the afflicted, so that the medium of life may have channels to flow through, and those who will may come, and drink thereof, and be healed of all ailments that have been inflicted through the powers of sin, to draw them home to thee.

Father, disease is the huntsman which thou hast started out to compel thy people to come home to thee; and when they flee to thy healing arms for shelter, shield, and buckler, let them find a place of refuge in the bosom of thy love. Put it into the hearts of thy chosen people that all diseases were determined of thee, to make an utter end of sin ; therefore, if the pain and sting of diseases have not been felt in this people enough to give them a tender, loving, and sympathizing feeling for sufferers, let them feel the piercing sting of diseases, and they will have a knowledge of pain.

Father, we know that divine hearts are equipped with these principles, but brutes are devoid of them. Let the brutes that are seated in the hearts of this people be destroyed, and create within them hearts of flesh. Thus the healing waters will have channels to flow through ; the deaf will hear ; the blind will see ; the dumb will speak ; the maimed will walk erect ; the halt will cease to limp ; devils will be cast out, and the diseased healed ; and those who are dead in sin will be raised to life by thy quickening power.

Father, we have seen what withholdeth ; let it flee away, and be no more. We will not accept those antagonists ; then why sufferest thou them to war against us continually ? Why not awake in thy almighty power and perform thy work ? Thou needest not the assistance of false hearts to do thy work ; then why not take to thee thy omnipotent power and accomplish it, overflow and pass over where the powers of perdition cannot come? As long as thou trustest false faces and masked hearts, corruption will exist, but as soon as thou showest thy omnipotent power and infinite manhood, there will be no more pain, strife, opposition, deceitfulness, sickness, hopelessness, nor fallacious judgment ; all will be purity, and the people will be one with me even as we are one.

Father, let us be exalted above the heathen in the earth, who regardeth not thy simple work and strange acts. Every step thou makest, and every course thou pursuest to carry out thy purposes, are errors, apparently. Thou hast made thy second advent to earth, to reign over all abominations therein ; why stayest thou thy reigning sceptre ? Thou art not pleased nor glorified with the conditions of thy divided kingdom. Mine eyes have seen, and my heart beareth testimony, that the opposing host of perdition keepeth thy kingdom divided against itself. I again appeal unto thee for a closer union, and an increase of zeal and courage, to finish the time of trials that are written, foretelling what thy Christ should suffer and encounter. Thou knowest that devils approveth not in holy, truthful discretion and equity; and for this cause, why prolongeth thou the time of thy reign? Wilt thou suffer hell to reign over me until it passes the point of toleration?

Father, am I raised up to make a continual proverbial taunting, to be a fugitive and vagabond in the earth? I have been cramped, and trodden under foot these many days, and the consummation of trials has come upon me, and I say there is enough done. The Devil and his host should be driven from the field of battle, and brought to an end, so that I be not pressed, and tried on this point inexpediently. Father, I know that I am composed of an everlasting, durable substance; but I should not be cast off in a forlorn state forever.

Father, if thou wilt only equip thy Christ with the full implements of war that are already prepared in thy kingdom, and endow him with thy omniscient wisdom and discretion, I will make an hasty and final end of the entire opposing regiments of perdition, and erase every principle through which they find entrance into the city of the New Jerusalem. Their time has been fulfilled, and I do abhor them in my presence, and this abhorrence is felt in me because thou hast stamped me indelibly with the pure principles of thy kingdom; and the principles of the Devil's kingdom are so adverse to those of the divine kingdom that there can be no harmony nor pleasure, as should be, until the mortal kingdoms are wiped out through disintegration. As long as one principle of perdition is left, it is only a messenger and telephone for Satan to make war against thy people, manifested in thy Holy Christ, characteristically. Destroy Satan's messengers, his telephones and telegraphic communications, with all of his agents, and there will be an end to non-unity.

Father, I acknowledge that this people are strangers, and sojourners into the land of promise, as all of their forefathers were. I acknowledge that the land is before us, but the heathen hold it in bondage; whenever they see us attempt to come in and take possession, that we may not inhabit this vast wilderness, they rise up in peace and craftiness, and impede every course we pursue which they do not understand. Father, thou art the creator of this trouble, thou art the continuator of it, and thou must be the annihilator of it; for this cause I shall not lay it to any one's charge, for thou purposed it, and thou must end it, and make thy name an everlasting glory.

Thou hast laid the foundation to this house, and thou must finish it; thou hast afflicted, and thou must heal; thou hast cursed, and thou must bless; thou hast made forlorn and friendless, and thou must befriend; thou hast called and chosen, and thou must establish; thou hast led us into snares of wickedness, and thou must deliver; thou hast made us despised, and thou must love. Thou hast made us fugitives and vagabonds, and a reproach among all who have heard of us, and thou must create honorable names and fame among all those about us. Thou hast made us small, and thou must enlarge; thou hast made us void of wisdom, and thou must make us wise according to thy glory. Thou hast divided us, and thou must bring us together in perfect union. Thou hast led us into hardships, and hedged up the true way, and thou must open and prepare the way before us, that we may go through. Thou hast made some of these hearts as hearts of brutes, and thou must make them hearts of saints. Thou hast made these hearts silent in praises, and thou must make them joyful, perform thy work, and establish thy promises to usward, and turn away thy burning vengeance and masked face, so that this people suffer no longer thereby.

When I fight against the antagonizing powers of perdition, thou strengthenest them; and when I strengthen, thou weakenest in a concealed way, which is to try and purge me, and make me clean from selfish propensities. Why dost thou not come straight forward, and perform thy work openly, harmonizing with the work thou hast clothed me to do, so that this people may find some reality in thy life? When thou art still, this people strive to be the same, which is right. Then thou stealeth off, and standeth so very high that they cannot reach thee, and then thine anger smoketh against them before they can approach thee; and when they get near thy located summits, thou vanisheth away, appeareth to be altogether vengeance and fire, and seemeth to be without base or summit. Why dost thou not get on a system, and cause thine anger to cease from consuming this people? It was thou who led them in this pell-mell way, unsystematically.

If our breaches are incurable, free us from the imprisonment of variation. Here we are in this hopeless state, and have not reached one point of regularity and system, to publish and establish thy marvellous works among men. How can thy kingdom unite when thou art divided against it? Canst thou wait any longer to see us put to perils and hardship, and driven into jeopardy? I want to see thy mercy that is promised to thy chosen people. Father, awake out of slumber, realize thy promises to usward, and put us off no longer.

I have reached the extreme point of faithfulness to lift up thy holy truth; and now I know it is useless to suffer here unless thou art interested, sympathizing, and merciful about the trouble this people are passing through faithfully to carry to the remotest end the work that thou hast laid heavily upon them. Thou hast clothed me with work to perform, and the way to do it is completely closed, and fortified by obstructions; still, thine anger burneth if it is not done, and if I appeal unto thee for thy course, — the perfect way to follow, to accomplish the work that thou hast laid heavily and grievously upon me, — thou directest not the holy way, neither tellest me the proper course to pursue.

If I pursue not, and search not for the way to accomplish my mission to mankind, the work which I came to do stands imperfectly. I find that I am completely forsaken and left alone, and am destitute of all help to perform a work that thou hast not yet made known of what it consists nor what is required of its members in order that they may find rest and favor in thy sight. This means that thou hast raised me up to be the leader and commander of thy righteousness without any apparent hope of triumph nor any system to travel by; and thou seemest to take no notice of our condition. Thou hast even taken away the name and title of the work that I was sent forth from thee to fulfil; and I find that we have nothing to proclaim that has one iota of rationality to make us systematical in profession among the people. Thou hast stripped us naked of everything that thou hast created, except evil pestilences, and hast left us here, it seems, to perish, and waste away to nothing. If thou hast any love at all for this people, it is now sadly needed; so rise up and give us an honorable name and title, systematically, harmonizing with divinity.

Father, I have no liking for damnified heresies, because I want the proper course and system of holy truth, so that this people be not treated as brutes for ever. Father, thou hast the power to save, and why dost thou not perform the work, and cause this gloominess to cease? These are human beings, so let me see thy love and sympathy for the human family. How can this cause ever be anything besides what it is today if I do no good for the people? If I do good for the bettering of the human race, they will do the same for me, as far as they have power, which will elevate and make honorable thy kingdom. Father, we are nothing now, as we are situated, for any one to take notice of us in honor of thy holy truth, because no one is benefited through me, to make them interested in me; and it seems as though thou hast no particular preference in the progress of divine righteousness. If thou hast, then change this hardship and rebellion, and accomplish thy work. Thou hast created every false way, every good way, and every evil thought; and why dost thou delay thy power in destroying that that thou hast created conflicting with immortality, after using the mortal to perfect the immortal creation, and not make a continual proverb of thy mysterious but simple power?

Thou hast created leviathan, the transcendent Lucifer, and also the unicorn, the mighty dragon, the fiery flying serpent, and the adder to bruise the heel; and thou must utterly destroy their powers that prevail over humanity, so that thou mayest accomplish thy perfect work, even as thou hast created them to fulfil thy purposes concerning the high reign of sin. These scientific powers, working in this people, are making them wholly depraved abjects. Every moment the science of perdition reigns over them, which is carrying them speedily on into the unfathomed depth of corruption.

I want to rise from this state and do good for the people; I want to destroy him who is destroying thy people. I was raised up to destroy the destroyer of humanity; as soon as they hear of me, they will flock to where my body is. I am filled with wrath and vengeance, because these antagonizing powers of science are allowed to detain me here in this concealed state; when the harvest is fully ripe, let me go, and I will arise and reap. Why is it that thou detainest me here sympathizing with nothing? Why not loosen me, and let me go about my work? Thou knowest that this is not my work in reality; then let me go, and I will accomplish my real work. Wilt thou hold me here until the loosened dragon destroys all thy people who have believed on thy name? I will answer, No; for I will not be detained here any longer to make nothing appear to be something. I shall uncover myself, and reign over the antagonizing science of perdition after fulfilling the Scripture to the extreme.

Father, I shall not linger here any longer being detained through fallacious ideas. This manner of work, that has existed with us these many days in an obscured state, will never result in anything if thou continuest to conceal thy power. I am not afraid to proclaim thy holy truth unto nations and people, kings and tongues, whose wisdom is bright, and countenances luminous and penetrating. Let me go, by realizing thy promises. Take away from me these strong bands of iron that thou hast bound me in — which iron bands are the fulfilments of thy righteous words handed down from generation to generation — so that all things that are written might be fulfilled at thy post-millennium. Move away from me all stipulations that thou hast connected with me and my mission corruptly, and leave me alone with thy entire kingdom, and I will realize the work that I came to do. I need not the help of man nor woman, but will accomplish the work with the elements of thy kingdom; only move away from me these impediments that thou hast laid within my way.

Thou hast obstructed my holy course of work, so let thy obstructions be far removed at once. Father, I am not commanding this to be done by and by, but it is to go into effect now; for I have been put off long enough, and will stand no more unreasonable imposition from these antagonists, as I have done, but shall proceed to make away with them. Father, I am determined to accomplish the real work I came to do, or cause all other work to be suspended, and cease to work at all. Thou knowest that the powers of corruption will never glorify thee; then why dost thou delay my eternal work, and continue to make me a full subject to the will and pleasure of devils? I am not raised up to glorify sin, and I shall not work to that end. My mission is to destroy the Devil, and burn up his works and kingdoms, and I shall not fall short of accomplishing the work. If thou hast chosen any one to be like me, make them what thou hast determined they should be, and cease from entertaining the things not beneficial to this cause.

That that thou has purposed in this people — that do; and show that thou art the God in these truths of omnipotent power. I have been faithful to the extreme to carry out thy purposes while facing the unreasonable perils, and declared thy righteousness in full unto a people who have not known thee; therefore I find that I have filled the measure, and am ready and willing to lay aside this manner of work thou hast clothed me in to do, — to cease from fighting this people, and cause thine anger and vengeance to cease from them.

Father, I demand of thee the establishment of thy promises, in faithfulness to ransom this people from the mental pit, even as thou hast been faithful in fulfilling thy promises in destroying the wicked and casting them into perdition. Thy redeeming promises are all recorded, so let thy quickening power flow through them, and let them be established and proclaimed among the nations. Father, show, through the revelation of truth according to thy redeeming promises, that we are thy elect, the chosen seed of righteousness. I am not pleading in the behalf of sin, but in the behalf of righteousness, and not the righteousness of men, but thine own righteousness, which is held fast in desolation because of the righteousness of men who are the walls of sin that besiege thy kingdom, and chain it down by the mighty powers of animal nature. Thy righteousness is not able to overcome but through thee, thy Christ; so place him upon his eternal throne, and he will accomplish the work he came to do. Thou hast created the doctrines of the Holy Christ, thou hast created the many doctrines and opinions of the antichrists, and thou hast created them all to carry out thy ordinations. Thou hast created the antichrists to try, purge, and refine thy Holy Christ through the antagonizing system he has passed, which was the seething process.

In order to try thy Holy Christ, those whom I have taken steps to save from trouble, thou gavest over to the sword; and when I gave some over to the sword, thou destroyest the power of the sword so that the work would not be done; but still I was compelled to give them over to the sword, and make attempts to redeem from the powers of sin according to the power that thou puttest in me. In the meantime thou art creating and injecting other sins to perpetuate the troublous times. I want the end of this trouble; for I have taken all the pleasure that I can take in it, and my pleasure shall now be in the reality of the work that thy Christ came to perform. Thou hast loosened the regiment of perdition to destroy the human race repeatedly; and I command this privilege to be abolished. I command thee to loosen thy Christ, to destroy the regiments of perdition, even as thou hast empowered them to destroy the holy people through the past ages even until now.

Why dost thou allow thine anger to burn continually against the human race? Why dost thou not let it burn against sin, and save the flesh for the everlasting inheritance promised to thy righteous seed? The mansions, or bodies of my brethren, are the land that thou hast promised to righteousness; so make thy full appearance to the world, and destroy the wicked who have the land in their possession. I am making these atonements for the development of the human race, through the destruction and cremation of the great adversary, the Devil. The people will delight in thy eternal way when they see it is real. Unveil thy face, which veil was put on through the concealed meanings of thy language, and show thyself unto the people as thou art; and they will flock to the mount to be cleansed of sin and iniquities.

Thou hast not been mindful of those who have suffered severely with me; this people are greatly neglected, and left here, in this state of apathy, it seems, to die. Father, I want all who have labored and suffered with me redeemed according as thou hast promised. Can this people continue in faithfulness when thou hast lingered on the verge of death on the non-fulfilment of thy blessed promises? They are cast down and discomforted, in waiting for thy redeeming love and transhumanizing power. They are sinking down to ruin, because they have not thy agents to redeem. Thou hast suffered thine indignation to burn continually against them, and hast made them the most insignificant creatures on earth; but according to thy promises, which are sure, this is the leading people of the earth, and the people through whom thou shalt show thy mighty, holy power.

I shall not be pacified on this matter any longer through promises; I will be pacified through the establishment of thy redeeming and blessed promises. All my forefathers fell short of thy real promises, because they were fearful in demanding the rights and privileges due to them, because they were not fully obedient to thy command. Through fear and trembling they suffered as we have; and travelled in darkness, not fully knowing thy purpose — which was similar to our travel these many days — and failed to enter the rest, because they had not the knowledge of thy purposes, neither had they the fulness of zeal to perform thy work for the perfection of humanity.

Thou wilt hearken unto the petition of the most zealous and faithful agent, who is laboring to accomplish a work for some good purpose; and with full pressure thou wilt hasten to their request. Thou hast raised up thy Christ through the request and pressure of the people; and he was rejected through the pressure of the people, and he must be received and reign through the pressure of the people. Thou art reigning on thy omnipresent throne omnipotently, and thou art holy and happy enough without the glorification of thy Christ, or saints; and if they do not compel thee to establish them in the earth in righteousness according to thy righteousness, the pressure of hell will reign forever.

The host of perdition has always been full of zeal and faithfulness to accomplish the work that they were commissioned to do; they were not ashamed to face the world for the establishment of their desires and aims, and they were not ashamed to beg for the enlarging and promoting of their kingdom. They are not too haughty to humble themselves to the saints to fulfil their time and purposes in warring against the truth ; and when they come in power they quickly declare independence. They have not been too selfish to deprive themselves of the luxuries of the world and the privileges they should have, in order to attain the full power to rule. They have not been too supercilious and fearful to make their aims and wants known to their enemies ; and through being enthusiastic and determined in the performance of their work, through the past dark ages of the world, they have excelled and ruled in their undertaking. They have not been backward in acknowledging their aims and intentions ; they showed themselves to the public just as they were, and by so doing, they have reigned, perpetrated the full victory, and held the leading power. They have devoted their time and labor consecratedly to search out the wisdom of the world; and they have explored the globe and found all the substances to reign during their time. They contain all the crafty wisdom of the world to continuate excellency ; and they have not been slack in obeying the commands of their antagonists to reach the goal of perfect corruption.

Thy Christ is like unto these antagonists in enthusiasm and courage, to annihilate these faithful zealots of perdition. Through the many words of these atonements, I have fully defined all things that thou hast created, and that now exist, and for what purpose they were created, showing that all have existed through thy power, and for this cause there shall be no more imputation of curses upon the human family because of sin. Thou hast continuated, in a dark and concealed way, all evil and all righteousness ; and I commend thee for the abolishment of all evil and the establishment of all righteousness, and the perpetuity of it. So let the thunder roll, and the lightning crash ; and let the healing waters that thou hast prepared for the nations pour down in torrents. Let thy healing be verified by works, which will be the establishment of thy promises.

Father, heal the diseased souls and bodies of all who come unto thee, and submit themselves unto thy will and pleasure to receive and learn thy holy truth and the understanding of thy marvellous works, and turn none away destitute of thy blessing, who come with the price of it. Father, bestow honor upon those to whom honor is due; show pity unto those to whom pity is due; have mercy upon those to whom mercy is due; and let it be fully manifested in me, and I will send it home, and where they are unworthy of it, it shall not go. Deliver those who are worthy of deliverance, I care not who they are; and if thy material eyes have not looked upon them, let them be recompensed all the same according to their works.

If there is anything conflicting with the progress of any person or persons, who are faithful and zealous to accomplish what thou hast given them to do, move every impediment out of the way, and bring them home to thee; and when they start home, let me see them through this atonement, which shall quicken their steps, and speedily advance them.

ATONEMENT OF THE LAMB TO COMPEL THE LORD GOD TO ACCOMPLISH HIS WORK AFTER BEING THE ORIGIN OF IT.

Thou Creator of life and death, and Maker of good and evil, hear this atonement, and hearken unto the multitude of words that I have discharged to show forth my love and sympathy toward the children of men. This is the first case of affliction thou hast placed into thy material hands, to make a manifestation of my faithfulness toward the children of men, and not only for this hast thou laid this case of affliction into thy material hands, but to show forth the damnified principles of these bulls and dogs who are sitting in these temples, showing unto me, through their fictitious influence and false affections, that they are Holy Christs, when they are the spirits of antichrists that thou foresaidst would come and deceive many. They have accomplished their work of deceivableness; so rid me of them, and let the principles of the Holy Christ occupy these temples. These are the temples of the Holy Ghost; suffer sin no longer to reign therein, by blotting them out, and thy Holy Christ will no longer be deceived by their fictions and craft.

I have learned, by experience, that I have here with me the chief scientists of perdition, star gazing, and prognosticating through fallacious divination, concerning thy mysteries of how thou shalt perform thy work and establish it among men. It is only the wisdom and strength, glory and honor, power, and riches, and blessings of the mortal world manifested in the one head, called "the man of sin."

The full scientific powers of the mortal kingdom are characteristically manifested here in the one material body; which powers have chosen the recording secretary for their great focus. Father, he has reached the apex of mental scientific wisdom, and the profound depth of depraved arts, which have made manifest the integral and leading powers of corruption. The manifest powers of this corruption in the focus have besieged the land with depravity, both mental and material.

Father, let this embodiment of mental depravity be destroyed from nature, so that thy kingdom may reign and be established among men. For this purpose thou hast raised up the figure of refined sin, to destroy the science and crafty works of sin, or the leading kingdom of utter darkness. Thou hast created and fashioned this man, the king of wizards, the metropolis city of wickedness, and the focalization of mortal science, namely, leviathan, the lion of mortality, who is the king beast of wickedness, and whose strength is mental. I have explored the globe of hell, and found all substances that create and worketh abomination; which creation worketh through mental pressure, according to the ardent desires of the heart.

Through the enchanting and sweet influence of the members of the mental pit, the woman was driven and detained in the wilderness, because she worshipped and conferred all honor upon this corrupt image, but rejected the tabernacle. I cannot accomplish the real work that I was raised up to do, until this mental pit is destroyed from the tabernacle of sin. I want thee to break the strong bands of the sweet influential powers that this corrupt image has bound the woman in who brought forth the man child; which image rules her arbitrarily in scornfulness, excessive nicety, and so on. She has, by putting on the same image, been a helpmeet for this mortal man, the image of corrupt science, all through the time of trouble, because she took up her abode in his kingdom, which definates the "wilderness." This was because she contained the principles harmonizing with the science of perdition; which compelled her to serve, glorify, and honor that man of sin. Thou hast shapened her thus, so that the Scriptures might be fulfilled, and the trouble prevail unto the end of the time spoken of.

We will now rise up and circumcise this ram, so that his seed no longer mingle and amalgamate with the holy seed. I declare that this image has not allowed this people to reach one point of holiness; their entire work has shown itself perfect through mortal science. Thou gavest the power for them to be endowed with this corrupt science, to make up the fulness and perfection of perdition, which appeared to them unawares, was transformed into angels of light, and destroyed the holy people wonderfully.

Thy Christ took this transformed dragon for his bosom friend in the two sexes; but in searching for the cause of the troubles and great perils, found him to be the origin and perpetuator of the trouble. This is the abomination that was set up on equality with the Holy Christ. This abomination was the mortal principles and substances contained in the material bodies of the people of the holy prince; and these principles and substances had perfect harmony with the righteousness of the holy prince until they were tried,— "whence the discord began." Through the powers of antichrists sitting in the temples of the Holy Ghost, showing through fictitious godliness that they were Holy Christs, the blasphemous dragon prevailed against the holy people in the most shrewd and crafty way, creating and perpetuating desolation.

Father, we have the proof of his detestable corruption; and his works during our time of hardship have proven to be an abomination and an abhorrence to all flesh. He was my best friend, when his abomination and blasphemy were manifested in the informal world; and when he ended his rage in this way, he showed his vengeance in his chosen people, who were connected with thy holy sanctuary through covenants. When thou hadst shown him to me, and his subtle schemes that he had machinated to prevail against us, I then turned to be his worst enemy, and fought against him.

He is the desperate enemy who is now sitting in thy temple showing, through peace and godlike strategy. that he is the god of power; and also opposing everything that is being done for the victory of the truth, because he exalts and magnifies himself and kind above all. Thy judgments have been passed on him, obtaining a great testimony through the prophecies that this subtle power, working hopelessly, carelessly, and independently, is the god and spirit of mortality, who rules over all people in this wise period. He does not want thy kingdom to reign, because it is the annihilator of his glory and kingdom. He is continually spewing out of his mouth poisons that create loathsome diseases ; and this prevents any good from being done for the children of thy people.

Thou hast placed into thy hands a case of disease to show thy goodness, love, and sympathy for the children of men ; then why is it that this diseased substance is not destroyed and erased from the victim ? Thou knowest all about it, for thou hast made me to know ; and I will solve the reality of thy knowledge, so that thou mayst no longer burden thy Holy Christ with unreasonable burdens that can be avoided, and thy work performed. Father, it is this abominable dragon whom thou hast impowered to continue these diseases. He cannot have things his way, and reign as he forethought; now he wants to slay all the children of thy people. He would rather die a material death than stoop and honor thee in thy kingdom, because it is small in appearance.

Father, thou canst see plainly, through the discretion of thy Christ, that his wrothfulness has retarded the progress of thy kingdom from the time he heard of thy marvellous work in choosing me to use an instrument for the redemption of thy people. I will again declare that his anger was first manifested in the informal world ; and when he entered thy fold, and was deceived in the satisfying of his damnable lust, he became wrothful, and raged in the metropolis city, and cursed thy holiness, and thought in his heart to do mischief to thy covenant. But thou hast put bands of iron on him (which was sound truth), so that he could not move from one side to the other ; and will now make an end of this embodiment of abominations.

Father, thou hast raised up thy Christ to promote and establish holiness in the earth ; so I command thee to make an acute and final end of this embodiment of scientific abomination, and I will show thy marvellous power unto the children of men. Father, I am not going to be detained by this prince of hell any longer ; I am going straight through with the undertaking put upon me, according to thy will and good pleasure. I want this poisonous monster taken out of the waters of life, so that the healing that thou hast laid upon me may be done, and the patient go about the work that thou wilt have him to do.

Father, this is the trouble that I am fighting now, the trouble that has obstructed the inflowing of the waters of life. Thou hast seen it. Why dost thou not remedy it, and let the building of the walls continue? Take away from me this case of disease, by effecting the requests of these atonements. I shall not linger here on the verge of reproaches ; I shall go through and promote thy truth, and establish thy righteousness among a people who have not known thee, though it was told to them. I will not wait here through pseudo-conception expecting the success of thy cause to look more favorable ; for the trouble is at the point of relapsing, and I have this day stretched forth my mighty rod to slay the origin and promoter of sin.

I shall not rest, nor cease from vengeance until I find a true friend who will lay down his life for his friend even as I have lain down my life for him. I shall, from this time and henceforth, travel by realities, and not by false appearances, and soft tones of voices. I shall make no more corrupt beings holy through judgments, when their abominable hearts and faces are masked ; but I require of thee thy entire weapons of war to slaughter and burn the inhabitants of perdition to ashes.

Father, thou knowest that John is unfit for divine and physical service until his corrupt embodiment is destroyed and cremated. This corrupt embodiment within him has worked evil from the time he heard of thy Christ's coming to reign even until now ; and if some good work does not spring up within him, I have, by the power of my mighty rod, slain him and cast him out of thy kingdom materially. If thou wantest the temple for any good purpose, take it and make it what thou wouldst have it to be ; for I have stretched forth my rod across the globe of hell, and its inhabitants are utterly damned from destroying thy holy people. I have destroyed the venomous sting and the poisonous germs which he has been empowered to emit into the waters of life, and made them of non-effect, so that there was no power nor virtue in them to heal.

This independent reptile is fearless as to what thou shalt do with him ; and for this cause I shall not be contentious about which way thou shalt perform thy work, and end his time warring against thy truth, stamping it under foot, and causing the land to moan. Thou hast pronounced judgments enough upon him, it seems, to condemn and destroy the world of abominations without holding further council on his case. His way is firm and substantial in seeking high and precious things, and despises small things. He dare not speak one word in the behalf of thy kingdom meaningly ; and that that he says is beautifully composed and framed by subtle art, and forced out of feigned lips. His obduration reaches beyond the limits of all rationaliy ; and his damnable doctrines have no foundation nor summit.

His greatness, kingship, scornfulness, deception, enchantment, unbelief, fearlessness, hopelessness, lustfulness, and all other abominations which he contains scientifically in a concealed way have no beginning nor end. As long as thou shalt equip him with gold and silver, and mortal things, his craft and stratagem must continue to deceive and be deceived. Strip him clean of mortal science and wisdom, and the lion will eat straw like the ox; which definates that he will be thankful and pleased to take his first lesson of simplicity, lay aside his foolishness, and serve thee through a newness of heart. Then he will appreciate, and be thankful for thy plain bread and water of life, which thou art giving out each day to bring thy people home to thee. Through leviathan's wisdom and Lucifer's science, he carries himself in a holy and perfect way, to shun thy rebukes, and to shun the edge of the sword; he has the full corrupt science of fear. He is always looking ahead to see what trouble is approaching him, to put on his perfect sheep's clothing to shun thy chastening rod; but when he is stripped naked of his science of corruption, his diseases will end.

He watches ahead, works it over in his sage mind, and finds out for surety what trouble is coming; and when he has done this, he starts his scientific craftsman to work to shun the trouble, and not to be overtaken, to continue his abominations. He is fearful when he is striving to shun the sword; but when it falls upon him his fear departs, and then he is fearless, stupid, unconcerned, and independent about what is done with him. This is the scientific workings of this embodiment of wizards; and for this cause I ask thee to let the creative words return to their creative power at once, which is the supreme ruling power of thy Christ; let the waters roll in mountains of life-giving power, and thy kingdom will no longer be subject to these powers of corruption.

Father, this case of disease that is in thy material hands has been moved in such a way as to receive a strong testimony through the agency of the physical physician. Father, what is the use of spending money for that that profiteth not? Thou canst abolish death in this case without the assistance of the physical medical science; rise up and work in thy supernatural medical science. Father, let the material use of medicine be cut off from this patient, through involuntary progression, and let the divine medical science of life awake through the power of instinct. Grasp that wrothful coughing beast, and take away his power at once. All that thou hast to do is to breathe into the nostrels of this patient the pure atmosphere of life eternal, and that tormenting and brutish cough will end, without even thinking of using the resistible and irritating remedies of physics.

Father, thou hast thy soothing and healing hands on that ravenous lustful dragon; renew thy grip, to stop his painful cough. Father, thine eyes have seen that the irritable breath of this patient is near the point to cease vibrating. I thank thee because thou knowest that I am a faithful and zealous enemy to that coughing dragon ; he destroys the organs of man and woman. Let me feed upon his mortal blood, whose system I have caused to cleave, that my soul may eat, and be satisfied ; and journey on and possess the land that he has in his possession.

Father, if he is going to destroy all of my mansions, let him be turned upon me, so that I may wipe him out of existence, and save the mansions for thy glory. I have slumbered with those who slept these many days, to awake in this day and put that monstrous death out of the earth. I am at thy will and pleasure, to do as thou hast determined in all things; but let that serpent who afflicts and puts humanity to death be destroyed by my rod. I thank, and adore thy name, and magnify thy power performed in a simple way in the achievement of the victory in making thy Christ the king and ruler of diseases.

Father, through the attainment of the victory which thou hast given me in the annihilation of the origin of diseases, thou hast put all diseases in fear of me ; and when they hear of my name, they will begin to tremble and seek other homes instead of the temples who are coming into my possession. All this wonderful work has already been done through the power of my rod of iron ; and thou shalt hasten the time to prove it by works, and verify thy supreme words of power which are stamped upon these pages.

Father, I am hasty in my decision because I have drawn thy almighty rod of iron, and if any prey falls within its reach contrary to the excellency of this cause and covenant, I shall slay it without warning. Let these words be driven to the heart of every enemy of thy kingdom ; my very heart thirsteth for their blood, for I shall see the last drop licked up by the fire gone out of my rod. Strengthen and increase the power and speed of my speech, and let it reach the fulness of power.

ATONEMENT OF THE LAMB TO SLAY THE SCIENCE OF PRIDE, JEALOUSY, AND SCORN FROM THE DAUGHTER OF ZION.

Father, I have seen the pride of the daughter of Zion; I have also seen her eminent science of jealousy, and her excessive scornfulness, which I detest and shall demolish by the fire that streams out of my rod. Father, change the course of the atmosphere of heaven, and let thy immortal breath breathe upon the slain of dry bones, that sinews and flesh may cover them, and life may come into them, and make them thy people according to the holy doctrine of the new covenant.

Caroline's principles are abnormal to the holy doctrines of this covenant. Thou hast spoken the words that created within her those repugnant characteristics, to use her a full subject to fulfil the Holy Scriptures at thy coming to reign over sin in thy chosen people. I do not confess that she was fashioned with those high and eminent principles of mortal science to bear the high and eminent principles of the feminine glory in the Godhead. These are thy express purposes for fashioning her as narrated, and I declare that it is good that it is so.

After fulfilling thy determination in the principalities of sin reigning within her, there must be a speedy change from the mortal state of eminence to the immortal state of eminent science. She is partial in her judgment court; and the eminent principles of mortal science must be subverted before she can be impartial in her discretion, be loving and sympathizing toward humanity, deny her own selfish wishes and condemned principles, lay down the old life, and live wholly for the perfect truth which was laid waste by the foreparents. I find that she is not devoted to divine purity; her devotion adheres to the science of pride, jealousy, and scornfulness, but these principles will never drink of life's pure waters, for they are an abomination. These principles and inclinations are the great current of mortality which hath continuated corruption; she has committed herself, her will and ways into my hands to reserve the good and destroy the evil, so that she may be created, fashioned, and transhumanized after the construction of this covenant. She has at last decided, and also confessed, that her way is darkness, misery, and death; and the way thou leadeth me is joy, life, and light.

When thy Christ descended to the earth to burn up sin and its works, thou hadst formed and resurrected the deadened, high, and eminent inclinations of the scientific workings of the Devil, which she contained in substance, which worked and ruled over the saints miraculously to make her one of the flaming swords around the spiritual land of Eden, because the mighty dragon sought to slay the man she brought forth. Father, I want a refraction of light to spring up within her at once through thy marvellous power, just as thou hast miraculously revived within her the kingdom of utter darkness, through the resurrection of abominable characteristics. I would that thou shouldst stamp her indelibly with thy entire feminine characteristics, and they will harmonize with those of the righteous man. Thus the two trees planted by the river of the water of life will draw water therefrom for the cleansing of human blood, and for the healing of the nations.

Father, the agreement and compounding of these substances in the two genders of transhumanity, and the affinity which these substances of truth will have for each other when compounded after being distilled from the immortal souls of the two sexes, will unite within the person to whom it is given, devastate corruption, and form within them, through a coagulation and adherence, the compounding of truths, restoring the waste and down-trodden principles of humanity, and besieging the walls of transhumanity against its spoilers and oppressors.

Before any one can be created expressly after the image and likeness of thy transhumanized body, the woman must be put to death in the wilderness, and cast into the crematory furnace, and both the woman and the wilderness be burned to ashes : and we will go in and tread down the wicked, made dust for the softness and glory to the soles of our feet. This sudden change will be the refraction of light, the final end of desolation, the reception of her reasonable service into the holy kingdom, the holy marriage supper of the Lamb, the preparation for bringing forth her children, and the establishment of the holy truth among the children of men.

Father, create within her, though the revivification of divine nature, thy flaming power of zeal, the true judgment and equity, to deal in love, truth, sympathy, and faithfulness with mankind, to restore and establish the true government and doctrines of humanity. Father, kindle the flame of truth within her soul, and burn up fallacious doctrines, false ideas, hopelessness, and all things within her incongruous to the laws and doctrines of thy holy covenant.

Father, quicken her desire with the fulness of the pure principles of thy kingdom, and the Son of Righteousness will soon translunarize the globe of sempiternity. Father, thou must work within her from this time, according to thy will, and subvert the letters of mortality that thou settest up within her nature and quickened, to use to represent and publish the book of sin in the fulness. Cause her to make a sudden change from this time by igniting the light fuel, which is the divine propensities that are sealed up within the bowels of her soul, which now is besieged by the power and strength that thou gavest unto abominations to prevail against the immortal soul.

Father, loosen her pure and everlasting seals of righteousness, that her beauty may be seen; which beauty all honorable beings of mankind will desire and seek after, for it is fair to the extreme. Father, let me not linger here in wait for the accomplishment of this atonement, but continue to unfold the realities of righteousness and unrighteousness, which will bring these words to pass. Father, let the spark of immortality kindle within her soul, and produce joy, life, and light, and the wilderness will consume away, and be no more. I am destitute of a material companion in the testimony of these truths; prepare her to be my companion in truth and righteousness.

PART VIII.

ATONEMENT OF THE LAMB TO DESTROY THE HASTY SPEED OF THE FLYING EAGLE.

Father, through this intercession, I shall stretch forth my mighty rod across the land of Egypt to destroy the Pharite host, the host of Babylon, all the ungodly people whom thou hast raised up during the past dark ages of the world to make the kings, princes, and chief rulers of perdition. Father, this eagle is the man stature, the image of abomination who, by stealth and stratagem, commanded and governed the regiment of perdition through lying words and deceivable acts, to lead thy people into Babylon, his kingdom, to lay waste through public disgrace thy holy city and sanctuary.

Father, he took thy people preys to his kingdom, and laid siege against them for many days, before we learned where we were situated and in to what manner of kingdom we had gone. Father, this sham of perdition was transformed into an angel of light through craft and deceit, to make his kingdom a continual snare to us; but thou hast seen our condition, hast turned the hearts of the rulers of his kingdom one against the other, hast established war between them, and hast slain those unfit for thy further purposes. This was thy marvellous power, manifested to deliver thy people out of the cruel and wicked kingdoms. Let the entire powers of the Babylonian's necromancers be annihilated and brought to an utter end, so that I may see it.

Father, this mighty power of deceivableness has prevailed over thy people through the man upon whom thou hast imputed the blessing of prosperity, to fulfil his time in a prosperous way deceiving thy holy people who are manifested in holy principles. This influential science of deceivableness performed such marvellous work that thy holy chosen principles were secluded to believe that he was possessed with the same principles. But thou gavest us wisdom to search him through and through, understandingly, and we found that the power that carries him is the antichrist, yea, and worse than an antichrist,—the great deceiver of mankind, the king of the bottomless pit. The spirit and characteristics that have carried him to finish up the time of transgression were the science of magianism, which practised the science of mesmerism through the art of lying, having power to speak and to make things that did not exist come into existence, and those things that are in existence become null and void.

This is the manner of dehumanized being that thy blessing of prosperity was imputed upon, to continuate abominations and keep thy holy kingdom divided against itself, by defending the flesh embodying this corruption. This angel of the bottomless pit had the full power of deceivableness between his two eyes, which is concealed by the lumination of mirthfulness; and this power can speak enchantingly on any matter in a firm and solemn manner, and at the same time be deceiving without any one's mistrusting that any such thing would fall from the lips of a man of his stamp, untruthfully. This branch of corrupt science is one of the controlling powers of sin that governs the people who live upon the earth. It was drilled out from the world by the horn of blood-kin and family circle, which is one of the chief branches of sin, and the assistant slayer of humanity.

Father, I would that thou shouldst slay these magicians that make up this great branch of iniquity, who are continually changing from one branch to the other, inventing and refining his science down to a more essential state in the arts of deception. Just as the science of holy truth was discovered and refined down to the essential degree, the mesmeric powers of iniquity have travelled in like manner to reach the superfine qualities of science to fulfil the time of prophecy. I commend thee to show, publicly, how mortal mental science can ever have an end, when it has been transformed and refined down to a substance equivalent to that of divine science. Can these that are with me in person be changed from the corrupt to the incorrupt? I will answer that they can, for they were fashioned thus, according to thy will and purposes, to make manifest, characteristically, the laws of the bottomless pit, which have, these last days of sin, in ruling the truth prevailed in its despotic power through the most advanced mental science.

Father, thou hast created these scientific, ruling, and attractive powers of perdition, so that abominations would be wholly spiritual in all of its many scientific branches of workings, to be equivalent to the holy science of life. I can see that those who are constructed with the science of perdition inhale the atmosphere of hell; and the atmosphere of perdition is the quickening spirit of antichrist, and the medium of life which moves over the sphere of antichrist, that has been refined down to a solid and substantial stratum and godlike system and power, and flows through these channels of corrupt and refined scientifical principles, which continuate the abomination and suffering of the flesh that they are planted within, perfecting the prevalence of the mental pit.

I do herein confess that the purity and high scientific workings of the holy truth have also reached the perfect state to rule over all mortal science and put an end to the destroyer of humanity, who keeps man from being like God in nature. Deceivableness of sin and vice has, through the powers of science, reached the apex of art in its lawgiver, whose laws and governments were made null and void at the post-millennium of Shiloh, — being interpreted, the second coming of the Holy Christ. — which fulfils thy words as follows: "The sceptre shall not depart from Judah, nor a lawgiver from between his feet, until Shiloh come: and unto him shall the gathering of the people be. Binding his foal unto the vine, and his ass's colt unto the choice vine; he washed his garments in wine, and his clothes in the blood of grapes: his eyes shall be red with wine, and his teeth white with milk."

The mystery unfolding the meaning of this prophecy reads as follows: —

"Thou, O king, sawest, and behold a great image. This great image, whose brightness was excellent, stood before thee; and the form thereof was terrible. This image's head was of fine gold, his breast and his arms of silver, his belly and his thighs of brass, his legs of iron, his feet part of iron and part of clay. Thou sawest till that a stone was cut out without hands, which smote the image upon his feet that were of iron and clay, and brake them to pieces, then was the iron, the clay, the brass, the silver, and the gold, broken to pieces together, and became like the chaff of the summer threshing-floors; and the wind carried them away, that no place was found for them: and the stone that smote the image became a great mountain, and filled the whole earth. This is the dream; and we will tell the interpretation thereof before the king. Thou, O king, art a king of kings: for the God of heaven hath given thee a kingdom, power, and strength, and glory. And wheresoever the children of men dwell, the beasts of the field, and the fowls of the heaven hath he given unto thine hand, and hath made thee ruler over them all. Thou art this head of gold. And after thee shall arise another kingdom inferior to thee, and another third kingdom of brass, which shall bear rule over all the earth.

"And the fourth kingdom shall be strong as iron: forasmuch as iron breaketh in pieces and subdueth all things: and as iron that breaketh all these, shall it break in pieces and bruise. And whereas thou sawest the feet and toes, part of potter's clay, and part of iron, the kingdom shall be divided; but there shall be in it of the strength of the iron, forasmuch as thou sawest the iron mixed with miry clay. And as the toes of the feet were part of iron, and part of clay, so the kingdom shall be partly strong, and partly broken. And whereas thou sawest iron mixed with miry clay, they shall mingle themselves with the seed of men: but they shall not cleave one to another, even as iron is not mixed with clay. And in the days of these kings shall the God of heaven set up a kingdom, which shall never be destroyed: and the kingdom shall not be left to other people, but it shall break in pieces and consume all these kingdoms, and it shall stand for ever. Forasmuch as thou sawest that the stone was cut out of the mountain without hands, and that it brake in pieces the iron, the brass, the clay, the silver, and the gold; the great God hath made known to the king what shall come to pass hereafter: and the dream is certain, and the interpretation thereof sure."

The exegesis unfolding the hideous phantom seen in days of old was the shadows of the four wicked kingdoms which stood in the people of the holy prince and rebelled against the holy kingdom in the annals of this doctrine. They are, namely, and successively in power and strength, as follows. Educational science is the king of mortal kings, signifying gold: the power that leads and governs: the sceptre of power, and the lawgiver of this advanced age. The glory, honor, and essential respect conferred upon woman by man, and upon man by woman, is the next most powerful kingdom of the world, signifying silver, which is ruled by the lawgiver. Avariciousness, that craves and seeks after the wealth of the world, is the third great kingdom, which is the grandeur and brightness of the four wicked kingdoms metaphored as brass, and governed by the first king.

Partiality, and the essential love and respect conferred upon blood-kin and family circle is the base of the four wicked kingdoms which is metaphored as iron mixed with miry clay, and also governed by educational science. John, the microcosm of the secular world by nature, was the focus of these four wicked kingdoms ruling in their supreme power over the holy kingdom through all deceivableness and adroitness; but educational science subdued the other three kings, and he ruled and kept them still in nature through the science of craftiness, upon which power the man Isaac was carried, in a spiritual way, to be faithful in his work. The strength and might of the four wicked kingdoms contained in the microcosm were governed scientifically by the wisdom and sentiments of educational science, which power held the inferior kingdoms in solitude peacefully by not allowing them to say a word in defence of their power, which enabled them to retain the ruling sceptre unto the end of the time prophesied of. By these four kingdoms' working within nature in such deceivable and crafty way, the man of sin, which is the focalization of these kingdoms, dwelt in this disguised temple, wielded the weapons of cruelty, and judged all things corruptly by making the true doctrines false and the false true, until the Scriptures were fulfilled.

I do confess, through the experience which I obtained during the great perils, while journeying around the worlds of mortality, that impure air cannot mingle with the pure atmosphere of heaven; if they are occupying together a portion of the same temple, one will keep the other in bondage, neither one will enjoy freedom. This matter has been thoroughly tried and proven,— that thy kingdom cannot mingle harmoniously with the animal kingdom, the Devil's race, for they were both crowded together in the same temple, supposing that all the substances within the temple were pure in purity and of the same degree in quality. The elements of thy kingdom have been confined and concealed within the microcosm through the troublous times of the saints by the prevailing powers of those four wicked kingdoms, which partly mingled with thy kingdom, but did not mingle to form a compound substance of the two substances. This caused the severe suffering and consumption of the corrupt body through constant griefs and burdens, finding all efforts of no avail until the Scriptures are fulfilled.

The elements of the holy and wicked kingdoms are at war within the microcosm, which continuates the apathy between soul and body, disagreeing, through judgment, on every point of truth until the body of death is destroyed and given to the burning flames of truth, which are leaping unto the skies to deliver the elements of holy truth out of the cruel hands of those wicked kingdoms. Now those impure substances must be burned, and the temple of flesh set free ; for these abominating powers have become a total curse to thy holy kingdom, and prevent its further advancement; and it cannot be lifted up in honor until these corrupt powers of science are no more.

I have found the chief object of the members of perdition, while sailing around the globe of the four rapid currents of sin. I have found that the ancient powers of perdition have no force in this advanced age except through transformation and metempsychosis of corruption. Through transmigration the holy truth, which has been sack-clothed during the past dark ages of the world, has concentrated and focalized into a polarizing ray of light, and has completed the translunary light of heaven. The pre-eternal, scientific workings of metaphysics, the powers of hell, have reached the same points and powers in its focus which were concealed and handed down through metempsychosis by the inheritance of depravity; and there is no way but through thy channel to exterminate the corrupt science of metaphysics. It is the exact similitude of the holy kingdom in its method of works; then how can they be distinguished one from another, if they continue to exist in the present state? Why dost thou not bring mortal science, that is warring against thy sanctuary, to an end? Deliver me from the powers of this dark scientific world.

ATONEMENT OF THE LAMB TO DIVULGE THE HIDDEN SECRETS OF THE SEVEN STREAMS OF CORRUPTION, AND LET THE WATERS BE DRIED UP.

Thou all-wise God of this covenant, hear, hasten to the demand of this atonement, and consider thy Israel's victory. There stands before me a thick black veil, which keeps concealed the modern hidden secrets of diseases. There are seven modern streams of corruption, which flow into one grand division to make up the grand central point of abominations, wherein all the smaller streams empty their contents for preservation. This grand division is the concealed mystery of death, wherein all the science and arts of death are taught to slay humanity; and this is called the "cold and icy stream of death," and no man is able to swim or sail across its rapids. No man in heaven, nor on earth, nor under the earth, and no man upon the sea is able to canoe himself across these turbulent waters, except through thy conquering rod which thou hast placed in the hands of thy second Moses, to smite it in the seven streams thereof, and make men to go over dry-shod.

Father, this is the time, and this is thy promised power to thy second Moses; and this is the thing thou shalt this day perform to show forth thy almighty power before Israel's face. When thou shalt have performed this thing, I will attain the state of wisdom and power, strength and honor, glory and riches, blessings, and divine righteousness. Let me see thy anthropomorphous manhood in these seven united powers in the eighth, namely, righteousness, by placing thy material eyes on the seven streams of corruption centred in the leviathan focus. Israel is this day waiting at the verge of its rapids for thy command to say, Cross over. Thy rod is fully sufficient to accomplish the work according as I have atoned. Let the seven pillars of fire range from the soles of thy feet to the highest substances in the kingdom of light and the kingdom of perdition. Let thy rod of iron make a plain manifestation of its power, by smiting the seven streams of corruption, which vast body is destroying humanity.

Father, force the seven streams of fire upon the seven streams of corruption, and consume and dry up the seven streams that make up abomination, so that men may cross over and not be driven back by its rapids any more. Father, awake, this day, and let the seven original streams of diseases be licked up by the fire of thy wrath and vengeance. Let the seven thunders utter their voices in this day on thy mysteries that have been kept hidden from men from the foundation of the world. Let hailstones, fire, and brimstone shower down in the focus of perdition, touching it in the seven streams, and dry up and consume the entire current of death.

Father, arise upon thy judgment throne this day, which is thy tabernacle of righteousness, and let the thunder roll, accompanied by lightning such as never was heard by flesh. Desert the tabernacle of flesh, by making it a tabernacle of word, spirit, and truth; and be thou the omnipotent God, and rule over god of gods. Let not thy material eyes look upon the temple of flesh, but search out the full utterance of corruption and incorruption. Rise up as a thief, and show a miracle that no man is able to look into until the great work is accomplished, and we are passed over this Jordan. Let us move on amid the waters of Jordan, and the science of this miracle will begin. Let the trumpet of divine science sound aloud — sound from the origin of science to its highest branches in every degree.

Father awake and smite this image of corrupt science by the loudest trump of divine science. How canst thou longer forbear? Wilt thou suffer this deleterious image to go pell-mell through the world until all humanity are destroyed by the power of his crafty and peaceful rage? The globe of hell is formal, and there are limits to its measurement and power; and I want to see the pit destroyed from the earth. How long wilt thou seek peace among the inhabitants of hell? How long wilt thou teach them to turn to thy holy way?

Father, canst thou convert the soul-workers of abomination to be soul-workers of righteousness? Why dost thou allow such unreasonable attempts to keep me in suspense? Canst thou see that this vast division of abominable science is envious against thy holy truth, and will not be reconciled with him? Father, these corrupt scientific principles in man can never see life; then why holdest thou me in bondage? This science will never turn to thy simple way; then let me go unto thy holy hill, where I may rest from the opponents of this great adversary of science.

ATONEMENT OF THE LAMB TO QUICKEN THE SEVEN ELEMENTS OF DIVINE MEDICAL SCIENCE, AND LET PROSPERITY BLOSSOM IN THE HANDS OF THE COMMANDER.

I, Samuel, the atoner for the progression and development of the cursed and down-trodden race of humanity — which curse is maintained because they reject the elements of divine truth — I do herein acknowledge my determination to accept the powers of eternal life in the fulness, and unanimously. I find, through searching into this case of disease, that the physical medical science is the semi-power of man's purity and material existence, to cleanse the material body for the temple of the Holy Spirit just as soap cleanses the clothing for the body, so that impure and offensive temples will not exist to cause the Divine Spirit to desert them.

I find that if the material body is filthy, the spirit of divine truth will not dwell therein. I find that if the spiritual body of man is depraved, the material body becomes affected with diseases. I find that divine fluid, which is in different styles of words with their proper spiritual meaning, is the clean raiment for the soul; and if we inhale the pure atmosphere of heaven, we are putting on clean raiment fashionable for the soul. The reception of divine truth, and the understanding of its true meaning, is called "the inhaling of thy immortal fragrant breath," which devotes the human race to perfect brotherly love and friendship toward their fellowmen.

I shall define this mystery more closely by saying that the soap and its agents are the cleansing power for the raiment of the material body, and the physical medical science is the cleansing power of the material body, both external and internal. The different words of divine truth, with their proper meaning, are the change of raiment for the soul; and the change of words is the newness of life; and divine truth is the cleansing power to keep the word clean and pure through the changes which it has to pass, acting in different cases and many purposes.

Father, I have found, by searching, that there are seven scientific doctrines of life eternal, and they are, namely, food and raiment, water and air, heat, and cold, and light. These seven doctrines of physical science are being fully perfected by the Lord God through the agency of the most advanced nations of the earth; and these same seven great doctrines are in the holy spiritual kingdom, and they are composed of the same substance, perform the same work, and have the same effect upon the soul that the seven elements that govern the terrestrial kingdom have upon the material body of man, and other creatures and substances.

The seven elements of physical science created every materia thing within the terrestrial kingdom; and without the agency of these seven elements was nothing made terrestrially. Without the agency of these seven elements, there could be no creation of members and substances for the inhabitation of the spiritual kingdom of the Lord God. The divine word is the Son crucible, and all the creative and destructive powers are in him. All the chemicals that are solid, ærial, and liquid are in the Son of Righteousness; and the different changes and degrees through which the son is passing are preparing the soil of humanity for the implanting of divinity to begin the divine creation of man in the image of the Holy God. The terrestrial sun passes through the different degrees of latitude to prepare the soil and every living thing for regeneration and creation.

The severe cold destroys the old roots of some herbs and buds of trees; and those that pass through the severe cold and yet live are regenerated; and those destroyed are no more, but others are created in their stead. The many changes are to bring forth a new harvest; and when it reaches the time and season for a new harvest, the sun enters the next degree through gradual changes, and the seven powers are within it, performing the work of creation and regeneration through moderate degrees. Each one of these seven powers is equipped with many thousands of chemical operators, which vary in size and strength just as they succeed in office and rank. The first is very powerful, the next not quite so much so, and so on, decreasing in size and power until they make up a number of ten thousand times ten thousand, and thousands of thousands.

All these many thousands of chemical agents are in the seven great doctrines of divine science. In the terrestrial world they are all governed by the sun ; and they perform their work by the power of the sun. In the celestial world the same amount of agents are at work under the control of the Son, which is the many grades and degrees of principles wrought in the Son ; and they are the many agents that are creating members for the celestial kingdom. Seeing that all these divine scientific medical principles are in the celestial kingdom, thou must endow thy Holy Christ with exploring wisdom to find each one of these many agents and put them in thy drug store in order, so that they may be issued correctly to heal the mortiferous diseases that are destroying the precious lives of mankind.

Why dost thou not come and make a change, through the quickening power of thy words, and put death out of this temple ? Why dost thou wait until life almost ceases to exist before thou accomplishest thy work ? Thou hast promised to redeem me from the powers of death in this case ; confirm thy promises now, for this mighty dragon will never be destroyed until thou becomest interested in his destruction. Now this case of affliction has gone as far as I will allow ; and I beg thee, with humbleness of heart, with honor, and with magnifying power, to awake to realities and let me return to the building of the walls of Jerusalem. I have taken every step on this case that thou hast stamped upon the ensign, and I have reached the origin of the trouble, both physical and divine ; therefore stop this plague, and free me from the mighty powers of his chains and castles.

When these atonements were made, the Holy God had intrusted to Samuel's care a case of material disease, which was consumption in its terrible form ; and this was for the spirit of divine truth to make atonements on, to utter the language and mysterious truths on all points of the diseases of the soul, and to pour out his wrath and vengeance in speech against the origin of diseases, to become the chief ruler of diseases. This case of affliction was George, the youth, whom the atoner had put to work with Isaac in the fruit store when the blessing of prosperity was imputed upon him.

ATONEMENT OF THE LAMB TO ATTAIN THE FULL POWER OF SPEECH IN THE UTTERANCE OF TRUTH IN THE COMPLETE BOOK OF LIFE.

I, Samuel, the commander of this people and the covenant of this people, attend unto thee, my Father, for what I am greatly in need, to face the world and proclaim thy truth in its fulness. Father, this is the thing of which I am greatly in need. I am dumb with silence because thou hast not taught my tongue to speak, neither hast thou prepared a people for me to speak to. I am but as a child who has never spoken. Now, Father, I shall ask thee to endow me with the fulness of thy wisdom that is connected with these truths, to place thy affluence of speech in my articulate organs, and to quicken my tongue to utter thy mysterious wisdom as pertaining to thy spiritual kingdom, because there is no other tongue to proclaim thy truth, that it may be established among the children of thy people.

There is no other heart made to retain and solve thy precious truths in the fulness, since all must be proclaimed and established through me and those yet to come like me. Then confer upon me the fulness of wisdom and the power of speech to represent and preside over the mysterious works and glory of thy kingdom. I will no longer keep thy name concealed, nor thy mysterious power covered from the children of thy people. I shall, from this time, speak with a new tongue, and show thy marvellous works through the mighty power of speech unto all whom thou drawest unto me. From this time thou wilt present to me, in speech, the utterance of the complete book of life, and I will declare it unto a people who have not known thee.

Father, I shall from this time give unto all whom thou drawest unto me for thy glory, thy precious words of truth ; and I shall have wisdom and knowledge to know thy people who are fashioned for thy glory. I care not what holy way they come, if they are interested in me, I am interested in them ; for they are the people whom thou shalt draw unto me, to make known thy mysterious power. Then loosen and free them from bondage,— all whom thou hast made ready to take interest in divine truth, — and enable them to stand before the son of man. Suffer none to come unto him but those who are found worthy ; and those who are not prepared to receive thy truth, to promote the interest of thy kingdom in this day, place bands of iron on, that they may continue in the way they now pursue until they are prepared to receive the truth as thou shalt divulge it. But put me not off in obtaining the quickening power of speech as it is now concentrated and contained in the complete book of life.

Father, as long as I am covered and secluded from the people, impurity and mysterious evils must exist around and about thy holy sanctuary; for all things covered and kept concealed are accounted evil. When I show myself as I am, the world will see no evil in me; and there will be no evil but that which is in them. But while I am concealed, I am deceiving those among whom I am travelling, for they take me to be as other men, when I am not as other men; and this false appearance and pseudonymous name are only used to carry out thy purposes.

If I show myself a righteous man, they will receive me as a righteous man; and this current of evil will no longer flow. I humbly implore thee to give me the full power of speech, that I may show myself as I am in thy glory. Let thy power of speech flow with the full current of righteousness, and the waters of Jerusalem will be restored to their perfect state and power. Standing waters are not wholesome; they cause all who drink of them to loath and die. Let the river of the waters of life flow continually, and the waters will be healed and cleansed. I mean that thou shouldst stream the waters of life through my mouth from this time henceforth.

Father, mend the leaky and waste places of Jerusalem, so that the waters may flow with full and high tide. Place thy material eyes on the broken cisterns, the leaky and waste places, and I care not where they are, I will rise up and repair them, and stop the waste of thy precious words. Thy words are wasted through giving them unto a generation who receiveth them not, but turneth away; and they flow down in the valleys, among the high hills and mountains, and bottomless channels, and are no more. And in those hollows and dry channels where they find bottoms, before evaporating, the waters become obnoxious and fill the air with offensive odor, so that the beast of the forest, and the cattle upon the hills, and the fowl that fly in the firmament, dare not drink thereof, because thou hath sent out the warning which declares that such waters are destructive to life.

Rocks and mountains, hills and valleys, plains and wildernesses, such as are in the material universe, are in this people's spiritual bodies, which were created by the floods of abomination; and this is the great waste of the waters of Jerusalem. Father, thou must make the mountains plains, the plains mountains, the valleys hills, and the high hills valleys; the rough ways make level and smooth, the crooked ways make straight, fill in the dry channels and hollows of the earth, make the earth, in rough and hollow places, smooth grassy plains, and hew out cisterns of thine own that will hold water.

As long as thou shalt suffer this mountainous, desolate, and barren world of sin to exist in connection with us, the great waste of the waters of Jerusalem will continue. There is no way to supply such a world as this with pure and free running currents of water, for the earth is filled with fissures and crevices which will imbibe all the waters that flow therein. This mortal world is filled with subterranean channels that cannot be filled. Seeing that this mountainous, rough, and rugged world is the land whereupon thy holy church shall be built, prepare it hastily for the erection and establishment of the holy church, and all other glorifications belonging thereto.

ATONEMENT OF THE LAMB TO DESTROY THE JEALOUSY OF PERDITION SO THAT PEOPLE MAY FLOW UNTO THE RIVER OF LIFE.

I, Samuel, the signet of this people,—who contain the twelve signs of heaven, to lead, govern, and point out the true way, by showing what is approaching, whether good or evil, — I attend unto thee, thou Almighty Prince of this covenant, concerning the great power of darkness which hangs heavily over the holy Jerusalem ; and its living waters do not flow freely. The great image of jealousy has fortified Jerusalem these many days, and has prevented any one from coming to the waters to drink that they might have life.

Father, this venomous serpent has ruled thy Christ and made him a slave to her, to carry out thy will and purpose in trying the holy truth thereby. It has tried thy Christ, purged and polished the substances of purity, until now I find it is no trial to him ; and the trials have gone to the full extreme. This jealous monster is no more a trial nor trials ; but from this sixth day of the ninth month of the year eighteen hundred and ninety-one, she is no more a polishing substance, but a desperado henceforth, until thou utterly destroyest her from the earth, so that the pure, loving, truthful, patient, obedient, and sympathizing jealousy shall inherit the land promised to thy saints.

This is the manner of jealousy manifested upon thy signet, and I shall accept none other than that manifested upon the signs of heaven. I shall unfold the twelve signs of heavenly jealousy, so that this people may see me as I am ; and these twelve signs of godly jealousy point toward those who are inclined the same way in honor of this life.

The signs of godly jealousy are, namely, love and honor, mercy and devotion, affection and sympathy, obedience and kindness, patience and truthfulness, sincerity and thankfulness. Where these twelve streams are flowing, there is perfect heavenly rest, peace, and satisfaction amid jealousy; and all currents that flow outside of these, to disturb the perfection of peace and rest, are abominations and the spirit of antichrist.

Father, seeing that this image of jealousy is now one of the greatest obstructions that impede the development of the people who are given to me for the support of this cause, take it away from me, so that those who are toiling faithfully for the support and aggrandizement of the holy truth may reach thy bosom of peace and rest, to renew their strength and confirm their hope by seeing the reality of thy Christ. As long as thou sufferest that detestable image of jealousy to exist, I must lie here in this supine state, powerless in advancing thy kingdom. Slay this power of evil, and the dawning light of day will soon make its appearance in the holy land.

The agreement of the dreadful powers of jealousy worketh in the two sexes of the epitome of sin and crimes : and if thou destroyest it from the female, thou wilt destroy the root and fœtus. I shall define it to no individual person; I shall destroy it from these two who are the full embodiment of the jealous dragon. Everything done by thee is nothing in the sight of this image of jealousy; and the properties of jealousy are still reigning in this people.

How long shall I stand before the judgment seat and make intercessions, redemption, and restoration for this people ? They have no power to change their natural propensities, for thou hast created within them the highest sovereign powers of sin in the building of their physique. Why dost thou not awake in them through the elements of eternal fire, and consume the abhorrible substances, so that they may be testimonies of the truth? I find that thou art utterly rejected, and art among a den of dragons. They take no pleasure in thee, except when thou turnest aside from truth, equity, and discretion ; and when thou turnest aside from righteousness to try them, the sun, moon, and stars of the Lucifer orb illume the globe of mortality in a moment.

As long as the most minute substances of perdition are manifested in the microcosm, hell must rise higher and higher to compete with thy kingdom seemingly, in magnificence and glory, in the dispensation of this doctrine. Inasmuch as thou hast in thy kingdom substances that do not wear down nor waste away by consumption, and are unexcelled, there is also the likeness of the same substances in the Lucifer kingdom; which shall cause thy kingdom to soar higher and higher after the establishment of this dispensation.

Thou hast explored and discovered the entire contents of the Lucifer globe, and found therein the same substances that are in thy kingdom; only thy kingdom is the victorious kingdom, which makes it greater in power. But hell is as high as thy kingdom, and has the same duration; and it is as deep as thy kingdom, and has the same propensities, only hell is eternal damnation, and thy kingdom is eternal salvation. The substance that upholds thy kingdom is informal; and the substance that upholds the Devil's kingdom is the same. Let us eject from our land the principles of the formal globe, so that we may rule over the land thou hast given us; and seal up the power and works of the informal substance until time shall be no more.

The formal globe of depravity is the part now opposing thy holy kingdom, and rejects everything said and done for the welfare of the cast-off and rejected elements of divine truth. The informal substances of perdition are the many sorts and different grades of sin and crimes now reigning over all nations, peoples, kings, and tongues that live upon earth, but disharmonizing with the formal globe of abominations individually, because the late subtlety of sin and crimes is to reign over its people in the eternal age. The existing laws and customs of sin and crime cannot mingle with their advanced brother, because they are too antique; they must be refined down to the late science of sin and crime before there can be harmony.

Lucifer is the supreme and scientific mortal God who shall govern and command the Abyssinian race during eternity, in not showing mercy to his faithful servants as hath been done during the past torments of the wicked. Thy Holy Christ is also endowed with the most advanced principles of righteousness, which were from the holy characteristics of all nations who have existed upon the earth and who now exist; and he cannot mingle with his antique brethren until they are refined down to the eternal science of life, and are stamped with the same principles. They must subdue, honor, and appraise thy holy truth, which is the stamping instrument, before they can be like him in reality.

As long as divine truths are rejected, thy kindom is rejected; and those whom thou hast chosen to be heirs of thy glory will suffer in the worlds of misery and woe : for the purest and most refined substances of the Lucifer kingdoms cannot inherit incorruption. I have found the subterranean channels belonging to the formal globe of hell, and have found the world void of form. I implore thee to close the womb that is giving birth to other members to inhabit the formal globe of perdition, and make the formal globe of perdition barren, even as thou madest the womb of the formal globe of incorruption barren these many days.

The essential power and perpetuity of sin are spiritual ; the essential power and perpetuity of righteousness are spiritual ; the divine birth in the holy language is spiritual ; the properties of the kingdom of Christ are spiritual, and the building of the Devil's kingdom in its essential existence is spiritual. Then deliver me from the spiritual kingdom of the Devil, and establish the holy kingdom in the earth, where the primary works, the chief corner-stone, and the church of hell are built in real spiritual existence, which must be done by transmigration. This must be done by transferring these pernicious scientific principles into wholly depraved earthly tabernacles, which exist upon the earth so that the eternal doctrine of divine truth may be established with all flesh, and abase the kingdom of darkness that is ruling in the informal globe. Thou hast prepared Abyssinian empires to swallow up the modern science of corruption, to establish by knowledge the doctrine of metempsychosis ; let me see it begin. I have looked beyond the black veil of time, and see the channel of righteousness and unrighteousness both upon the motor of transmigration.

Father, let thy mighty and eternal blessing of prosperity spread its broad wings over thy chosen and faithful people, and make manifest thy real blessedness forever. Thy real blessedness is in the inheritance of thy holy kingdom ; and when the heirs of the eternal age put on thy raiments, they will put on thy real blessing of eternal prosperity. Because sin is the everlasting curse and damnation of the wicked, divine righteousness is the eternal blessing of the righteous, and the everlasting burning and torment of the wicked.

Father, open thine arms of love to receive all who seek thee ; but eject the souls of the wicked, and cast them into animal bodies to be rewarded for the evil they have done in sinning against thy sanctuary. Father, awake to their redemption those who have denied the world mentally, and are bound by the chains and castles of sin materially, so that they may be one with me even as we are one in righteousness. According as thou hast thought, let thy purposes be carried into effect in delivering thy righteousness from the will of the cruel powers of the heathen of the earth. Let thy full favor be toward me, to lift up thy kingdom out of the hands of bloody men, those who take no pleasure in divine righteousness.

Let me rise hastily to a higher degree in the advancement of thy kingdom. Let me not linger here, for this is still the verge of perdition ; so increase thy speed and power that I may soon reach the holy land. Let the fiery pillar appear upon the firmament of heaven ; let the waters flow, and my speech will be quickened, this existing scene will flee away, and the scenes will be such as have not been presented to this people. The scenes that now are presented to my sight are such as I have looked upon from childhood : so take away the existing scenes, insert the eternal blissful scenes, and this people will enter thy perfect rest.

ATONEMENT OF THE LAMB TO ABOLISH EDUCATIONAL SCIENCE AND ESTABLISH THE REALITIES OF DIVINE SCIENCE.

I, Samuel, the embodiment of divine science, intercede and plead in the behalf of thy holy truth, that he may be delivered from the great division of educational science. This great division of mortal educational science is embodied in John in its mighty power partly mingled with thy divine science, which is manifested in the understanding that he has of thee through the scientific use of the alphabets ; still he is exiled from home and does not return home to thee. Let this unquenchable fire ignite in the natural letters, and burn them to ashes.

Father, this image of science is searching thee day by day, and from time to time, to enter thy rest through the science of the letters, when there is no taste in him for thy holy truth. Awake from slumber where thou art sleeping in his flesh in the elements of divine truth, and consume that book of mortal science ; rain upon the dry and thirsty land, and the taste of divine science, which is planted in him, will take root and spring up.

The science of perdition has reached maturity, and the inhabiters thereof have made themselves ready to sow another harvest to surmount thy holy truth in wisdom by searching thee out by mortal science. The truth concerning thee is the seed to sow within the soil of divine nature. How shall men become immortal when the soil of nature is mortal, and the seeds and roots of mortality are planted within their natures? I will liken the body of man unto the earth, which man prepares for grain growing: he prepares the soil for planting before he sows the grain ; the preparation which is made through plowing up the earth destroys the rapid growth of herbs. When the earth is fallowed the wheat is sown without dividing the grains, and they produce a new harvest at the end of the season: but if he divide the grain in many parts and sow it into the earth, it will perish and decay in the earth.

The unwise sower visits the earth and watches the appearance of the grain in another form, but it cannot be seen; he consults the wise and experienced sower to find the cause of the seed's not regenerating, and when the wise and experienced sower examines the seed he finds that the grain was broken in many parts before being sowed by the unwise sower. The wise sower instructs the unwise sower how the earth should be fallowed, and the grain again sown into the earth just as he purchases it from him who sells it. When this is done his grain produces a new harvest, and yields abundance ; then he calls himself a fool and no longer lays the blame to him from whom he purchased the seed. So must the seed of immortality be sown into the earthly body without dividing it into many parts. Divine truth, when given by the seven angels, is the seeds of eternal life presented to man to sow into his heart to produce a new life.

If the holy words of God are received into the heart without being picked to pieces, regardless of its real meaning and forthcoming power and work, it will soon spring up an entirely new body ; which fœtus begins to form and grow by the power of nature within itself, and brings forth in due time the true form, meaning, and power of its life and existence.

The truth first dies in the soul, and when it makes its appearance it is a quickened body, the real meaning of the word of God when given to man in a mysterious form. But if the words of divine truth are picked in many parts, the true meaning severed, and a false meaning added, when it is received into the soul it decays and makes the depraved nature more fertile for the increase of demons and heresies. This creates offence within the soul, and it turns against the seven angels, by declaring that the words of God given in the fulness are unable to create eternal life and redeem from death. When the soul gets to this junction, the news rings in the ears of the competitors of divine truth, whereby they find full access into the soul, where they congregate with an imitation of the real truth, which is nothing but chaff and dross filled with magic power ; and in the meantime the seeds and roots of depravity are rapidly increasing in growth.

The soil that is productive of the integrity of morality is productive of divine integrity, providing the tendencies cleave to divinity. If a man is composed of honorable and refined qualifications, and is upright and loyal to the laws of the moral gods in honor of the Divine God, he is the soil which has been prepared by the agricultural instruments called the "physical scientific truth." These culturing instruments of natural science till the qualities, plant the seeds of godly virtue, and convey him on, step by step, higher and higher, overcoming and rising above unpolished qualities, until at last he steps into the state of redintegration.

ATONEMENT OF THE LAMB TO CIRCUMCISE THE UNCIRCUMCISED WHO ARE AMALGAMATING WITH THE RIGHTEOUS SEED.

I, Samuel, who contain by doctrines the covenant of the people, appeal unto thee, my Father, for speedy deliverance from the powers of the uncircumcised, who are amalgamating with the righteous seed. Father, thou hast this ram in the proper place to circumcise him ; thou hast fully seen the rage of his ravenous lust, so draw out thy sharp instrument and circumcise him, which is to take away from him the regenerator of abominations that is giving birth to the contaminating seed of darkness. There is no love nor reverence in this image for the daughter of Zion unless she yields up her material body to quench the burning flame of his ravenous lust. I find that this uncircumcised ram is making a brute of the daughter of Zion, he is making an harlot and a common prostitute of her. Until this uncircumcised power is taken away from this man, he cannot love and honor her in a holy way. He shall first learn to love, honor, and reverence thy holy truth wherein dwelleth the realities of the daughter of Zion.

Let the temple of flesh be delivered out of the cruel hands and tormenting powers of his rapacious lust. Take this rapacious beast away from me, for he is despising and trampling thy truth under foot and causing the building to cease. Deliver John from the will of his mighty power, he who is his agent to make manifest the strength of the spiritual power of the unclean beast. Compel him to lay aside his nonsense, and return to the work that thou hast chosen him to do. Shall I continue to make atonements on the destruction of this king of unclean beasts? I will answer, No; for he is near his end and none shall help him.

I do herein describe the manner of love and adoration that men shall obtain for the daughters of Zion when they enter the circumcised family. They will first love, honor, and magnify thy holy truth, thy simple and high ways of righteousness, with all their heart, mind, soul, and strength; and then they will love, honor, and delight in the spirit of the daughters of Zion, but will not love them in the lust thereof. Thy love bestowed upon the circumcised worketh no selfish craves nor excessive desires to obtain any certain thing for the gratification of the flesh, neither spite, grief, nor enmity; for the desires of the circumcised race are calm and peaceful, loving and affectionate.

This man has no such purity existing within him; this image is nothing but a mass of abomination, and, lastly, hell. He has no appetite nor taste for thy truth and judgment, but still he is equalizing himself with thee in thy righteousness. He has conceived the idea that if he has the opportunity to fulfil his desire, and satisfy his damnable lust, he would be satisfied to turn to thee; but this is a necromancing lie and one of the doctrines of hell.

Thou hast said to this people: "Blessed are they which do hunger and thirst after righteousness; for they shall be filled." This ravenous beast hath opened his poisonous mouth to swallow up thy people, and cause the building to cease; but I shall not linger here in wait to see what his intentions are, nor to see what help he is to this covenant. Nothing that glorifies this abominable image is good for this cause; and when the temple embodying this image is glorified over anything besides thy holy truth, it is destructive to this covenant.

ATONEMENT OF THE LAMB TO ABASE THE HAUGHTY AND HIGH LOOKER, AND SLAY UTTERLY THE MAGNIFIED SPIRIT OF LEVIATHAN.

I, Samuel, the contents of the hierarchy of divinity, commend thee, my Father, to make an hasty riddance of the magnified spirit of leviathan, who continuates the infamy and obscure gloominess; and has power to force into the minds of this people that thy works are small and insignificant, and not worthy of one's faithfulness. These mental propelling agents of depravity are the seed that is continually being brought forth by him and his companion, who embodies the substances which have perfect harmony to beget depraved abjects.

The images that this people bore have briefly repeated the historical parts of the apostolic Bible concerning Mary and Joseph's flight into Egypt until the death of Herod. The female has also repeated the trials of Sarah, being taken away from Abraham because he refused to say that she was his wife; and for this cause the Egyptian king took her to himself for wife. She has also repeated the trials of Isaac, being sent into Egypt. King Abimelech saw that Isaac's wife was fair, desired her, and questioned him concerning her, to know whether she was his wife; and fearing that he would meet death at the hands of the Egyptian, he said, "She is my sister."

The image that Caroline put on at the postliminy of Christ held the offices of all the wives of all godly men assigned to the apostolic epochs to repeat their work in a spiritual light. There was made a spiritual repetition of Noah, building the ark, and the eight persons and every living creature going into the ark, to be reserved in judgment, and convey them over into the new land; for the revelator is the eighth person, the embodiment of the seven righteous branches, and the books of the apostolic Bible which he opened before the floods of abominations began were the ark in which the eight persons and living creatures were reserved to reach the new land when the raging billows of abominations subsided after being cleansed by the strength and purity of these doctrines. Amen.

There were many more atonements made, reduced to writing, and recorded; but the atoning lamb saw it a necessity to leave them out on account of the time it would occupy, and the expense it would incur. For this reason the atoning lamb came to an abrupt decision to cut short the atonements and revelations which caused the great triumph of these doctrines in overpowering the satanic race, so as to cause to issue from his nature that manner of sound and infallible truth which will be of more value to the foundation and circulation of this book, and for the welfare of the readers, although the elementary principles of divine psychology are involved in the part uttered in the opening of the seven seals.

This permits me to take a scholarly discourse to reveal the wisdom that characterizes the higher plains, the existence of man in the transhumanized life, and to bring to sight a few more mysteries yet concealed ; also to reveal the aims of the higher mortal beings, who exist in errors far in advance of the baser sins and crimes practised by the common people, and the history of this people. After I have done this, I will rise still higher to prove by language the superiority of the power and purity of the life and wisdom conferred upon the revelator beyond that of the wisdom, power, and purity of the refined classes of mankind. This course of revelation shall run along the horizon of educational science, which will fully circumvolve the natural brain lobe, and show all the evils and crime therein contained.

This will show how the spiritual metamorphic change took place within the soul of the revelator; which enabled him to receive the fulness of godliness to step upon the free sod of the transhumanized life, to discover the perfect doctrines of life, and to find their proper names and offices. It can be understood that the atonements and revelations herein revealed fortified and redeemed from death and suffering the faithful members of the holy prince ; which atonements are strictly universal in love and sympathy, the power to redeem all mankind who receiveth the divine word, spirit, and truth as being the Saviour of the world, the Lord God, omnipotent in power, omniscient in wisdom, and omnispective in researches and observations.

The metamorphic change took place within the soul of the revelator after mingling with, and purging by judgments, the kingdoms of the world, beginning on this wise June 17, 1891. The antagonizing and noxious principles of the world, which were seated in the people of the prince with such potential power, and priorly had failed to relent and succumb to the doctrines of civilization — these the holy prince put force upon amain, and compelled them to go into the secular world, and work faithfully for the material support of the holy kingdom, or else be severed from the holy kingdom and its forthcoming blessings and privileges, which shall be greater than the suffering.

The revelator passed through the metamorphic change by the power of a prophecy which the Eternal God-revealed to direct the way: and the revelator passed through the metamorphic change with joy, peace, and praises, to produce the change in him to be willing to force from mingling with him that man of sin who was the focalization of the kingdoms of the world and its spiritual pollutions in the most substantial and venomous way. For this reason the excruciating pain took place in the soul of the man of sin to set the temple in motion among the people in the temporal world ; and this was the thing that he was so desperately opposed to doing before this prophecy went forth.

The prophecy which produced the metamorphic change within the souls of the revelator and the Son of Perdition reads as follows : I, the Lord God, prophesy on the glorious day, time, and season that the sanctuary shall desert the present locality; and the time, day, hour, and minute the sanctuary shall arrive at his new building, where he shall be stationed forever. The sanctuary shall begin to prepare his goods for transportation June 17, 1891 ; and shall remove the first load of furniture into his new house on the eighteenth of the month; and on the nineteenth of the month, at sharp seven o'clock at eve, the entire belongings of the sanctuary shall be conveyed to the new house, at which time the metamorphic change shall set in, which is the forming of the embryo in the matrix.

The embryo of the immortal soul will increase marvellously in growth from this time onward; and by the power of a miracle will reach the state of maturity in the matrix on the twenty-seventh of the month, at fifteen minutes past three o'clock. At this time the life from the Lord God will come into the creature, or soul, and just at this time it will turn over on its right side, causing much pain which shall last only a short time. On the twenty-eighth of the month, it shall raise itself up on the left side, keeping all its members in a rapid motion through the day, and shall make the temple somewhat restless the following night ; but the temple shall be made able to endure unto the end of the time. On the twenty-ninth of the month the creature shall stand upon its feet at eight o'clock at eve, and shall make a mighty attempt to pass through the matrix, but shall fail at the time.

The soul shall lay dead and lifeless from this time until July 1, at half past two o'clock at evening, at which time the mighty power of my kingdom, with its entire belongings, shall circumvolve the mortal cycle. At this time the Father and Son of immortality shall unite, and form the spiritual compound substance of sempiternity, which is the unquenchable fire, the immortality of the human soul, the perfect salvation of the saints, the second resurrection of the dead. And the man child shall stand upon his feet, and the fulness of life shall be given to him ; and like a gush of water and a streak of lightning, the creature shall pass hastily through the matrix, instantaneously overcoming the animal race, and make its advent to the paradise and Eden of the Lord God, which is the uniting of genuine and pure humanity with the eternal divine and physical laws.

The termination of this prophecy left not a scintilla of desire in the man of sin to dwell any longer as a recording secretary in the private service of the holy city and sanctuary; neither had he any further desire to strive for competition and superiority, as he had done. The vengeance of the terrible God, unmixed with mercy, which came upon him, a fatal and sudden blow, during the time of this prophecy, fulfilled the cycle of time prophesied of in the eleventh chapter of Revelation, involving the entire chapter concerning the six hundred and threescore days. This time was fulfilled, beginning the first of March, 1889, and the great sovereign of sin prevailed over the holy city and sanctuary until this number of days was fulfilled, after going to the extreme by the overspreading of abomination.

This means the number of days the man of sin sat in the temple, ubiquitously, with finite power, to fulfil the time of prophecy on the seven seals in a blind and mysterious way, before the essential truth could be discovered, to eclipse and overpower his many cunning arts and his dexterity. It also fulfils the doctrinal prophecy proclaimed by the apostle Paul, saying: "Now, we beseech you, brethren, by the coming of our Lord Jesus Christ, and by our gathering together unto him, that ye be not soon shaken in mind, or be troubled, neither by spirit, nor by word, nor by letter as from us, as that the day of Christ is at hand. Let no man deceive you by any means: for that day shall not come, except there come a falling away first, and that man of sin be revealed, the son of perdition; who opposeth and exalteth himself above all that is called God or that is worshipped; so that he as God sitteth in the temple of God, shewing himself that he is God." — 2 Thess. 2.

As soon as the Son of Righteousness obscured and overpowered the man of sin, and before the overspreading of abomination, the revelator made an enthusiastic appeal unto the Almighty God, to bless him with an honorable name and title of the work which he was sent forth to accomplish. And the Holy Spirit instilled into him the title of "Divine Psychology," which comprises the seven infallible doctrines of the human soul; and this title was used on the souls of those who are assigned to this revelation until the title became practical after the overspreading of abomination ; which relapsed upon the holy city and sanctuary on this wise, after the Holy King overpowered, condemned, cast down from heaven, and renounced that man of sin, and declared him to be unfit for the office of recording secretary.

This renouncing movement continued a short time, when the holy prince was humbled through the power of sympathy, and resolved to take the man of sin again into the private and holy limits of the sanctuary. When he resumed work in the privacy of the sanctuary, he abhorred the work, became grieved at heart, and was unable to continue as before : then the holy prince again sent him away into the world to work for the support of the sanctuary, but this time was not compelled to use so violent a force to send him away, although griefs and burdens were his most frequent visitors after leaving the sanctuary.

The feelings of the man of sin taught him that his work within the private limits of the sanctuary was unfinished, and that he had other work to accomplish with the revelator ; so the revelator made another mighty ardent appeal unto the Lord God to bless him with some kind of work to do among the people in honor of the title with which he had been blessed. The Holy Spirit issued a commandment declaring that he should begin the holy title among the people, by publishing the work he had accomplished in secret, in monthly issues, in pamphlet form. As soon as this was declared, the revelator made an appeal to the Almighty, in order to secure work with him for the recording secretary, if it was so ordained.

The work that the holy prince allotted to him was recording the writings, and attending to the printing and the sale of the books. Immediately after he recorded the writings of the first book, and an application had been sent in for copyright, the man of sin again stood up and overpowered the flesh, and condemned and loathed the idea of doing the recording, or of taking any part in the work. This caused the flesh to become overwhelmed with the king of griefs, burdens, and despondency; and he wanted to compel the flesh to seek death at his own hands, and put himself out of the way, because so many unsuccessful attempts had been made, and fruitless efforts put forth to deliver him from the powers of that man of sin that it seemed useless to suffer any longer in vain attempts. This caused an error in the application for copyright. which delayed matters.

The revelator then made a sacrifice of the step which he had taken to publish his writings, and gave it up to failure if the writings were not beneficial to mankind. He then turned and used the weapons of word, spirit, and truth on the man of sin; and the more he worked to slay his prevailing griefs, the more the flesh had to suffer. Seeing that there was no hope of saving the flesh from that mighty power, the revelator made a sacrifice of both soul and body, and then stood up in vengeance and renounced him upon oath, and sent him from his presence into the world, to work for himself and not for the sanctuary. He was to mingle customarily with the people of his class, to live the life that they live, and to die the death that they shall die; and in the meantime he should preach of the impossibility of his kind ever being allowed to receive the perfect salvation to mingle with the holy seed. The holy Jerusalem then imprecated a fatal curse upon the Son of Perdition, and made the flesh to see and understand that his general composition then was equal to that of an ox or a horse, by telling him he had no soul, because his natural soul was utterly condemned, driven from the presence of God, damned, ruined, and lost forever.

When the Son of Perdition was forced into this crisis, he utterly lost all hope of retaining or regaining his office at the sanctuary to deceive, mislead, and obstruct the true course as he had done. This blow caused the Son of Perdition to fall down slain in the lowest regions of humanity, where he rapidly yielded up the ghost, so that he was unable to stand up in arms against the holy kingdom to make war, and reject the perfect truth through peace and stratagem, as he had done. The Almighty God empowered the revelator to pursue this course to defeat the aims of the man of sin, and to take away his ruling sceptre, and slay him, to free the flesh from his will and power; and this manner of work was accomplished through the utter destruction of his hope.

While it shows that in that state and condition the man of sin was bluntly whirled to work continually, as long as he lived apart from the holy city and sanctuary, and to live on a level with the lowest animals, it was a blow too hard and scientific for him to receive and live through to overpower the flesh when God saw fit to reclaim it from the ruins of perdition. This the merciful God did by the power of the seven doctrines of the human soul when the man of sin had lost his ruling sceptre and the piercing sting. Not as the first, nor as the latter, did he receive the flesh: but he continually stretched forth his almighty redeeming hand-writing in the utterance of psychology, and brought him up from the wretched state of the Abyssinian gulf into the land of the living, and gave the flesh the privilege of progressing up where he could offer unto the Lord offerings in righteousness.

Not very long after the man of sin was driven from the presence of the holy king, the revelator received the copyright applied for and he commenced putting his writings into print. He had three separate issues published monthly, and circulated them among the people, and then caused the publication of them to cease. A small circular was issued with these books, which gave the conditions of the work that Christ would do among the notoriety while the books were in circulation to fulfil that time as it was determined.

Through involving the millennium embassage as a teacher of the seven doctrines, it caused the covenant to drift back entirely into the millennium doctrines and customs of living and how to live, accepting in many instances the sinful customs of men, and in other instances rejecting the pure and rational truth. This brought in discord and desperate conflict between the two eras, which were the laws of the common salvation in its impure state, warring against the perfect salvation united with the purity of the common salvation, and disguising itself in the great change of its method of working, and of demonstrating the power of Christ among men.

To fulfil God's purposes, this then mystery destroyed the power of both eras hastily, after the new era began to circulate among the people, so that every moving power within it was soon wax cold, and the momentum stood still. This discord caused the holy prince to cease his public work. When this was done he rejected and renounced the millennium embassage for the welfare of the truth, that purity would be maintained at the next public issue, and the sounding of the eternal trump. Then the Holy God issued a commandment to publish the entire writings in one edition, which prolonged the secret trials of the holy Jerusalem.

This ends the historical adventures of the New Jerusalem, the holy city and sanctuary, in the strongest hazardous events in fulfilling the time determined against sin and spiritual wickedness which overpowered all the wicked kingdoms that move over the surface of humanity. The fulfilment of the cycle of time to give birth to the holy doctrines of life did also cleanse the holy city and sanctuary after mingling with the seed and customs of men. This is the beginning of the holy public doctrines of life, and the beginning of divine creation.

FROM THE MORTAL LIFE TO DEATH AND FROM DEATH TO THE RESURRECTION OF THE DEAD; ADMITTANCE INTO THE TRANSHUMANIZED LIFE, AND ITS MODE OF LIVING.

The inspiring power of God's wisdom instilled into the soul of mankind suffices with gratitude, and harmonizes with both divine and physical endowment in the entity of the two genders of humanity. Man, in his perilous state, which abounds between entity and non-entity, has no taste nor progressive thoughts tending homeward; because suffering and death are the only alternities, which must carry him home from whence he is carried by reason of fear that pierces the mortal man, whose name is death.

After the uncivilized man has left the borders of life, and plunged precipitously into depravation, the lifeless percentage of immortality revives in its true tenor, survives mortality, and vaporizes the genuine soil of humanity with the unction of divinity until life and aspiration are set ablaze in every secret chamber of the immortal soul. While this strange and irrational movement is in operation, the soul of sophistry is destined to the state of supination, consumptively; and the pernicious customs of the secular life are wasting away through acknowledging the evil craves and desires which carried the soul into the state of apathy.

The wasting away of the depraved life and its tendencies is produced through confessing the evil craves and inclinations of the inner man, and through believing and receiving the rudiments of truth as pertaining to both good and evil as revealed from heaven through the man whom God raised up for this purpose. This is the momentum of both downward and upward progress of the inner man. The mortal soul is commissioned to work in accordance with the ordinations of the omniscient God, to establish friction between its endowment and the endowment of immortality, so that the friction between the two moving bodies would produce a substance stronger, purer, and more durable than the substances in action in the so-called pure and impure bodies; for a living body cannot be so corrupt but what friction will produce some pure substance, which will be of value when the original bodies are consumed, and the dross of both bodies have mingled agreeably, and the purity has done the same.

While the strange and irrational movements are in progress between the two mighty bodies, the corresponding corpuscules of both physical and divine ingredients are coming together ordinately, and adhering each kind to its kind, fashioning and composing the transhumanized soul and body, with each active member in its proper place as was fixed upon the soul of sophistry. On the other side the corresponding corpuscules of mortality, which are more durable than some of its kind, are falling together successively and adhesively, composing its body both physical and spiritual; which will condemn and cause to cease, in the civilized era, the material suicides, fellonious crimes, and man-slaughter prevailing in the world of moral and immoral beings.

Sin, which is the similitude of morality, and the competitor of transhumanity, will exist and work upon an entirely different and higher basis of crime in its chosen members in the eternal age: which shall be powerless over the just in every material and spiritual sense, and shall be powerless over its own kind in a material sense. This compels the civilized world to cause to cease and be annulled every law enacted upon brutal punishment, such as are now enforced upon capital crime perpetrators. As soon as the statutes that enforce brutal punishment upon humanity are made null and void, capital crime will cease rapidly, and have an end.

The execution of material bodies shall cease, because this restriction of law, which enforces brutal punishment upon crime committers, has created the fulness of indignation and maliciousness in the human soul after being driven from their habitations by brutal and unmerciful execution of human flesh. The souls of these, when re-embodied, determine despitefully to carry out and continue their desperate crimes, by the forcible impulse of their thoughts, which overpower humanity to wreak their vengeance by retaliating upon their enemies who show no mercy to human flesh that falls suddenly into the snare of brutal capital crime.

Brutal capital punishment exasperates the souls of men to continue capital crime, because this law was of old, when the world was far from its now civilized basis. The brutal capital punishment now in existence was ordered and established by the antique typical commandments of the Holy God, to establish the holy and civilized spiritual commandments, after mankind reach the fulness of obedience and fear in fulfilling the type of the real, which is spiritual. The fear of the typical commandments has come to the full in humanity; and the fearlessness of the spiritual and typical commandments has attained the fulness of power in humanity, whence the friction is produced with power, between the true and the false, to create the perfect human soul, the eternal salvation of man.

The material habitation of the inner man is the being upon whom modern punishments are imposed for spiritual crime, such as disappointment of aims in life, accidents, distress, despondency, sickness, grief, burdens, aches and pains, incurable chronic diseases, and death. The grievances that prevail in the sphere of humanity are continually issuing from some rational resource, which is far beyond the comprehension of carnality; and for this cause such have power to continue in the world, where the light of genuine truth hath not appeared to produce light.

The intermingling of genuine truths with the world of sophistry keeps sophistry and genuine truths in the state of ambiguity and obscuration, so that neither is able to behold the injury the one does to the other. The long worn cares and conflicts that dwelt close by sophistry and genuine truths at many times deadened and mutilated the fear and trembling that existed in one because of the brutality that concealed itself in the other to be exercised against its antagonist. At many times neither dared to make open opposition against the other; and neither dared to take steps to publish and establish their laws, doctrines, and mode of living.

Rising still higher in the civilized world, and understanding more and more of its mode of living, which is contained in its laws, doctrines, and commandments, I would write of a higher thought, and a closer walk with the genuine truths in man's eternal existence; which will cause the members of the holy dispensation to issue in freedom, peace, satisfaction, and prosperity, to learn what is required of them to magnify, honor, and obey the Omniscient Being in their works, conversations, and dealings with men.

After the pure human soul has succumbed and received the fulness of word, spirit, and truth in approaching the perfect salvation, there are no other works nor conditions required of them, in the holy dispensation, but to live in harmony with their own choice and desires; which will be the will and pleasure of the Holy God manifested in them, because the fleshly man is dead.

The condemned and ruined souls have no power to revive and usurp power over the immortal soul. After receiving the full doctrines of the genuine truths, the soul and body are no more slaves of the seven doctrines, but they are free agents; and the genuine truths become the servants of the members of truth, as each one desires to live, whether to seek a companion, or to remain single and continue an agent of the holy truth, as was in the outset. It will not be a curse nor a conflict upon and against the members of the holy era to seek their counterparts in the world in harmony with their talents, if they are so led irresistibly by the demands of their own natures and condition, where such step is strengthening to health, prosperity, talent, and to the prolongation of life, while in wait for the world to reach that state of holiness, or civilization, for the members of the holy era to become united with their kind.

As the new dispensation must live materially in the holiest customs of the old era, the members of the holy age must be blessed and justified in living in perfect conformity with their leading and controlling desires, whether united connubially or single in the world. When the civilized age becomes the leading government of the people, both spiritual and physical, the connubial union will be upon the full basis of friendship, love, and truth, with the members of its own dogma. Such will purge and purify the temporal world as the spiritual is pure; but the genuine civilization cannot become a normal method of living until there be a radical change in the physical world, as pertaining to its leading laws and doctrines, and the general welfare of the people in living an honorable life.

These truths are revealed to the world to show by a flood of prophecies, and prove by a doctrinal dogma, that there shall be a radical change in the established customs of both divine and physical laws; but in no case shall this doctrinal dogma desire nor attempt to establish itself materially while it conflicts against the leading and established laws of nature. The works and teaching of these doctrines shall harmonize with every civilized physical statute; and they shall move by the power in themselves to be established just as the laws of the physical world are revised, to prevent a conflict between the two.

Journeying on to a much higher scope of the civilized dispensation, I would relate that no member nor members shall, under any circumstances, be held in bondage against their will and pleasure to pay tribute unto these doctrines. Neither shall any person nor persons connect themselves with the holy doctrines with the purpose of organizing a body of members to compel the world to see the progress of the new era, and that this is the people of the living God. Neither shall any one be forced to receive and come under the teaching of these doctrines through excessive fear, and upon an irrational basis of motive and impure aim. All things shall be made perfectly clear concerning these doctrines, before each one who will can come under its teachings in full; and they must derive this understanding from the principal authority before their insight be considered valid.

Persons of insane minds, or devoid of sound, active reason, shall not be allowed to come under the teaching of the holy doctrines. No person who has been cast out of society because of immoral conduct shall be received a proselyte of the holy doctrines. No male nor female shall be received a proselyte of the holy doctrines who has been unfaithful, without a just cause, in a wicked sense to mother, father, sister or brother, son or daughter, husband or wife; or who has wronged any one brutally, and has not confessed and repented of his demeanors. No person of a dangerous and deeply seated chronic disease shall be allowed to become a proselyte of the holy doctrines merely to receive physical health, and then turn from the true way, and they shall not be received under any circumstances in a dangerous state of physical disease.

All persons placing themselves in the saving hands of the holy doctrines must do it because they love its truths, privileges, and doctrinal dogma beyond that of all others. No person under legal age, whether male or female, shall be allowed to become a proselyte of the holy doctrines without the full consent of his guardians; neither shall any person nor persons contribute means for the support of the holy doctrines, if under age, married or single, or bound, without the consent of those to whom they are subject, legitimately. No persons shall be allowed to become teachers of the holy doctrines, except those who are proven to be chosen and ordained by the Holy God to do this manner of work; and who forsake all other vocations of life.

No persons shall be allowed to become proselytes of the holy doctrines who do not believe in their entire method of teaching the true life in both divine and physical matters. No person shall be allowed to become a proselyte of the holy doctrines who does not believe in the truism of both divine and physical truths, as is revealed by the spirit of judgment and equity. No persons shall be allowed to become proselytes of the holy doctrines unknown to their friends or relatives with whom they are associated in the important walks of life. No person shall be allowed to become a member of the holy doctrines merely to find a companion among the members of the holy doctrines.

There shall be no limited charge made in teaching the seven doctrines of life, such as putting a limited fee upon each member who comes under the teachings of the holy doctrines; because each one who is worthy of the higher doctrines, and who is received a member of the holy dispensation, will have the teachings in his heart, and, ruled by the true conscience, will know what to give to the support of the holy doctrines in return for what the truth has done for him, what it is still doing, and what it shall continue to do. The perfect truth is the government of the people, the support of the people, the life of the people, and the eternal salvation of the people; and the people are the support of the true government, and will sustain that which upholds them and defends them in justice, judgment, and righteousness.

How the Union of the Seven Doctrines Constitute Transhumanity; Why Sin Cannot Find Any Place in Transhumanity; How the Life of the Transhumanized Soul is Superior to that of Refined Classes of Mankind.

Moving on by the pacific flow of revelation unto the sphere which contains the translunary light and the lesser lights of wisdom, I must judge all things rightly, so that all things that God hath created and made will hold their proper offices, and receive the due honor and respect, not allowing the baser substances to mingle with the purer substances, neither allowing the baser to fall into the office of the purer substances, nor to receive the honor of the purer substances. This will keep pure and untarnished forever the transhumanized soul and its tabernacle, whatever name it may come under.

I have disclosed to the civilized world that the transhumanized soul is the concentrated focus of the seven doctrines of the human soul, which is the redeemer of mankind. Then there is no other human being in existence, nor can any other human being exist to equal the focus of the seven doctrines. Men can be cleansed from all sins, and be as pure in substance, yet they cannot equal the transhumanized soul as it exists in the fulness ; because the life and blessings, joy, peace, perfect satisfaction, and the eternal wrath of God proceedeth from this being; because if men live in harmony with the involuntary doctrines that move over the surface of this holy being, they will be blessed and prosper at whatever thing they turn their hearts and hands, to perform that which is good for their success, both spiritual and physical. On the other hand, if men should machinate evil against this being, or agree with judgment against the same, or strive to deceive this being, the entire world cannot sustain them effectually in striving to confer upon them peace, prosperity, and satisfaction in their aims in business matters, or whatever thing it may be.

This shows that when one is dealing with the embassador of the seven doctrines, it is not like dealing with the embassadors of the Christian era; neither is it like dealing with the subordinate members of these doctrines, because success is in its supreme power when one deals with these truths justly, with honest motives in every respect. The power to execrate and throw down from prosperity is also in its supreme power if one should wilfully fall short of dealing justly with the holy embassador, which warns the people to be wholly honest in their motives and dealings with the holy doctrines. It were better had they never come near; for if they do the like it will curse their business and whatever they put their hands to do.

It is better for all persons having their greatest pleasures and hope centred in the world, to fulfil their pleasures and hope honestly therein, and not to attempt to deceive the embassador of the holy truths in any way, for he cannot be deceived. There is an omnispective eye and omniscient wisdom watching over and looking into the heart of each person who aims to enter the holy era, and also those who are associated with it, to see if they are sincere in what they say or do, as pertaining to the higher truths.

If you have no taste nor desire to receive the perfect truths to live in a godly manner, do not seek that life, neither strive to mingle with the holy seed. One can desire to receive the higher truths which will eventually create the taste for the perfect doctrines. If one should receive the truth seemingly when they have no taste for the same, they injure their soul by doing the like, and fall short of the glory of God and that which they might have obtained in the world, by being unfaithful to their trust and desire. The world and the holy doctrines have no fellowship ; neither is there any prosperity for those who strive to involve the world with the perfect doctrines of life.

In order to give due warning to the forthcoming members, that they may not walk blindly into the snare of utter destruction I would add that no one should venture to live the life of the holy seed without first counting the cost and coming to a final conclusion that they are tired of the world and cannot live any longer therein When one reaches this degree of knowledge there are no dangers to walk into while approaching the holy doctrines. The reason why the world in man, when it has not satisfied its craves among its kind, is liable to fall into utter destruction is because the world verily is envious against God in the higher doctrines ; and if the envious world should connect itself with the holy era, when it is not ready to be harvested, the soul will turn wholly against the true doctrines of life ; which would compel the holy king to condemn and cast into perdition the entire soul, which will produce apathy and throe. This caution will prevent any one from persuading his dear friends and relatives to join the army of the living God.

If a person or persons should be blessed with the true spirit, after living a vicious life, and should turn abruptly from depravity, and seek life of the holy doctrines, they will not be rejected, it matters not what they have done, nor how they have conducted themselves in the world, when they have turned suddenly and wholly to the perfect doctrines of life : for God's love and cleansing truths are able to take away their sins and free them from crime, if they turn entirely away from the vicious life, and walk in the newness of life.

All depraved conduct does not proceed from nature ; and the most desperate crime perpetrators are ruled by spirit, which does not proceed from matter. The crimes that are perpetrated materially are the overruling powers of sin, which proceed from a vicious spirit. The spiritual crimes that overrule the true soul and throw it into a state of throe are distilled from nature without spirit which creates mental disorder, which issues from evil thoughts, craving desires, and free-thinking facilities, while material crimes proceed from an irrational spirit. If such persons should turn to the holy doctrines of life they would turn soul and body. Meantime the person who is depraved by nature would have to work out his salvation by the consumption of nature, and by gradual degrees, which will continue until every depraved inclination and lustful desire stands up in mental disorder. Meanwhile the holy truth will judge and condemn the vicious freaks just as fast as they stand up and oppose the true life and its mode of living.

The judgments shall not be pronounced upon a person living in harmony with his desires and inclinations, in connection with these doctrines, until such become a conflict in living, or become a burden mentally, or become noxious to the holy truth in some way.

How Prayers Are Fulfilled when One Becomes a Member of the Holy Doctrines.

The merciful and sympathizing God does herein reveal to the civilized world the insurmountable power and unimpeachable doctrines that shall remove the strain from the people of God, that they may cease from struggling to enter the rest which was prepared for them before the world began. The prayers of those who are blessed to receive the word, spirit, and truth of the seven doctrines of the human soul are fulfilled, and they are no more the instrument of power, as was in the old era. As soon as one connects himself with the perfect doctrines, he is in an entirely new beginning of life in every sense of the word; for instead of prayers of the saints, atonements availeth, and are the supreme power of Christ, which shall ever ascend unto God for the redemption of his people.

When a person reaches the state to receive the teachings of the eternal truths, the day of grace is fulfilled; because this time and duty were only put upon man to fulfil and pay the price of holiness, and for transgressing the holy law, the doctrines of the perfect life. Then there were many degrees of suffering for the mortal image to pass through before sin was made perfect in its mission, and came to the full in humanity. The world has reached that scope of the perfect day where everything that has ever wielded the weapons of cruelty has come to the ultimate degree, both in depth and height, width and length. This shows that both sin and divine righteousness are ready to be harvested. Whether or not persons have taken an active part in the prevailing custom of praying according to the so-called Christian worship, they belong to the praying world, and they are members of that era: they are also partakers of its sins and pollutions. and they are also to be partakers of the future peace, happiness, and all blessings belonging thereto.

The atonements are in the utterance of the seven doctrines, and these seven doctrines shall atone for its people involuntarily, and cause the formality of praying to cease among its sons and daughters; which shall in no wise condemn the prayers and worships of those who are disconnected with the holy era. Those who become members of the holy age shall not bring in their blood-kin to be blessed, loved, and respected equally with the members of the holy era; neither shall it be in the hearts of the holy members to bring in their blood-kin to receive the blessings which the holy truth confers upon its members, simply because they are their blood-kin. If any one does the like intentionally, it shall be a curse to him; and he shall not prosper in doing the like. If he bring in his blood-kin by subtlety, the one who doeth the like merely for the sake of blood-kin shall not escape unpunished when he is brought before the council of the living God.

The holy seed shall work as faithfully for the salvation of non-relatives as they shall for their own blood-kin. No partiality shall be shown on account of blood-kin. All who would come unto life eternal must die from the glory and the lust of the world, and after death come into judgment to receive the just recompense according to their inclinations and motives, regardless of personal friends or relatives.

No one among the holy seed shall be highly honored because of money or wealth, education or talent, or whatever trade he may have naturally acquired, or have already received. All among the holy seed shall have equal honor and respect. I care not what their talent, learning, or wealth may be. There shall be no special honor conferred upon those who for this purpose make large contributions for the support of the holy doctrines. This will prevent any one from buying blessings and privileges contained in the New Jerusalem, and still strive to retain the body of death.

Those who contribute to the support of the holy doctrines must not do so with the hope of the holy doctrines being partial in their judgments, when they stand up to judge and burn up the works of sin within them. There can be no partiality shown to the works and substances of sin, I care not what sacrifice a person may make of his belongings and his own body; for sin is seated in nature, and it must be consumed before the eternal king of glory can come in. Amen.

The Interpretation and Location of the Names Millennium and Post-Millennium: the Forthcoming Punishment, the Torment for the Motives and Deeds of the Wicked; the Forthcoming Recompense and Happiness for the Deeds and Motives of the Righteous.

As I am indued with wisdom which surmounts and darkens that of both ancient and modern mythology, in revealing the long hidden and sought-for secret concerning man's future happiness, peace, rest, and also his misfortune, misery, and woe, which now is present in both lives to his unconsciousness, I find it essentially important to give a brief explanation and location of the unknown worlds of both sin and iniquities, and peace, prosperity, and happiness.

After men have lived out and fulfilled their desires, and are dead from the life, pleasure, glory, honor, and prosperity centred in the secular world, they then enter into the millennium world, which lies contiguously to the temporal world. The millennium world is the perfection of all the high and simple workings of the perfect man of sin in the two sexes. Millennium is that intermediate world and kingdom where the natural Christ appeared and wrought miracles, signs, and wonders, thousands of years after his crucifixion, ascension, and decension to the people who believed on his name, and his power to make mankind more civilized at his first advent to humanity.

When Christ made his second advent to humanity, to reign plenipotently over the principalities of this world, and to utterly destroy from humanity every particle of sin, he gathered his elect out of the millennnium kingdom, purged them thoroughly, and made them heirs of his glory in the post-millennium kingdom, which means that when Christ appeared the second time, without sin unto salvation, he chose his messenger out of the customs of the secular world, and stamped within that being the entire principles, holy deeds and motives of the saints who were existing in the religious worlds intermingled with huge images of fallacies. This means that the Holy Christ passed through the bowels of the millennium hell, accompanied by his chosen people, and gathered the heirs of his glory, and carried them with him to heaven, to share with him in his glory in the holy age, called the "post-millennium kingdom," or, "the transhumanized kingdom."

The post-millennium kingdom is situated contiguously to the millennium kingdom, which is entirely ultramundane, both to the temporal and the millennium world; therefore, all the immortal characters, deeds, and motives of the people of Christ who heretofore existed in the religious worlds are carried over to the new world, which made the millennium kingdom an everlasting hell for the wicked, and also a torment to the people of the transporting world, who linger therein for life, restraint, and prosperity, although there are high and simple ways to escape all the woful and miserable things contained in the millennium kingdom that strive to surmount the true wisdom, obstruct the path of rectitude, and eject the judgment and understanding of the transhumanized sovereign, if one is willing and will be guided by the revelation and doctrines of the embassador of the new world, which lays just beyond the millennium.

The seven doctrines are plenipotent, and will surmount, stamp under foot, and remove every impediment that exists in the millennium hell, which opposes the progress and prosperity of the emigrants who are bound for the land of transhumanity. The people who are organized to receive eternal life in the material body have great tastes and desires for the noble and the grand things of the secular world, both in greatness and simplicity; and when they go so far, their desires go beyond the glory and contents of the temporal world, by having libidinous tastes and desires for what the world does not contain.

While passing through the millennium kingdom, you see and behold all precious and magnificent things, which are pleasing to licentiousness but pernicious to the immortal life while in the animal kingdom, because they contain the glory and honor of that wicked man, and for this great reason they must be utterly rejected while in that kingdom, so as to escape the pollutions of the world, because the same glory, honor, and pleasure, but pure and holy, are in the transhumanized world, and will be given to the heirs of Christ when the Omniscient seeth that you stand in need of them. If one should hesitate over the glory and splendor reigning in the millennium kingdom, while en route for the eternal world, the glory contained in the animal kingdom will adhere to his mortal soul, delay his progress, cast him into castles, erect hells in his soul, and create severe suffering where such could be avoided if the journey were continued without hesitating.

When the soul reaches the millennium world, the seven doctrines are set to work by the omnipotent power; and they work in spirit and nature like the blood and breath, which is a perfect machinery to destroy the mortal soul, or life, and bring in the perfect life, the salvation of the wicked, the immortal soul.

The embassador of the perfect age shall not handle the seven doctrines deliberately to perform the work in revealing the eternal truths and life to persons who come under the creation of the seven doctrines. He only has to receive the truth from persons who seek eternal life, concerning their desires, choice, conditions, deeds, and needs: and he then reveals to them what they are required to do, or to leave off doing, to overcome the world, in order to receive eternal life at the end of the world in their souls. When every step is made toward the embassador truthfully, sincerely, and honestly, the seven doctrines begin to work within the soul of the person like a perfect piece of machinery, which performs the work which is needful or desired without taking thought how the work is being done, or without a struggle or very great strain.

The millennium world is the everlasting punishment for the wicked motives and deeds of both the great and the simple, who live in that kingdom and refuse to turn from the will of the world and live in honor of the eternal life. The mental disorders that begin and prevail, while passing from death unto life, issue from the millions and millions of depraved souls who are spiritualized and embodied in nature, and which must be raised from the dead to be judged, condemned, and cut off from among the just, to redeem the immortal soul.

The millions and millions of false souls who stand up out of the earth in opposition to the eternal life are the millions and millions of false doctrines, faiths, and opinions contained in the millennium kingdom, and are propelled mentally through the mind, and presented to the sojourner's understanding in harmony with the false ways. There are also millions and millions of holy souls, centred in the seven doctrines of life, working in the spirit and nature of man to lay siege against that wicked one, to produce light to see all the cunningness and changes of sin, which it invents to induce the true souls into misery and woe. . All the embassador has to do to make the work a perfect success is to point the true course, and declare and distinguish the difference between the true and false ways; and the sojourners only have to hear and receive the truth in every change that he shall make to direct them through the nethermost.

The seven doctrines will undoubtedly work by the power in themselves to fortify the true souls against the science of perdition, and guide them safely on to the land of rest. At times, while passing through the nethermost, apathy sets in, and the soul loathes the continual inflowing of the seven doctrines, because of the solitary life which souls are compelled to live in order to overcome, and escape the punishments and woes of the millennium sovereign.

As long as man's hope, craves, trusts, and motives are mortal, everything that appears to his soul to comfort is the agents of mortality that animate the souls of sophistry and prolong the time of suffering. After one has escaped the punishments, miseries, and woes of the temporal and millennium worlds, he enters into the eternal world, and learns and feeds from the "Lamb's Book of Life." This is to show and prove to the heirs of the perfect age how their work and life begin and prosper in the temporal world materially, and how they are to live in connection with those who have not this manner of doctrine.

The doctrines of the "Lamb's Book of Life" give back to man those things which were condemned and cleansed, while leaving the vanity and glory of the world to put on the new man ; and the many temporal things that are returned to humanity are undefiled, and will prosper in both hands and hearts of those who attain to this state. Then both temporal and spiritual things will perform their work in perfect order, and act each thing or kind in its proper office.

UTTERANCE ON THE SEVEN ESSENTIAL DOCTRINES OF THE MORTAL SOUL, CALLED METAPHYSICS.

Wisdom has hewn out her seven pillars of scientific wisdom in both the mortal and immortal souls. There is the same number of prime doctrines on both sides to produce sufficient proofs to both the godly and the ungodly, so that both classes will follow their own inclinations, to receive their just reward, whether tending to happiness or unhappiness. Then the mixtures which have heretofore existed in the holy and wicked kingdoms will cease to mingle.

In this day and time, where wisdom has reached the highest degrees in humanity, the man of sin, the finite power of spiritual wickedness, works on a different and more civilized and honorable method than it did during the past dark ages. The name of the leading sovereign, the focus of that man of sin, is, namely, "Metaphysician," whom the world class a brother of psychology; but not so until the metaphysician is purged and cleansed, and then becomes willing and receives the true revealed God. The unpurged and uncivilized metaphysician is the great central point, the plenipotence of that man of sin, the polished and lettered Son of Perdition, who contains seven prime self-acting doctrines, which constructed the millennium hell, the spiritual punishments for mankind, in striving to reach the eternal world.

The chief subdivisional doctrines of metaphysics are as follows: theosophy, sophistry, logic, theology, politics, ethics, and false philosophy. There are millions and millions of truths found in these false and corrupt doctrines: but as a sample of every essential truth which exists in metaphysics is carried over to the new world in perfect purity, there is no way wrought out for the man to be saved who leans to the teachings and understanding of the duties of right and wrong, while he receives the mixtures of good and evil contained in the seven doctrines of metaphysics. I do not say that there are no eternal truths in the laws and doctrines of metaphysics, for there are divers truths found therein; and there are also divers errors, which place the man of sin and customary divinity dwelling together in the very same spirit, body, and nature. For this cause, the endless truths found in the laws and doctrines of metaphysics were gathered into the soul of the New Jerusalem, after passing through the general judgments, being tried, purged, purified, and refined by fire.

The same doctrines, but purely prepared, are in the image of the immortal soul, and are active and ready to perform their work to arrange physical modes of living after separating the false from the true; which manner of laws and doctrines must work within each and every man's soul until the errors are purged out, and the true laws and doctrines are given to humanity unmixed with base substances. This explanation is to show and prove to the human world that there are no laws, doctrines, powers, nor professions that are honorable anywhere in the limits of the temporal or religious worlds, to save mankind from the rapid increase of misery and woe. I care not how pure their motives and determinations are; and it matters not how high they are blessed to soar into the grandeur of metaphysics.

After man has attained to all the wisdom and grandeur that the world contains, he is but mortal and miserable, and has no staid peace nor resting-place, any more than the ignorant and the poor ; and if there is any difference between the contentment of the two classes, the poor and the ignorant are the most free from care.

There is no safe hope nor continual treasure in either of the old temporal and religious worlds, for which man is to strive alone to obtain contentment, peace, and rest ; because everything found therein is perishable, changeable, and complicated, even if the long-sought-for treasures should by chance fall into one's possession. This is because the whole machinery that keeps in motion the religious and business worlds is associated with trickery, schemes, fraudulence, bribery, deception, and robbery ; yet no human being can exist corporeally without receiving his support from the world, because the means to purchase food and raiment, and other necessities of life, must come from the sinful world.

Sin does not exist in the means that issue from the sinful world for the support of the true souls, because sin exists only in the people who are reigning over the things with which God has blessed them, — talents and knowledge to discover and invent for the glory of his elect ; only the inventors and discoverers are making bad usage of the earthly glory, by using it selfishly, and fail to send the glory and honor to whom it is due. For this reason, the Creator of the earthly glory has prepared the fulness of heavenly glory and honor — so that mankind may have something of worth to strive for beyond the glory of the world — by making complete sacrifices of the glory of the world, so that man's selfish glory, honor, aims, and desires will die, and by so doing will cleanse them of their selfish wants, aims, desires, and libidinousness.

This will realize the long-looked-for end of the world, the general judgments, when those who have lived in godly manner unto the end of these things shall be taken out of the sinful world and carried by the angels of the second resurrection unto life eternal, which is beyond the glory, honor, aims, and desires of man. Then everything which once was set up in the heart of man in its sinful existence and power will be returned in purity, and in glory, praises, and honor to the Creator of them. Then the eternal king will be existing in his fulness in humanity, and reigning in the spirits of his people, where sin once reigned. Then everything that issues from the temporal and divine worlds will come through the eternal king, the cleansing power to the quickened flesh.

The man of sin reigns in humanity despite laws, doctrines, motive, sincerity, fidelity, or anything else, until the laws, doctrines, customs, sincerity, fidelity, and motives of men are dead. And when there are no more places found in the people of Christ for the customs and glory of men, then the king of glory comes in, sweeps and embellishes the temple, and quickens it to the perfect life ; but not for man to be perfect, but for God to be perfect in him, which is to use man to his glory, honor, and pleasure in all things, and, in the meantime, the man be pleased, reconciled, and glorified in the same glory, and take pleasure in God's glory and pleasure. Then man will have on God's image and likeness, which will raise him from the dead and stupid state, and quicken to the eternal desires, reasons, wisdom, love, obedience, fidelity, sympathy, understanding, and every true character to fill the vacancy in spirit and nature which formerly was occupied by the mortal soul.

The work which is required to bring man to this state and privilege does not impair the true human mind one iota ; but it brings man up out of the worlds of mania, idiosyncrasy, and insanity, so that the true thoughts and reasons can act when necessary. When men obtain eternal wisdom and understanding of how to live and how not to live, they are looked upon by some natural, thinking men as being *non compos mentis;* while, in reality, the natural man is an idiot, and *non compos mentis*, because he cannot think truly, purely, neither discretely, for he is filled with mixtures of both false and true reasons. believes in unreasonable things, and rejects reasonable things.

There is no limited time for the proselytes of the perfect life to receive eternal life. or to be freed from sin, any more than their time is limited in the world for them to live and enjoy life, be educated, become great, rich, and famous among men. When men are set free from sin by the power of the true laws and doctrines of life, and put on the life of Christ, they will have a knowledge of it as much as the natural man knows when he reaches manhood, and obtains talent, education, honor, and wealth. When one presents himself to be a servant of the holy doctrines of life, he takes no thought of the end of sin, nor of his existence at the end of the world.

Men should not conform themselves to the glory and pleasure of the holy king simply because they want to receive life ; but they should pursue this course because they love the life of the holy king, and have no other life nor desire ; and they are determined to live the true life as long as they live, if all others turn from it. A person or persons answering this description will receive the truth rapidly, and end the world in them speedily after coming under the teachings of the seven holy doctrines, because they are instrumental and devoted to the true life, just as the man of sin is to the life which he is determined to live in some people.

The natural and fearful man, who does right in the sight of men, does so because he is afraid of going to hell, according to the superstitious doctrines of the pit, when they expire materially; and they think also that they will be taken to heaven, when they are doing right against their own free will merely because they are afraid of the contagious conceptions and false ideas concerning the burning pit. Such characters are already in torment, yet they are striving blindly to shun it, because their motives and every effort are corrupt.

The heirs of the perfect age shall live right according to the righteousness of the holy king, and not according to men's judgment and understanding of right and wrong; and by so doing they will die from the glory, styles, and customs of men, which are the sins of the world, and its spiritual glory. Then you will be prepared to meet the holy king, and make peace with him; and will continue to live and reign on earth with the holy kirgdom set up in the quickened body. This realizes the very same work that the natural man is vainly and unreasonably hoping without faith to receive, though the real work of man's final redemption takes place within and spiritually; only the natural and unreasonable man is blinded by his own false conceptions and opinions, by searching for the Lord's wisdom and ordinances by the wisdom of men's laws and doctrines, which proceed from the science of the metaphysician, who pursues the false courses to make humanity woful and miserable, because such is the Devil's mission to humanity.

The holy king has fully and amply warned men to shun the ways leading to demolition, and to seek the life beyond that of the charms of the world; and because they fail to hearken unto the voice of their true friend, their enemies pursue and overtake them, and wreck their vengeance upon them, because they are not true, faithful, and obedient to their friend.

The only way to be successful in both earthly and heavenly undertakings is to be true, faithful, and obedient to the one or the other, and not to aim to pretend to be what you are not, for you will never succeed nor reach a good end. Whatever your faith or work is, be faithful, straightforward, honest, obedient, and true, and you will prosper in any undertaking that is tending to immortality.

THE LIGHT OF THE BRILLIANT STAR.

I.

The Lamb, the Lamb, the conquering Lamb,
    Was worthy to take the book,
And has opened the seven seals,
    Whereon no man could look.

All glory to God's holy name
    For the miracle he has done.
He took a man of sinners born,
    And made of him a son.

He is the power: he has the keys
    To heaven, death, and hell.
He is a prophet, priest, and king:
    His name is Samuel.

You enemies to God's own Son,
    What are you going to do?
You cannot slay my Lord again,
    For he will not let you.

The Lamb that was slain has come now to reign
    In righteousness forever:
He came, do you see, to save you and me,
    To set up his spiritual kingdom.

By faith I can view the land of the blest,
    Where sorrow and sin cannot enter.
I cannot be lost if I believe on the Son :
    He promised me life eternal.

II.

Emmanuel, the fountain, the fountain of blessing!
I need not blush when I speak his name.
This is the reason now I am singing, —
It came from the fountain that never runs dry.
    Glory and honor be to the Father!
    Glory and honor be to the Son!

I am so happy, I have a Saviour
    Mighty to stand the storms all alone.
He is a rock in this time of danger,
    Where we can hide when our own strength is gone.

Pharaoh is raging, that is his mission;
    God has a purpose in all that is done.
Samuel, our captain, is fighting our battles;
    He has the spiritual sword in his hand.

He came to save his Israel from bondage,
    Destroy the Egyptians, and give us the land.
If I have patience, be humble and faithful,
    I shall inherit the land of the blest.

What difference to me if temptations
    Do rise and follow me here?
My Saviour has power to keep me,
    And give me a home over there.

My Saviour is more than a mother;
    His love is stronger to me.
He knows my weakness and trouble,
    He knows the secret of heart.

I have no words to express me;
    Eternity won't be too long
To sing of his goodness and mercy,
    For all for me has been done.

THE END.

www.ingramcontent.com/pod-product-compliance
Lightning Source LLC
Chambersburg PA
CBHW022102230426
43672CB00008B/1253